T3-BNT-969

WHOLLY FOR GOD

Selections From The Writings Of William Law

EDITED BY ANDREW MURRAY

DIMENSION BOOKS

BETHANY FELLOWSHIP, INC.
Minneapolis, Minnesota

Wholly for God
Extracts from the writings of William Law
Compiled by Andrew Murray

This edition published in 1976 by Bethany Fellowship, Inc.
Reproduced from the 1894 edition published by James Nisbet
& Company of London.

Library of Congress Catalog Card Number: 76-6622

ISBN 0-87123-602-8

DIMENSION BOOKS
Published by Bethany Fellowship, Inc.
6820 Auto Club Road, Minneapolis, Minnesota 55438

Printed in the United States of America

FOREWORD

The writings of William Law have been to me the key which unlocked the door into the true treasure chamber of what Paul called "the mystery of godliness." I had come some distance by grace through faith, both into the initial new birth experience and on into what is sometimes spoken of as "the second work of grace," "sanctification," "full salvation," or "enduement with power," by which Galatians 2:20 ("not I, but Christ liveth in me") had become a transforming reality.

But, as Paul wrote to the 'topline' saints of Ephesus, who already knew Christ in a saved and Spirit-filled relationship, they still needed "the eyes of their understanding to be enlightened," so William Law was the beginning of that enlightenment to me, carrying me into what I would daringly call the ultimate of understanding. Here at last was, in reality, what it is all about!

It was through extracts from his writings, authored by Andrew Murray, that I came to find William Law. I grew up under Andrew Murray. But here was a discovery. Murray must have felt the need of lifting the veil just a little into his own true sources of depth insights in "the way of God more perfectly." For William Law's unfoldings of the truth within the truth go way beyond any of Murray's published writings; and I think in the wisdom of God, Murray's commission was to interpret them in more readable and palatable form for the majority of God's people, who maybe are not meant to pursue to the ultimate.

As soon as a friend handed me *Wholly for God*, I scented the source of the river. That was about 35 years ago. I found Law difficult. His presentation of ultimate truth was too ultimate for me at first. Its concepts went more deeply into "the nature of things" (one of Law's favorite terms)—who God is, who Christ is, who man is—than any mere surface understandings I already had, which had not before seemed surface to me.

Then I found that William Law himself was an illumined man only because he had come across the writings of the German cobbler, Jacob Boehme. William Law was a high church legalist, knowing nothing of grace. In his student days at Oxford, together with John Wesley, he belonged to a group called The Holy Club. Law with his writing gift then wrote what is considered an English classic on a level with *The Imitation of Christ,* which he called *A Serious Call to a Devout and Holy Life.* This book offers the reader the hopeless ladder of good works to attain perfection. That was the only William Law that John Wesley knew, so after Wesley had his illumination in grace, he always regarded Law as someone to be avoided as ignorant of grace. He never knew the transformed Law.

Jacob Boehme's writings opened this whole new world of depth revelation to Law. Law is really the expositor in simpler form of Boehme's glowing, but sometimes almost unintelligible, outpourings. Jacob Boehme is, of course, acknowledged by all the great investigators of truth—scientists (Sir Isaac Newton owed some of his basic concepts on gravity to Boehme), philosophers, theologians—as one of the greatest "seers" of all time, yet always with the Scriptures as his ultimate source. I must admit I have received more pure light from a few sayings of Boehme than from whole books by other authors. However, he is difficult to understand and much goes beyond me, whereas anyone can read William Law, though there again it took time for me to soak into his glorious presentation of God "the eternal will to all goodness," to the depth understanding of the Fall, wrath, atonement, and the total meaning of the new birth. You may not find it easy to follow through, even with this *Wholly for God*, but oh what riches if you do! In William Law, Jacob Boehme, and some others, for me "the winter is passed; the time of the singing of the birds has come."

I am very thankful that Andrew Murray let us in on his secret springs, and that Bethany Fellowship has undertaken the reprinting of this choice volume.

Norman Grubb
International Secretary Emeritus of
The Worldwide Evangelization Crusade

CONTENTS

CONTENTS

INTRODUCTION

A FEW words, first of all, to let my reader know what has given rise to the publication of this volume. Last winter Dr. Whyte of Edinburgh gave a lecture on WILLIAM LAW, in which he directed attention to the treasures to be found in the writings of this almost forgotten, though, as he styles him, "quite incomparable author." With many others I owe Dr. Whyte a debt of gratitude for this introduction to one of the most powerful and suggestive writers on the Christian life it has been my privilege to become acquainted with. The present volume is a proof of my high appreciation of his teaching, and my desire to let others share with me in the profit to be derived from it.

Not long after the delivery of the lecture, a volume of selections was published, with the title *Character and Characteristics of William Law, Nonjuror and Mystic. Selected and Arranged, with an Introduction by Alexander Whyte, D.D.* (Hodder & Stoughton.) I would not have thought of now publishing this volume, were it not that I hoped that the special point of view from which these extracts have been made would prove an attraction to some, and introduce LAW to readers to whom the larger volume would never find its way. That point of view I have expressed in the title as the True Christian Life. I know of no writer who equals LAW in the clearness and the force with which the claims of God on man are asserted. God is all; God must have all; God alone must work all: round these central truths all his teaching gathers. In their light he convicts the religious world of the hollowness and terrible self-deception of the Christianity it professes. He proves to the believer no less how little he has lived as one who is wholly devoted to God in every action of common life, how little he has made exalted and eminent piety, and devotion to God, his one study, in the same way that a man of the world does with his business. And what is more, in his later works he lays bare the root and source of all this evil in the unconquerable power of self, and shows how nothing but the mighty, immediate, and perpetual operation of God on the soul can give deliverance, and how nothing but the having the very spirit and humility, and love of the Lamb of God within can ever satisfy either God or our own heart. I feel confident that the teaching will be a stimulus and a strength to many.

WILLIAM LAW was born in 1686, and died in 1761, at the age of seventy-five. After completing his studies, he entered Holy Orders, and for five years held a Fellowship in Cambridge. At the end of that time, in 1716, he lost his Fellowship, owing to his refusal to take the oath of allegiance to George I. His loss of all hope of preferment in the Church has been its great gain. The closing of the door to active work set him free for that life of contemplation and prayer of which we reap the fruit. His forsaking all for what he deemed faithfulness to conscience helped to intensify that separation from the world, and that whole-hearted allegiance to God and His will for which he was to be such a witness and advocate.

His earliest books were controversial, 1717–1726, and at once gave him a name as an author. His first practical works were—*A Practical Treatise upon Christian Perfection* (1726) and *A Serious Call to a Devout and Holy Life* (1729). It is by the latter of these works that LAW is best known. The first short paragraph of the book contains the text into the exposition and application of which the writer throws his whole soul : "Devotion is neither private nor public prayer ; but prayers, whether private or public, are particular parts of devotion. *Devotion signifies a life given, or devoted, to God.*" Throughout the volume he never wearies of illustrating and applying the two statements of his text. He sees men deceiving themselves with the thought that prayer is devotion : he proves to them, that as words are less than actions, prayer is the least part of devotion : devotion consists in a life given up to God. And what this means, he puts in such a light, both from Scripture and the very nature of things, that every serious reader must confess that he has but little realised how wholly God expects us to live for Him, and how nothing less than a life with the spirit of Christ's commands and example animating us at all times and in every action is what God asks and accepts. The word "*wholly unto God*," which recurs unceasingly, is the keynote of the book.

As I have read and re-read the first ten chapters of the book, and felt how difficult it is to realise, even intellectually, this absolute devotion to God, I have

more than once thought that if a minister were to try
and reproduce in his preaching their substance, the
result would in more than one way be a surprise to
him.   He would be surprised to find how difficult it is
to get a clear and full grasp of that high standard
of living, which he cannot but admit is nothing more
than what Christ demands.   He would be surprised
at his own want of success in conveying to his hearers
the same impression of intense and entire devotion to
God's will and pleasure as the one object of life.   He
would probably be surprised at discovering how, while
he thought he had preached holiness and the imitation
of Jesus Christ, he had given but a very faint impression of the unworldly, the heavenly life, which it
is the duty of every Christian to lead.   He would
possibly be most of all surprised at finding how little
his own life had really aimed at, not to say had
attained, the true ideal, set before us in Christ Jesus.

It was not many years after the publication of this
book that an event took place which exercised an
unexpected influence on the life of LAW.   This was
his becoming acquainted with the works of the German
mystic, JACOB BOEHME or BEHMEN.   Though at first
he found much in the writings of Behmen that
appeared unintelligible, he came so completely under
his influence that he gave himself up entirely to the
study and the exposition of his teaching.   The mystic
element had always been strong in LAW'S nature.
One of the chief marks of the mystic is, that he seeks
to pierce through all the appearances of nature to the
Great Being who lives and moves in it all.   *The Serious
Call* is proof of how LAW had learnt to see God in
every thing, and how he sought to bring men to let

God in very deed be their ALL.   Behmen taught LAW
what he had only faintly seen before, that God not only
is All, and must have All, but that He alone must do
All.   In different works written after this time,
between 1737 and 1740, the influence of Behmen
was distinctly visible, and the substance of his teaching
given.

Then there follows an interval of nine years (1740–
1749), during which he published nothing.   He appears to have given himself to that intense contemplation and fellowship of the Unseen, which is the
only way in which eternal things can come with their
full power into the spirit, and can so impart themselves as real existences, that in what is spoken and
written, the weight and the fire of the Eternal makes
itself felt.   One cannot but observe this in the
works written by LAW after this season of silence.
They were—*The Spirit of Prayer* (Part I. in 1749 ;
Part II., 1750) ; *The Way to Divine Knowledge*,
preparatory to a new edition of the works of Behmen,
1752 ; *The Spirit of Love* (Part I., 1752 ; Part II.,
1754).   In all these books, though some of them are
quite small, one feels that a man is speaking who
does not deal with thoughts and conceptions of the
truth, but in whom the vision of the spiritual world
has been opened, and through whom the fire of the
sanctuary sheds its light and warmth.   One feels
impelled to pause and read again, and to confess that,
though the meaning be clear and plain, there is a
something behind that draws us on to long for the full
possession and experience.   Of these later works, *The
Spirit of Prayer* and *The Spirit of Love*, Dr. Whyte
says : " Christopher Walton does not exaggerate one

iota when he says that LAW's readers will rise up from
these books, saying, These are the two best books in
the world ! . . . I have laid down these books again
and again, saying with Walton, In their way, and
on their subjects, show me another two books like
them in all the world."

And yet I fear that, with many who might be
induced to begin reading them, it might happen as it
did to me, when *The Spirit of Prayer* came into my
hands some years ago, in regard to prayer, as it is
ordinarily taught, I found absolutely nothing. Dis-
cussion in regard to the origin of nature and matter
and sin, that were not at once easily apprehended, and
that appeared to have no direct bearing on the subject
of the book, deterred an unprepared reader, and the
book was laid aside. And so I have thought it might
be a help to give such extracts from these books, as
would bring his more direct teaching on the spiritual
life within the reach of all. It will, I am sure, be the
means of leading some to get the original works, and
study LAW's teaching on the Kingdom of Grace in its
deep and wondrous unity with the Kingdom of Nature.[1]

The spiritual insight into the truth of God acquired by LAW, under Behmen's guidance, made its
influence very marked and felt on his practical teaching. The difference between *The Serious Call* and *The
Spirit of Prayer* or *The Spirit of Love* is very great.
The former is from beginning to end a plea for God,
in which every duty of the Christian life is exhibited
and insisted upon with the voice of authority, and the
motives to obedience are urged with all-convincing

[1] *The Spirit of Prayer* (Part I.) and *The Spirit of Love* have
been published in shilling volumes by Griffith & Farran.

argument. But there is one thing wanting. To the question of the struggling soul who feels its impotence, and asks for strength to cast aside its bonds, and fulfil what is demanded of it, he gives no answer. Of the power that comes to faith, nothing is directly said; of the grace which the Holy Spirit works, mention is scarce made. In the later works the tone is entirely different. The utter corruption and impotence of our nature, the absolute necessity of a new birth as an operation of God's mighty power in the soul, the indwelling of Christ in us, are preached in demonstration of the Spirit and in power. And these are passages in which the nature, the simplicity, the necessity, the alone efficacy of faith as making us partakers of the life and power of Christ, are set forth with singular beauty.

How deeply it was felt by some in LAW's own day that there was something wanting in *The Serious Call*, is evident from what took place with JOHN WESLEY. His biography tells us that he had been some twelve years a minister before he found that salvation by faith of which he afterwards became such a preacher. During the years preceding what he counted his conversion, Wesley had frequent intercourse with LAW, and looked up to him as a teacher. When brought to see how salvation is by faith alone, he wrote LAW a letter, reproaching him for never having taught him this precious truth. Wesley tells him that for two years he had been preaching after the model of *The Serious Call* and *Christian Perfection*, and that the result had been to convince the people that the law of God was holy, but that when they attempted to fulfil it, they found themselves without power. And he asks LAW, " Why did I scarce ever hear you name

b

the name of Christ? Never so as to ground anything upon faith in His blood."

LAW answers: "You have had a great many conversations with me, and you never were with me for half an hour without my being large upon that very doctrine which you make me totally silent and ignorant of. . . . I have been governed through all that I have written and done by these two common, unchangeable maxims of our Lord: ' *Without Me ye can do nothing.*' ' *If any man will come after Me, or be My disciple, let him take up his cross and follow Me.*'" These two texts were without doubt the spirit of all LAW taught. *Christian Perfection* and *The Serious Call* are little else than an extended exposition of the second of the two. And as to the former, he did indeed insist upon the necessity of Divine aid. And yet we can quite understand how Wesley, when once he came to the light, could complain that LAW had never pointed out to him the unique place that faith holds in God's plan of salvation. If we are to judge by his writings, LAW, while holding that we are saved by faith, had not yet himself learnt what self is, and what the vanity is of all self-effort, and what the wondrous power of Christ is in him that believes. I have already alluded to the striking passages in his later works so infinitely beyond what he had ever written before.

These statements in regard to the difference between the earlier and the later works of our author will account for my not having, in these selections, adhered to the chronological order. I thought that, in beginning with *The Spirit of Love*, and setting before my readers some of the ripest, richest fruit first, I would tempt them on to search for the tree on which that fruit grew. That tree they will find in *The Spirit of Prayer*, and its teaching on Regeneration and the Birth from Heaven. In the strength of the faith of what God will do, we may then go on to *The Serious Call*, with its solemn, heart-searching exposition of true Christianity. That book will teach us what the tending and pruning, the digging and dressing, is that is needed to enable the tree to grow and bring forth fruit to perfection.

This order is that which is found in more than one of the New Testament Epistles. The high state and calling of the Christian in Christ is first expounded; then the reader is led on into everyday life, and shown what are the conditions of the maintenance and enjoyment of the grace bestowed in Christ. Or, as we have it in Ephesians, the first half lifts us into the heavenly places with the life in the Holy Spirit; the second brings us down to the practical duties of life on earth, with its cares and duties. I am in hopes that even so, after the reader has been encouraged and quickened in the heavenly atmosphere of *The Spirit of Love and Prayer*, he will go down at the hand of *The Serious Call* into the valley of humiliation, to see what is still wanting in his life, spirit, and conduct, and to prove that the previous teaching of what God and faith can do indeed enable a man to live and love as God would have him do.

LAW is known as a mystic. Dr. Whyte calls him the greatest of English mystics. The deeper insight into spiritual truth which his later works reveal, and the higher life of which they testify, he all attributes to the teaching of the great German mystic, as he

calls him, " The heavenly illuminated and blessed man,
Jacob Behmen."

That we be not, on the one hand, led unaware
into error, nor, on the other, be prejudiced against
truth by undue apprehension, it may be well for us
to consider what this word " mystic " means.

In mysticism, as in everything human, there is an
admixture of good and evil. Some writers give
prominence to what they consider its errors and
dangers, and count mysticism in principle to be
untrue and unhealthy.

In the Preface to Vaughan's *Hours with the Mystics*,
the author writes : " Mysticism, though an error, has
been associated, for the most part, with a measure of
truth so considerable, that its good has greatly outweighed its evil." The statement that what is at
heart *an error* should effect so much more good than
evil, cannot but strike one as somewhat strange. It
would be surely more correct to say : Mysticism,
because it is at root a truth, its good has, notwithstanding a considerable amount of error, greatly outweighed
its evil. The writer of *Hours with the Mystics* would
wish the word applied to the error in mysticism alone,
and thinks that St. John ought not to be called a mystic.
In this case we should need another word to express
that special element which is so marked a character-
istic of the apostle.

" Others, looking at its good, which even, according
to Vaughan, so greatly outweighs the evil, noticing
how many of the noblest and holiest of us have
breathed its spirit, and remembering what the wonderful attraction its teaching often has for the most
earnest and thoughtful minds, maintain that there

must be truth in its root-principle, and that its errors must be put to the account of human weakness, and the difficulties of the high problem with which it deals.

Lange says (*Herzog-Schaff Cyclopædia*) :—

"Mysticism has been defined as belief in an immediate and continuous communication between God and the soul, which may be established by means of certain peculiar religious exercises; as belief in an inner light, which may almost dispense with the written revelation. This definition identifies mysticism too closely with its extravagances, its more or less unsound developments, and overlooks that *there is a mystical element in all true religion, both objectively in the revelation and subjectively in the faith.* According to common acceptation, mysticism is simply a one-sided development of that element."

It is evident from what has just been said, that it is not easy to define what mysticism is. It is not a system of doctrine. It is found in all religious systems ; in heathenism and pantheism, as well as in Christianity. With the Church of Christ it is not a sect or party ; every Church has its representatives. In every complete Christian character there is an element of mysticism. It is the outgrowth of a certain disposition or temperament, which ever seeks for the deepest ground or root of spiritual things.

The close connection between the words *mystic* and *mystery* will help us to understand what it means. In all religion, in all existence, there are hidden mysteries : for these the mystic has a natural affinity. In all the mysteries of revelation there is a human side, which the mind of man can master and reduce to a system.

There is another, the Divine side, which human reason cannot grasp or express, but which opens itself to the faith that, in contemplation and worship, lives in the Invisible. The mystic believes in a Divine light and power that comes on the soul that makes these its special object. The moment we attempt to formulate what the spiritual faculty is that receives this communication, in how far it may be counted a real revelation of God's Spirit, and what its relation to the inspired word, we come upon controverted ground. What we have said is enough to indicate very generally what distinguishes the mystic from the ordinary Christian.

It may help to prepare the way for reading these extracts from LAW with profit, to mention some of the chief characteristics of his teaching, as they mark the true and healthy mysticism, from which the Church has nothing to fear, and a measure of which is necessary to a full and all-sided development of the gifts of the Spirit. As long as mysticism is regarded as a system which aims at making all whom it can reach into nothing but mystics, it is no wonder it should be looked on with apprehension. But if once it be understood that mystics have a special gift and calling in the body of Christ, that, like all specialists, their value consists in their devoting themselves to one side or sphere of the Divine life, thereby to benefit those who have not the same gift or calling, and that the result of what they attain must become the common property of those members of Christ's body whose talents point them to other parts of the great field of Christian life and duty, prejudice will be lessened, and the immense benefit acknowledged which the Church has from the presence and life of those who so intensely witness for the Unseen and Incomprehensible.

1. The great mystery of the universe is GOD. The mystic seeks for God. To know God, to realise God, to live here on earth in conscious fellowship with Him, to love God, is his highest aim. "That God may be all," is the truth to which all others are subordinate. The words of Scripture, "*For whom* are all things, and *through whom* are all things," stand in the very forefront of its theology. "FOR WHOM ALL." Whether it be in nature or grace, in time or eternity, all things exist only for God, as the medium through which He can show forth His power and goodness, and so be glorified in the beauty and happiness of His creatures. "AND THROUGH WHOM ALL." All things glorify God only, because He alone works in them whatever is good and right. Just as these two truths hold in nature, so it is the one aim of religion to make them true in our lives. Man can live ALL FOR GOD as by faith he yields himself to expect ALL THROUGH GOD. To know and enjoy and honour God thus, must be the one object of existence; to aim at it and increasingly to attain to it, is true religion and true happiness. LAW will wonderfully help us to realise this. His *Serious Call* will teach us what *all for God* means. His later books, what *all through God* can be to us.

2. The mystic insists especially on the truth that the organ by which God is to be known, is not the understanding but the heart; that only love can know God in truth. Man was made in the image of God. We know God first in His works. From these we rise to His attributes, and form our conceptions of how these constitute the perfection of Him we seek to know.

But behind and beyond these attributes there is the Infinite and Incomprehensible Being, who hides Himself in a light that is inaccessible. Even so there is in man, who was made in the image of God, an outer life of thoughts and feelings, of words and actions. From these we go inward to the powers from whence they come—the understanding, the affection, the will. But then behind these, there is the deep centre of the soul, what Scripture speaks of as the spirit, and at times as the heart, in which life has its secret roots, where its hidden character is found, and from whence all the issues of life proceed. This is that inner hidden sanctuary of man's nature which corresponds to the mystery of the Divine Being, whose likeness he bears, and which God created specially for Himself to dwell in. This is that hidden depth which none but He who searches the hearts can fathom or know. This is the seat of that renewing of the Holy Spirit, in which the birth of the Divine life creates a man anew. Reason can form its conceptions, and frame its image of what God must be; but the Hidden, the Incomprehensible One Himself, reason cannot touch. As He is in Himself, so His working in man: His dwelling and His dwelling-place in the heart are a mystery too.

One of the great reasons that our religion is so powerless, is that it is too much a thing of reason and sense. We place our dependence on the intellectual apprehensions of truth, and the influence these exert in stirring the feelings, the desires, and the will. But they cannot reach to the life, to the reality of God, both because they are in their nature unfitted for receiving God, and are darkened under the power of sin. Mysticism insists upon this — and presses

unceasingly the cultivation of the spiritual faculty
which retires within itself, and seeks in patient
waiting for God by faith to open the deepest recesses
of its being to His presence.

How true and yet how little understood what LAW
says: "Man's intellectual faculties are by the fall in
a much worse state than his natural animal appetites,
and want a much greater self-denial" (*Character*, 57).

"When the call of God to repentance first rises in
thy soul, thou are to be retired, silent, passive, and
humbly attentive to this new risen Light within thee,
by wholly stopping, or disregarding the workings of thy
own will, reason, and judgment. It is because all
these are false counsellors, the sworn servants, bribed
slaves of thy fallen nature, they are all born and
bred in the kingdom of self; and therefore if a new
kingdom is to be set up in thee, if the operation of
God is to have its effect in thee, all these natural
powers of self are to be silenced and suppressed, till
they have learned obedience and subjection to the
Spirit of God' (*Spirit of Prayer*, § 28).

"If nothing can do any good, be any happiness or
blessing but only God Himself in His holy Being, and
if God cannot communicate Himself to you under
a notion, or an idea of reason, but only as a degree
of life, good, and blessing, born or brought to life in
your soul, then you see that to give yourself up to
reasoning and notional conceptions is to turn from
God, and wander out of the way of all Divine communication" (*Character*, p. 224; see also pp. 185,
197).

We can now understand why such high value is
attached to the contemplative life, to stillness of soul,

and to the practice of the presence of God. It is as the insufficiency of our own powers of thought is deeply felt, and their activity is restrained, that the deeper the hidden powers of our nature can take their place, and faith can exercise its highest function as a faith of the operation of God, who raised Christ from the dead. The door is opened for God to become our inward life as truly as self has been our very inmost life.

3. Another point in which the mystic seeks to enter into the hidden mystery of God, is the nature of redemption. There are two views we find in Scripture, each the complement of the other. In the one, the simpler, more outward and objective, Christ as our representative did a certain work for us which He now in heaven applies to us. In the other, the knowledge of Him as an outward person and of His outward work is considered as but the means to an end, a preparation leading up to the inward experience to His indwelling in us. LAW says, "A Christ not in us is the same as a Christ not ours;" and opens up with wonderful clearness and power what this Christ in us and faith in Him means. He shows how, in the very nature of things, nothing less can restore that life of God which we lost in Adam, than a Christ whose life and disposition live in us as truly as that of Adam does.

If we ask what Christ in us means? his answer is, that that which constituted *Him* the Christ, made Him acceptable to God, and enabled Him to restore within us the perfection we lost, that *that* is what He must be in us. What constitutes Him the Lamb of God is His meekness, His humility, His resignation to God's will. And no faith in an outward Lamb of God, on the cross or on the throne, can possibly save us, except as it restores us to that humility before God, that resignation to His will, which is, whether in heaven or earth, the only possible way of entrance into God's presence.

" Our salvation consists wholly in being saved from ourselves, or from that which we are by nature. In the whole nature of things, nothing could be this salvation or Saviour to us, but such an Humility of God as is beyond all expression."

" Every man has within him a redeeming power, the making of the heavenly life, called the Lamb of God. This is the great trial of human life, whether a man will give himself up to the meekness, the patience, the sweetness, the simplicity, the humility of the Lamb of God. This is the whole of the matter between God and the creature " (*Character*, pp. 57, 66).

" Death to self is a man's only entrance into the Church of Life, and nothing but God can give death to self. Self is an inward life, and God is an Inward Spirit of Life; therefore, nothing kills that which must be killed in us, or quickens that which must come to life in us, but the inward work of God in the soul, and the inward work of the soul in God. This is that *mystic religion*, which, though it has nothing in it but that same spirit, that same truth, and that same life, which always was and always must be the religion of all God's holy angels and saints in heaven, is by the wisdom of this world accounted to be madness " (*Character*, etc., p. 60; see also the very beautiful passage on the only way of dying to self being by receiving the patience, meekness, humility, and resignation to God's will which was in Christ Jesus into our hearts—*Spirit of Love*, Part II.).

It is just this element of mysticism that has formed its great attraction to those who truly thirst for God. Sin would be nothing if it were not sin *in us*, inspiring and ruling our inmost life. And Christ cannot be a complete Saviour until His indwelling and inworking be as real and full as that of sin. I am confident that there will be no thoughtful reader of LAW, who really hungers for the bread of heaven, but will lay down the book with the grateful acknowledgment that he has a deeper insight into the real nature of Christ's work and indwelling, and a stronger hope of the attainment of what so often appeared to be beyond his reach.

4. Just one more of the special teachings of mysticism. It is summed up in the expression that we must come away out of the manifold to the simple, out of multiplicity to unity, from the circumference to the centre. The thought runs through its whole system, and is the key to the right apprehension of much of its teaching.

This truth holds in reference to *God*. Until a soul learns to see how entirely God is the centre of all, how God is to be met and found and enjoyed in every thing, so that nothing in heaven or earth can for one moment separate from Him, it never can have perfect rest. And rest in God is the first duty and the true bliss of the creature. You have Christians who devote themselves most diligently to the study of God's word, who are delighted with every new truth they discover, or every new light in which an old truth is set before them, and who yet scarce ever meet the one Divine

Word, who speaks in power within them. You have others who are consumed with zeal and labour, and yet know not what it is through all to have their rest in God. We need to be brought from the circumference to the living centre; there we shall be rested and refreshed, and endued with the power of a Divine strength to do our work in the power of the eternal world.

This truth holds in reference to *sin* In LAW's books we have a remarkable illustration of this, in the distinct advance to be seen in his teaching.

In *The Serious Call*, individual sins, whether of life or heart, are uncovered and exposed with convincing power. Nothing less than entire conformity to God's requirement and Christ's example is held up as our only standard, or hope of being found meet for admission to heaven. But there is nothing like the laying the axe to the root of the tree, the tracking of sin to its one source and beginning, as we have it in the later books. Behmen's teaching had opened up to him the meaning of the fall, and the entire corruption of human nature, and had shown him that there is but one deliverance from sin, and that is the deliverance from self. From all the manifold sins he had learnt to look to the one sin—incarnate self. He points out how the four elements of self or fallen nature—covetousness, envy, pride, wrath—"are tied together in one inseparable band; they mutually generate and are generated by each other; they have but one common life, and must all of them live, or all die together" (*The Spirit of Love*, Part I.). "Self is the whole evil of fallen nature." "Self is the root, the tree, and the branches of all the evils of our fallen state." "Self is not only the seat and habitation, but the very *life* of sin; the works of the devil are all wrought in self; it is his peculiar *workhouse*; and therefore Christ is not come as a Saviour from sin, but so far as self is beaten down, and overcome in us" (*Spirit of Prayer*, § 32).

It is as the soul in this light is led to turn from the hopeless multiplicity of its sins, by which it has been distracted, to the one source of all, that it will learn how hopeless its efforts are, and see its need of a death to self in the death of Christ as its only hope.

This truth holds especially also in regard to *faith*. LAW says (*Spirit of Love*, Part II.): "I would have you believe that the reason why you, or any one else, are for a long time vainly endeavouring after, and hardly ever attaining these first-rate virtues, is because you seek them in the way they are not to be found, in a *multiplicity* of human rules, methods, and contrivances, and not in that *simplicity* of faith in which those who applied to Christ immediately obtained that which they asked of Him."

It is as the soul is led to see that in God is the unity and centre of the universe and of our life, and thus that sin is nothing but our having turned from this God to self, and that therefore our one need is the deliverance from self, that it will discover in Christ a new meaning, and will understand how in the very nature of things nothing can save us but the simplicity of faith. Christ becomes to us the man who lived the life of God for us in human nature, and who brings salvation from self by Himself being born into us, and giving us a life of God in which self is swallowed up as darkness is swallowed up in light. This life must be received; and to receive it nothing avails but a true desire and a simple faith.

LAW makes clear that in the Christian life there are two stages—that of babes, and that of men; that in the earlier stage our great duty is to remove hindrances, and to prepare the way for God to set up His kingdom; and that it is only as we are faithful in the earlier stage that we shall be fitted for attaining the *full outbirth* of the Divine life within us. " Now, this way of attaining goodness (by rules and precepts), though thus imperfect, is yet absolutely necessary in the nature of the thing, and must first have its time, work, and place in us. Yet it is only for a time, as the law was a schoolmaster to the gospel." All this effort is only to bring a man to such a total despair of all help, from human means, as to make him turn to God from whom alone life can come. Faith becomes the one thing needful. " When the Virgin Mary conceived the birth of the Holy Jesus, all that she did toward it herself was only this single act of faith and resignation to God : ' Behold the handmaid of the Lord ; be it unto me according to thy word.' This is all that we can do toward the conception of that new man that is to be born in ourselves. The truth is easily consented to. But this is not enough : it is to be apprehended in a deep, full, practical assurance, in such a manner *as a man knows and believes that he did not create the stars*, or cause life to rise up in himself. Then it is a belief that puts the soul into a right state, and that makes room for the operation of God upon it."

Oh, blessed simplicity of the Christian life ! May we all learn its blessed secret. Let God be all to us. Let Christ be all, as our way to God, as God working and dwelling in us. Let faith be all to us, the simple

and unceasing turning of our souls to Christ Jesus;
and out of the multiplicity of our strugglings and
wanderings we shall by faith enter into the rest of
God.

Just one word more in conclusion. There is a
great deal in our modern habits of reading, and in our
religious literature, that is not favourable to the cultivation of that habit of mind which is needed to read
Law with pleasure or profit. Let me advise all those
who hope by a cursory perusal to master his thoughts,
to lay the book aside. But if we are prepared in
quiet meditation to give time to the words of a man,
who had, more than most, the powers of the invisible
opened up to him and resting on him, to do their
work in us, we shall, I am confident, be richly
rewarded. And I am much mistaken if there will
not be many of the readers of this volume who turn
back time after time to dwell again on words, which,
though they appear so simple and plain, yet will be
increasingly felt to be full of the power of God and of
eternity.

ANDREW MURRAY.

Wellington, 31st Oct. 1893.

THE SPIRIT OF LOVE

FIRST PART

THE SPIRIT OF LOVE

FIRST PART

———◆———

MY DEAR FRIEND,—You say, "There is nothing in all my writings that has more affected you than that spirit of love that breathes in them; and that you wish for nothing so much as to have a living sensibility of the power, life, and religion of love. But you have this objection often rising in your mind, that this doctrine of pure and universal love may be too refined and imaginary; because you find that, however you like it, yet you cannot attain to it, or overcome all that in your nature which is contrary to it, do what you can; and so are only able to be an admirer of that love which you cannot lay hold of.

This objection will fall into nothing, as soon as you look at it from a right point of view; which will then be, as soon as you have found the true ground of the nature, power, and necessity of the blessed spirit of love.

1. The Spirit of Love in God.

Now, the spirit of love has this original. God, as considered in Himself, in His holy being, before any thing is brought forth by Him, or out of Him, is only

3

an eternal will to all goodness. This is the one eternal,
immutable God, that from eternity to eternity changeth
not, that can be neither more nor less, nor any thing
else, but an eternal will to all the goodness that is in
Himself, and can come from Him. The creation of
ever so many worlds, or systems of creatures, adds
nothing to, nor takes any thing from, this immutable
God: He always was, and always will be, the same
immutable will to all goodness. So that as certainly
as He is the Creator, so certainly is He the Blesser
of every created thing, and can give nothing but blessing, goodness, and happiness from Himself, because He
has in Himself nothing else to give. It is much more
possible for the sun to give forth darkness, than for
God to do, or be, or give forth, any thing but blessing
and goodness.

2. The Spirit of Love in the Creature.

This is the ground and original of the spirit of
love in the creature; it is, and must be, a will to all
goodness, and you have not the spirit of love till
you have this will to all goodness, at all times, and
on all occasions. You may indeed do many works
of love, and delight in them, especially at such times
as they are not inconvenient to you, or contradictory
to your state, or temper, or occurrences in life. But
the spirit of love is not in you, till it is the spirit of
your life, till you live freely, willingly, and universally,
according to it. For every spirit acts with freedom
and universally according to what it is. It needs no
command to live its own life, or be what it is, no more
than you need bid wrath be wrathful. And therefore,
when love is the spirit of your life, it will have the

freedom and universality of a spirit; it will always live and work in love, not because of this or that, here or there, but because the spirit of love can only love, wherever it is or goes, or whatever is done to it. As the sparks know no motion but that of flying upwards, whether it be in the darkness of the night, or in the light of the day; so the spirit of love is always in the same course; it knows no difference of time, place, or persons; but whether it gives or forgives, bears or forbears, it is equally doing its own delightful work, equally blessed from itself. For the spirit of love, wherever it is, is its own blessing and happiness, because it is the truth and reality of God in the soul; and therefore is in the same joy of life, and is the same good to itself, everywhere, and on every occasion.

3. The Perfection of the Spirit of Love.

Oh, sir, would you know the blessing of all blessings? It is this God of love dwelling in your soul, and killing every root of bitterness which is the pain and torment of every earthly, selfish love. For all wants are satisfied, all disorders of nature are removed, no life is any longer a burden, every day is a day of peace, every thing you meet becomes a help to you, because every thing you see or do is all done in the sweet, gentle element of love. For as love has no by-ends, wills nothing but its own increase, so every thing is as oil to its flame; it must have that which it wills, and cannot be disappointed, because every thing naturally helps it to live in its own way, and to bring forth its own work. The spirit of love does not want to be rewarded, honoured, or esteemed; its only desire is to propagate itself, and become the blessing and happiness of everything that wants it. And therefore it meets wrath, and evil, and hatred, and opposition with the same one will as the light meets the darkness, only to overcome it with all its blessings. Did you want to avoid the wrath and ill-will, or to gain the favour of any persons, you might easily miss of your ends; but if you have no will but to all goodness, every thing you meet, be it what it will, must be forced to be assistant to you. For the wrath of an enemy, the treachery of a friend, and every other evil, only helps the spirit of love to be more triumphant, to live its own life, and find all its own blessings in a higher degree. Whether, therefore, you consider perfection or happiness, it is all included in the spirit of love, and must be so, for this reason, because the infinitely perfect and happy God is mere love, an unchangeable will to all goodness; and therefore every creature must be corrupt and unhappy, so far as it is led by any other will than the one will to all goodness. Thus you see the ground, the nature, and perfection of the spirit of love.

4. The Absolute Necessity of the Spirit of Love.

Let me now, in a word or two, show you the necessity of it : now the necessity is absolute and unchangeable. No creature can be a child of God, but because the goodness of God is in it; nor can it have any union or communion with the goodness of the Deity, till its life is a spirit of love. This is the one only band of union betwixt God and the creature. All besides this, or that is not this, call it by what name you will, is only so much error, fiction, impurity, and corruption, got into the creature; and must of all necessity be entirely separated from it, before it can have that purity and holiness which alone can see God, or find the divine life. For as God is an immutable will to all goodness, so the divine will can unite or work with no creaturely will, but that which willeth with Him only that which is good. Here the necessity is absolute; nothing will do instead of this will; all contrivances of holiness, all forms of religious piety, signify nothing without this will to all goodness.

For as the will to all goodness is the whole nature of God, so it must be the whole nature of every service, or religion, that can be acceptable to Him.

For nothing serves God, or worships and adores Him, but that which wills and worketh with Him.

For God can delight in nothing but His own will, and His own spirit, because all goodness is included in it, and can be nowhere else.

And therefore every thing that followeth **an own will**, or **an own spirit**, forsaketh the **one will** to all goodness; and whilst it doth so, hath no capacity for the light and Spirit of God. The necessity, therefore, of the spirit of love is what God Himself cannot dispense with in the creature, no more than He can deny Himself, or act contrary to His own holy being. But as it was His will to all goodness that brought forth angels, and the spirits of men, so He can will nothing in their existence, but that **they should live and work, and manifest that same spirit of love and goodness which brought them into being.** Every thing, therefore, but the will and life of goodness, is an apostasy in the creature, and is rebellion against the whole nature of God.

There is no peace, nor ever can be, for the soul of

man, but in the purity and perfection of its first created nature; nor can it have its purity and perfection in any other way than in and by the spirit of love. For as love is the God that created all things, so love is the purity, the perfection, and blessing of all created things; and nothing can live in God but as it lives in love.

5. Self crucifies Christ.

Look at every vice, pain, and disorder in human nature; it is in itself nothing else but the spirit of the creature turned from the universality of love to some self-seeking or own will in created things. So that love alone is, and only can be, the cure of every evil; and he that lives in the purity of love is risen out of the power of evil, into the freedom of the one spirit of heaven. The schools have given us very accurate definitions of every vice, whether it be covetousness, pride, wrath, envy, etc., and shown us how to conceive them as notionally distinguished from one another. But the Christian has a much shorter way of knowing their nature and power, and what they all are, and do, in and to himself. For, call them by what names you will, or distinguish them with ever so much exactness, they are all, separately and jointly, just that same one thing, and all do that same one work, as the scribes, the Pharisees, hypocrites, and rabble of the Jews, who crucified Christ, were all but one and the same thing, and all did one and the same work, however different they were in outward names. If you would therefore have a true sense of the nature and power of pride, wrath, covetousness, envy, etc., they are in their whole nature nothing else but the murderers and crucifiers of the true Christ of God. Not as the high priests did many hundred years ago, nailing His outward humanity to an outward cross, but crucifying afresh the Son of God, the holy Immanuel, who is the Christ that every man crucifies as often as he gives way to wrath, pride, envy, or covetousness, etc. For every temper or passion that is contrary to the new birth of Christ, and keeps the holy Immanuel from coming to life in the soul, is, in the strictest truth of the words, a murderer and killer of the Lord of life. And where pride, and envy, and hatred, etc., are suffered to live, there the same thing is done as when Christ was killed and Barabbas was saved alive. The Christ of God was not then first crucified when the Jews brought Him to the cross; but Adam and Eve were His first real murderers; for the death which happened to them in the day that they did eat of the earthly tree was the death of the Christ of God, or the divine life in their souls.

6. Of Christ our Redeemer.

Christ had never come into the world as a second Adam to redeem it had He not been originally the life, and perfection, and glory of the first Adam. And He is our atonement and reconciliation with God; because, by and through Him, brought to life in us, we are set again in that first state of holiness, and have Christ again in us, as our first father had at his creation. For had not Christ been our first Father, as a birth of life in Him, Adam had been created a mere child of wrath, in the same impurity of nature, in the same enmity with God, and in the same want of an atoning Saviour, as we are at this day.

For God can have no delight or union with any creature, but because His well-beloved Son, the express image of His person, is found in it.

This is as true of all unfallen as of all fallen creatures; the one are redeemed, and the other want no redemption, only through the life of Christ dwelling in them. For as the Word, or Son of God, is the Creator of all things, and by Him every thing is made that was made, so every thing that is good and holy in unfallen angels is as much through His living and dwelling in them, as every thing that is good and holy in redeemed man is through Him. And He is just as much the Preserver, the Strength, and Glory, and Life of all the thrones and principalities of heaven, as He is the Righteousness, the Peace, and Redemption of fallen man.

This Christ of God hath many names in Scripture; but they all mean only this, that He is, and alone can be, the light, and life, and holiness of every creature that is holy, whether in heaven or on earth. Wherever Christ is not, there is the wrath of nature, or nature left to itself, and its own tormenting strength of life, to feel nothing in itself but the vain, restless contrariety of its own working properties. This is the one only origin of hell, and every kind of curse and misery in the creature. It is nature without the Christ of God, or the spirit of love, ruling over it. And here you may observe, that wrath has in itself the nature of hell; and that it can have no beginning or power in any creature, but so far as it has lost the Christ of God. And when Christ is everywhere, wrath and hatred will be nowhere. Whenever, therefore, you willingly indulge wrath, or let your mind work in hatred, you not only work without Christ, but you resist Him, and withstand His redeeming power over you; you do in reality what those Jews did when they said, "We will not have this Man to reign over us." For Christ never was, nor can be, in any creature, but purely as a spirit of love.

In all the universe of nature nothing but heaven and heavenly creatures ever had, or could have, been known, had every created will continued in that state in which it came forth out of and from God. For God can will nothing in the life of the creature but a creaturely manifestation of His own goodness, happiness, and perfection. And therefore, where this is wanting, the fact is certain that the creature hath changed and lost its first state that it had from God.

7. Of Purification.

Every son of fallen Adam is under the necessity of working and striving after something that he neither is nor hath; because the life of man has lost its first unity and purity, and therefore must be in a working strife, till all contrariety and impurity is separated from it, and it finds its first state in God.

Purification, therefore, is the one thing necessary, and nothing will do in the stead of it. But man is not purified till every earthly, wrathful, sensual, selfish, partial, self-willing temper is taken from him. He is not dying to himself till he is dying to these tempers; and he is not alive in God till he is dead to them. For he wants purification only because he has these tempers; and therefore he has not the purification which he wants till they are all separated from him. It is the purity and perfection of the divine nature that must be brought again into him; because in that

purity and **perfection** he came forth from God, and could have no less, as he was a child of God, that was to be blessed by a life in Him, and from Him. For nothing impure or imperfect in its will and working can have any union with God; nor are you to think that these words, the purity and perfection of God, are too high to be used on this occasion; for they only mean that the will of the creature, as an offspring of the divine will, must will and work with the will of God, for then it stands and lives truly and really in the **purity** and **perfection** of God; and whatever does not thus is at enmity with God, and cannot have any union of life and happiness with Him, and in Him.

8. The Spirit of Love the Universal Good.

Now, **nothing wills and works with God** but the spirit of love; because nothing else works in God Himself. The Almighty brought forth all nature for this only end, that boundless love might have its infinity of height and depth to dwell and work in; and all the striving and working properties of nature are only to give essence and substance, life and strength, to the invisible hidden spirit of love, that it may come forth into outward activity, and manifest its blessed powers; that creatures born in the strength, and out of the powers of nature, might communicate the spirit of love and goodness, give and receive mutual delight and joy to and from one another. All below this state of love is a fall from the one life of God, and the only life in which the God of love can dwell. **Partiality, self, mine, thine,** etc., are tempers that can only belong to creatures that have lost the power, presence, and spirit of the **universal good.** They can have no place in heaven, nor can be anywhere, but because heaven is lost. Think not, therefore, that the spirit of pure, universal love, which is the one purity and perfection of heaven, and all heavenly natures, has been, or can be, carried too high, or its absolute necessity too much asserted. For it admits of no degrees of higher or lower, and is not in being till it is absolutely pure and unmixed, no more than a line can be straight till it is absolutely free from all crookedness.

9. Love is of God.

To return to our chief subject: The sum of all that has been said is this: All evil, be it what it will, all misery of every kind, is in its birth, working, and extent nothing else but nature left to itself, and under the divided workings of its own hunger, wrath, and contrariety; and therefore no possibility for the natural, earthly man to escape eternal hunger, wrath, and contrariety, but solely in the way as the gospel teacheth, by denying and dying to self. On the other hand, all the goodness and perfection, all the happiness, glory, and joy that any intelligent, divine creature can be possessed of, is, and can be, from nothing else but the invisible, uncreated light and Spirit of God manifesting itself in the properties of the creaturely life, filling, blessing, and uniting them all in **one love**, and joy of life.

And thus again: no possibility of man's attaining to any heavenly perfection and happiness, but only in the way of the gospel, by the union of the divine and human nature, by man's being born again from above, of the **Word and Spirit** of God. There is no possibility of any other way, because there is nothing can possibly change the first properties of life into an heavenly state, but the presence, and working power, of the Deity united with and working in them. And therefore the "Word was made flesh," and must of all necessity be made flesh, if man is to have an heavenly nature.

Now, as all evil, sin, and misery have no beginning, nor power of working, but in the manifestation of nature in its divided, contrary properties; so it is certain that man has nothing to turn to, seek, or aspire after, but the lost spirit of love. And therefore it is that God only can be his Redeemer; because God only is love; and love can be nowhere else but in God, and where God dwelleth and worketh.

10. The Spirit of Love not a Notion, but a Nature.

Now, the difficulty which you find in attaining to this purity and universality of the spirit of love, is because you seek for it, as I once told you, in the way of reasoning; you would be possessed of it only from a **rational** conviction of the fitness and amiableness of it. And as this clear idea does not put you immediately into the real possession of it, your reason begins to waver, and suggests to you that it may be only a fine notion, that has no ground but in the power of imagination. But this, sir, is all your own error, and as contrary to nature as if you would have your eyes do that which only your hands or feet can do for you. The spirit of love is **a spirit of nature and life**; and all the operations of nature and life are according to the working powers of nature; and every growth and degree of life can only arise in **its own** time and place from its proper cause, and as the genuine effect of it. Nature and life do nothing by chance, or accidentally, but every thing in one uniform way. Fire, air, and light do not proceed sometimes from one thing and sometimes from another; but, wherever they are, they are always born in the same manner, and from the same working in the properties of nature. So, in like manner, love is an immutable birth, always proceeding from the same cause, and cannot be in existence till its own true parents have brought it forth.

How unreasonable would it be to begin to doubt whether strength and health of body were real things, or possible to be had, because you could not by the power of your reason take possession of them! Yet this is as well as to suspect the purity and perfection of love to be only a notion, because your reason cannot bring forth its birth in your soul. For reason has no more power of altering the life and properties of the soul than of altering the life and properties of the body. That, and that only, can cast devils and evil spirits out of the soul, that can say to the storm, " Be still," and to the leper, " Be thou clean."

The birth of love is a form or state of life. Reason can no more alter or exalt any one property of life in the soul, and bring it into its perfect state, than it can add one cubit to the stature of the body. The perfection of every life is no way possible to be had, but as every flower comes to its perfection, viz. from its own seed and root, and the various degrees of transmutation, which must be gone through before the flower is found. It is strictly thus with the perfection of the soul; all its properties of life must have

their true natural birth and growth from one another.
The first, as its seed and root, must have their natural
change into an higher state; must, like the seed of
the flower, pass through death into life, and be blessed
with the fire and light and spirit of heaven, in their
passage to it; just as the seed passes through death
into life blessed by the fire and light and air of this
world, till it reaches its last perfection, and becomes a
beautiful, sweet-smelling flower. And to think that
the soul can attain its perfection any other way than
by the change and exaltation of its first properties of
life, just as the seed has its first properties changed
and exalted till it comes to have its flower, is a total
ignorance of the nature of things.

11. The Birth of Love.

Hold it, therefore, for a certain truth, that you can
have no good come into your soul, but only by the one
way of a birth from above, from the entrance of the
Deity into the properties of your own soulish life.
Nature must be set right, its properties must enter
into the process of a new birth, it must work to
the production of light, before the spirit of love can
have a birth in it. For love is delight, and delight
cannot arise in any creature till its nature is in a
delightful state, or is possessed of that in which it
must rejoice.

And this is the reason why God must become man
it is because a birth of the Deity must be found in the
soul, giving to nature all that it wants, or the soul
can never find itself in a delightful state, and only
working with the spirit of love. For whilst the soul
has only its natural life, it can only be in such a state

as nature, without God, is in, viz. a mere hunger, want, contrariety, and strife for it knows not what.

Hence it is, that that which is called the wisdom, the honour, the honesty, and the religion of the natural man, often does as much hurt to himself and others, as his pride, ambition, self-love, envy, or revenge; and are subject to the same humour and caprice; it is because nature is no better in one motion than in another, nor can be so, till **something supernatural** is come into it.

We often charge men, both in Church and State, with changing their principles; but the charge is too hasty; for no man ever did, or can, change his principles, but by a birth from above. The natural, called in Scripture the old man, is steadily the same in heart and spirit, in every thing he does, whatever variety of names may be given to his actions. For **self** can have no motion but what is **selfish** which way soever it goes, or whatever it does, either in Church or State. And be assured of this, that **nature** in every man, whether he be learned or unlearned, is this **very self,** and can be nothing else, till a birth of the Deity is brought forth in it. There is therefore no possibility of having the spirit of love, or any divine goodness, from any power of nature or working of reason. It can only be had in its own time and place; and its time and place is nowhere but where nature is overcome by a **birth of the life of God** in the properties of the soul. And thus you see the infallible truth and absolute necessity of Christian redemption; it is the most demonstrable thing in all nature.

The Deity must become man, take a birth in the fallen nature, be united to it, become the life of it, or the natural man must of all necessity be for ever and ever in the hell of his own hunger, anguish, contrariety, and self-torment; and all for this plain reason, because nature is, and can be, nothing else but this variety of self-torment till the Deity is manifested and dwelling in it.

12. Dying to Self the only Way to the Life of God.

And now, sir, you see also the absolute necessity of the gospel doctrine of the cross, viz. of dying to self, as the one only way to life in God. This cross, or dying to self, is the one morality that does man any good. Fancy has as many rules as you will, of modelling the moral behaviour of man; they all do nothing, because they leave nature still alive, and therefore can only help a man to a feigned, hypocritical art of concealing his own inward evil, and seeming to be not under its power. And the reason why it must be so is plain: it is because nature is not possible to be reformed; it is immutable in its workings, and must be always as it is, and never any better, or worse, than its own untaught workings are. It can no more change from evil to good than darkness can work itself into light. The one work, therefore, of morality is the one doctrine of the cross, viz. to resist and deny nature, that **a supernatural power,** or divine goodness, may take possession of it, and bring a new light into it.

In a word, there are, in all the possibility of things, but two states, or forms of life; the one is nature, and the other is God manifested in nature; and as God and nature are both within you, so you have it in your power to live and work with which you will, but are under a necessity of doing either the one or the other. There is no standing still; life goes on, and is always bringing forth its realities, which way soever it goeth.

In a word, goodness is only a sound, and virtue a mere strife of natural passions, till the spirit of love is the breath of everything that lives and moves in the heart. For love is the one only blessing, and goodness, and God of nature; and you have no true religion, are no worshipper of the one true God, but in and by that spirit of love which is God Himself living and working in you.

But here I take off my pen, and shall leave the remaining part of your objection to another opportunity. I am, etc.

King's Cliff, *June* 16, 1752.

THE SPIRIT OF LOVE

SECOND PART

THE SPIRIT OF LOVE

SECOND PART

THE FIRST DIALOGUE

BETWEEN

Theogenes, Eusebius, and Theophilus

---

1. Of the Divine Love.

Theogenes.

DEAR THEOPHILUS, this gentleman is Eusebius, a very valuable and worthy curate in my neighbourhood; he would not let me wait any longer for your second letter on the Spirit of Love, nor be content till I consented to our making you this visit. And indeed we are both on the same errand, and in equal impatience to have your full answer to that part of my objection which you reserved for a second letter.

Theophilus.—My heart embraces you both with the greatest affection, and I am much pleased at the occasion of your coming, which calls me to the most delightful subject in the world, to help both you and myself to rejoice in that adorable Deity, whose infinite being is an infinity of mere love, an unbeginning, never-ceasing, and for ever overflowing ocean of meekness, sweetness, delight, blessing, goodness, patience, and mercy; and all this, as so many blessed streams breaking out of the abyss of universal love. Father, Son, and Holy Ghost, a triune infinity of love and goodness, for ever and ever, giving forth nothing but the same gifts of light and love, of blessing and joy, whether before or after the fall, either of angels or men.

2. Nature only Exists to manifest the Goodness of God.

Look at all nature, through all its height and depth, in all its variety of working powers, it is what it is for this only end, that the hidden riches, the invisible powers, blessings, glory, and love of the unsearchable God may become visible, sensible, and manifest in it and by it.

Look at all the variety of creatures, they are what they are for this only end, that in their infinite variety, degrees, and capacities they may be as so many speaking figures, living forms of the manifold riches and powers of nature, as so many sounds and voices, preachers and trumpets, giving glory, and praise, and thanksgiving to that Deity of love, which gives life to all nature and creature.

For every creature of unfallen nature, call it by what name you will, has its form, and power, and state, and place in nature for no other end but to open and enjoy, to manifest and rejoice in some share of the love, and happiness, and goodness of the Deity, as springing forth in the boundless height and depth of nature.

Now this is the one will and work of God, in and

through all nature and creature. From eternity to eternity He can will and intend nothing towards them, in them, or by them, but the communication of various degrees of His own love, goodness, and happiness to them, according to their state, and place, and capacity in nature. This is God's unchangeable disposition towards the creature; He can be nothing else but all goodness towards it, because He can be nothing towards the creature but that which He is, and was, and ever shall be in Himself.

3. God is an Immutable Will to all Goodness.

Theogenes.—Indeed, Theophilus, both Eusebius and myself find ourselves incapable of thinking any otherwise of God than as the one only good, or, as you express it, an eternal immutable will to all goodness, and which can will nothing else to all eternity, but to communicate good, and blessing, and happiness, and perfection to every life, according to its capacity to receive it.

Had I an hundred lives, I could with more ease part with them all, by suffering an hundred deaths, than give up this lovely idea of God.

For to know that love alone was the beginning of nature and creature, that nothing but love encompasses the whole universe of things, that the governing hand that overrules all, the watchful eye that sees through all, is nothing but omnipotent and omniscient love, using an infinity of wisdom to raise all that is fallen in nature, to save every misguided creature from the miserable works of its own hands, and make happiness and glory the perpetual inheritance of all the creation, is a reflection that must be quite ravishing to every

intelligent creature that is sensible of it. Thus to
think of God, of providence, and eternity, while we
are in this valley and shadow of death, is to have a
real foretaste of the blessings of the world to come.

4. Of the Twofold Life of the Creature.

Theophilus.—To inquire or search into the origin of
wrath, is the same thing as to search into the origin
of evil and sin: for wrath and evil are but two words
for one and the same thing.

The creature can have no beginning or sensibility
of wrath in itself, but by losing the living power, the
living presence, and governing operation of the Spirit
of God within it; or, in other words, by its losing that
heavenly state of existence in God, and influence from
Him, which it had at its creation.

Now no intelligent creature, whether angel or man,
can be good and happy, but by partaking of, or having
in itself, a twofold life. Hence so much is said in the
Scripture of an inward and outward, an old and a new
man.—For there could be no foundation for this distinction, but because every intelligent creature, created
to be good and happy, must of all necessity have a
twofold life in it, or it cannot possibly be capable of
goodness and happiness, nor can it possibly lose its
goodness and happiness, or feel the least want of them,
but by its breaking the union of this twofold life in
itself. Hence so much is said in the Scripture of the
quickening, raising, and reviving the inward new man,
of the new birth from above, of Christ being formed
in us, as the one only redemption and salvation of the
soul. Hence also the fall of Adam was said to be a
death, that he died the day of his sin, though he lived

so many hundred years after it; it was because his sin broke the union of his twofold life, and put an end to the heavenly part of it, and left only one life, the life of this bestial, earthly world in him.

Now there is, in the nature of the thing, an absolute necessity of this twofold life in every creature that is to be good and happy; and the twofold life is this, it must have the life of nature and the life of God in it. It cannot be a creature, and intelligent, but by having the life and properties of nature; that is, by finding itself to be a life of various sensibilities, that hath a power of understanding, willing, and desiring : this is its creaturely life, which, by the creating power of God, it hath in and from nature.

Now this is all the life that is or can be creaturely, or be a creature's natural, own life; and all this creaturely natural life, with all its various powers and sensibilities, is only a life of various appetites, hungers, and wants, and cannot possibly be anything else. God Himself cannot make a creature to be in itself, or as to its own nature, any thing else but a state of emptiness, of want, of appetite, etc. He cannot make it to be good and happy, in and from its natural state; this is as impossible, as for God to cease to be the one only good. The highest life, therefore, that is natural and creaturely, can go no higher than this; it can only be a bare capacity for goodness and happiness, and cannot possibly be a good and happy life, but by the life of God dwelling in and in union with it. And this is the twofold life, that of all necessity must be united in every good, and perfect, and happy creature.

See here the greatest of all demonstrations of the absolute necessity of the gospel redemption and salvation, and all proved from the nature of the thing. There can be no goodness and happiness for any intelligent creature, but in and by this twofold life; and therefore the union of the divine and human life, or the Son of God incarnate in man, to make man again a partaker of the divine nature, is the one only possible salvation for all the sons of fallen Adam; that is, of Adam dead to, or fallen from, his first union with the divine life.

5. Of the Folly of Deism.

Deism therefore, or a religion of nature, pretending to make man good and happy without Christ, or the Son of God entering into union with the human nature, is the greatest of all absurdities. It is as contrary to the nature and possibilities of things, as for mere emptiness to be its own fulness, mere hunger to be its own food, and mere want to be its possession of all things. For nature and creature, without the Christ of God or the divine life in union with it, is and can be nothing else but this mere emptiness, hunger, and want of all that which can alone make it good and happy. For God Himself, as I said, cannot make any creature to be good and happy by any thing that is in its own created nature; and however high or noble any creature is supposed to be created, its height and nobility can consist in nothing but its higher capacity and fitness to receive a higher union with the divine life, and also a higher and more wretched misery when left to itself, as is manifest by the hellish state of the fallen angels. Their high and exalted nature was only an enlarged capacity for the divine life; and therefore, when this life was lost, their whole created nature was nothing else but the height of rage and hellish distraction.

A plain demonstration that there can be no happiness, blessing, and goodness for any creature in heaven or on earth, but by having, as the gospel saith, Jesus Christ made unto it wisdom, righteousness, sanctification, and peace with God.

6. Of the Twofold Life of Man.

And the reason is this : it is because goodness and happiness are absolutely inseparable from God, and can be nowhere but in God. And, on the other hand, emptiness, want, insufficiency, etc., are absolutely inseparable from the creature, as such ; its whole nature cannot possibly be any thing else, be it what or where it will, an angel in heaven, or a man on earth ; it is and must be in its whole creaturely nature and capacity a mere hunger and emptiness, etc. And therefore all that we know of God, and all that we know of the creature, fully proves that the life of God in union with the creaturely life (which is the gospel salvation) is the one only possibility of goodness and happiness in any creature, whether in heaven or on earth.

Hence also it is enough certain, that this twofold life must have been the original state of every intelligent creature, at its first coming forth from God. It could not be brought forth by God, to have only a creaturely life of nature, and be left to that ; for that would be creating it under a necessity of being in misery, in want, in wrath, and all painful sensibilities. A thing more unworthy of God, and more impossible for Him to do, than to create numberless earthly animals under a necessity of being perpetually pained with hunger and thirst, without any possibility of finding any thing to eat or to drink.

For no creaturely life can, in itself, be any higher or better than a state of want, or a seeking for some thing that cannot be found in itself, and therefore, as sure as God is good, as sure as He would have intelligent beings live a life of goodness and happiness, so sure is it that such beings must of all necessity, in their first existence, have been blessed with a twofold life, viz. the life of God dwelling in, and united with, the life of nature or created life.

Eusebius.—What an important matter have you here proved in the necessity and certainty of this twofold life in every intelligent being that is to be good and happy. For this great truth opens and asserts the certain and substantial ground of the spiritual life, and shows that all salvation is and can be nothing else, but the **manifestation** of the life of God in the soul. How clearly does this give the solid distinction between inward holiness and all outward, creaturely practices. All that God has done for man by any particular dispensations, whether by the law, or the prophets, by the Scriptures, or ordinances of the Church, are only as helps to an holiness which they cannot give, but are only suited to the death and darkness of the earthly, creaturely life, to turn it from itself, from its own workings, and awaken in it a faith and hope, a hunger and thirst, after that first union with the life of the Deity, which was lost in the fall of the first father of mankind.

7. Of the Immediate Operation of the Deity in the Life of the Creature.

Theophilus.—How unreasonable is it to call perpetual inspiration fanaticism and enthusiasm, when there cannot be the least degree of goodness or happiness in any intelligent being, but what is in its whole nature, merely and truly the breathing, the life, and the operation of God in the life of the creature? For if goodness can only be in God, if it cannot exist separate from Him, if He can only bless and sanctify, not by a creaturely gift, but by Himself becoming the blessing and sanctification of the creature, then it is the highest degree of blindness to look for any goodness and happiness from anything but the immediate indwelling, union, and operation of the Deity in the life of the creature. Perpetual inspiration, therefore, is in the nature of the thing as necessary to a life of goodness, holiness, and happiness, as the perpetual respiration of the air is necessary to animal life.

For the life of the creature, whilst only creaturely, and possessing nothing but itself, is hell; that is, it is all pain, and want, and distress. Now nothing in the nature of the thing can make the least alteration in this creaturely life, nothing can help it to be in light and love, in peace and goodness, but the union of God with it, and the life of God working in it, because nothing but God is light, and love, and heavenly goodness. And therefore, where the life of God is not become the life and goodness of the creature, there the creature cannot have the least degree of goodness in it.

8. Of the Need of the Perpetual Operation of the Spirit of God within us.

What a mistake is it therefore to confine inspiration to particular times and occasions, to prophets and apostles, and extraordinary messengers of God! and to call it enthusiasm, when the common Christian looks and trusts to be continually led and inspired by the Spirit of God. For though all are not called to be prophets or apostles, yet all are called to be holy, as He who hath called them is holy, "to be perfect as their heavenly Father is perfect, to be like-minded with Christ," to will only as God wills, to do all to His honour and glory, to renounce the spirit of this world, to have their conversation in heaven, to set their affections on things above, to love God with all their heart, soul, and spirit, and their neighbour as themselves.

Behold a work as great, as divine, and supernatural, as that of a prophet and an apostle. But to suppose that we ought, and may always be in this spirit of holiness, and yet are not, and ought not to be always moved and led by the breath and spirit of God within us, is to suppose that there is a holiness and goodness which comes not from God; which is no better than supposing that there may be true prophets and apostles who have not their truth from God.

Now the holiness of the common Christian is not an occasional thing, that begins and ends, or is only for such a time, or place, or action, but is the holiness of that which is always alive and stirring in us, namely, of our thoughts, wills, desires, and affections. If, therefore, these are always alive in us, always driving or governing our lives, if we can have no holiness or goodness but as this life of thought, will, and affection works in us, if we are all called to this inward holiness and goodness, then a **perpetual, always existing operation of the Spirit of God within us** is absolutely necessary. For we cannot be inwardly led and governed by a spirit of goodness, but by being governed by the **Spirit of God Himself.** For the Spirit of God and the spirit of goodness are not two spirits, nor can we be said to have any more of the one than we have of the other.

Now if our thoughts, wills, and affections need only be now and then holy and good, then, indeed, the moving and breathing Spirit of God need only now and then govern us. But if our thoughts and affections are to be **always holy and good,** then the holy and good Spirit of God is to be **always operating** as a principle of life within us.

The Scripture saith, "We are not sufficient of ourselves to think a good thought." If so, then we cannot be chargeable with not thinking and willing that which is good, but upon this supposition, that there is always a supernatural power within us, ready and able to help us to the good which we cannot have from ourselves.

The difference then of a good and a bad man does not lie in this, that the one wills that which is good, and the other does not; but solely in this, that the one concurs with the living, inspiring Spirit of God within him, and the other resists it, and is and can be only chargeable with evil because he resists it

Therefore whether you consider that which is good or bad in a man, they equally prove the perpetual indwelling and operation of the Spirit of God within us, since we can only be bad by resisting, as we are good by yielding to, the Spirit of God; both which equally suppose a perpetual operation of the Spirit of God within us.

9. The Teaching of the Established Church on Perpetual Inspiration.

Eusebius.—How firmly our Established Church adheres to this doctrine of the necessity of the perpetual operation of the Holy Spirit, as the one only source and possibility of any degree of divine light, wisdom, virtue, and goodness in the soul of man, how earnestly she wills and requires all her members to live in the most open profession of it, and in the highest conformity to it, may be seen by many such prayers as these in her common, ordinary, public service.

O God, forasmuch as without Thee we are not able to please Thee, grant that Thy Holy Spirit may in all things direct and rule our hearts.

Again, We pray Thee that Thy grace may always prevent and follow us, and make us continually to be given to all good works.

Again, Grant to us, Lord, we beseech Thee, the spirit to think and do always such things as be rightful, that we, who cannot do any thing that is good without Thee, may, by Thee, be enabled to live according to Thy will.

Again, Because the frailty of man, without Thee, cannot but fall, keep us ever, by Thy help, from all things hurtful, and lead us to all things profitable to our salvation, etc.

Again, O God, from whom all good things do come,
grant to us Thy humble servants, that by Thy holy
inspiration we may think those things that be good.,
and by Thy merciful guiding may perform the same.

But now the true ground of all this doctrine of the
necessity of the perpetual guidance and operation of
the Holy Spirit lies in what has been said above, of
the necessity of a twofold life in every intelligent
creature that is to be good and happy. For if the
creaturely life, whilst alone or left to itself, can only
be want, misery, and distress, if it cannot possibly
have any goodness or happiness in it, till the life of
God is in union with it, as one life, then every thing
that you read in the Scripture of the Spirit of God,
as the only principle of goodness, opens itself to you,
as a most certain and blessed truth, about which you
can have no doubt.

10. Of the Seed of Heaven bred in every Man.

Theophilus.—Let me only add, Eusebius, to what you
have said, that from this absolute necessity of a twofold
life in every creature that is to be good and happy,
we may, in a still greater clearness, see the certainty
of that which we have so often spoken of at other
times, namely, that the inspoken word in Paradise,
the bruiser of the serpent, the seed of the woman, the
Immanuel, the holy Jesus (for they all mean the same
thing), is and was the only possible ground of salvation
for fallen man. For if the twofold life is necessary,
and man could not be restored to goodness and happiness but by the restored union of this twofold life into
its first state, then there was an absolute necessity,

in the nature of the thing, that every son of Adam should have such a **seed of heaven** in the birth of his life, as could, by the mediation of Christ, be raised into a birth and growth of the first perfect man. This is the one original power of salvation, without which no external dispensation could have done any thing towards raising the fallen state of man. For nothing could be raised but what there was to be raised, nor life be given to any thing but to that which was capable of life. Unless, therefore, there had been a **seed of life,** or a smothered spark of heaven in the soul of man, which wanted to come to the birth, there had been no possibility for any dispensation of God to bring forth a birth of heaven in fallen man.

The faith of the first patriarchs could not have been in being, Moses and the prophets had come in vain, had not the Christ of God laid in a state of **hiddenness** in every son of man. For **faith,** which is a will and hunger after God, could not have begun to be, or have any life in man, but because there was something of the divine nature **existing** and hid in man. For nothing can have any longing desire but after its own likeness, nor could any thing be made to desire God, but that which came from Him, and had the nature of Him.

The whole mediatorial office of Christ, from His birth to His sitting down in power at the right hand of God, was only for this end, to help man to a life that was fallen into death and insensibility in him. And therefore His mediatorial power was to manifest itself **by way of a new birth.** In the nature of the thing nothing else was to be done, and Christ had no other way to proceed, and that for this plain reason, because life was the thing that was lost, and life, wherever it is, must be raised by a birth, and every birth must and can only come from its own seed.

But if Christ was to raise a new life like His own in every man, then every man must have had, originally, in the inmost spirit of his life, a seed of Christ, or Christ, as a seed of heaven, lying there as in a state of **insensibility or death,** out of which it could not arise but by the mediatorial power of Christ, who, as a second Adam, was to regenerate that birth of His own life which was lost in all the natural sons of Adam the first.

But unless there was this **seed of Christ** or spark of heaven **hidden** in the soul, not the least beginning of man's salvation, or of Christ's mediatorial office, could be made. For what could begin to deny self, if there was not something in man **different** from self ? What could begin to have **hope** and **faith** and desire of an heavenly life, if there was not **something of heaven hidden** in his soul, and lying therein as in a state of inactivity and death, till raised by the mediation of Christ into its first perfection of life, and set again in its true dominion over flesh and blood.

11. The Mystery of the Inward Life.

Eusebius.—You have, Theophilus, sufficiently proved the certainty and necessity of this matter. But I should be glad if you knew how to help me to some more distinct idea and conception of it.

Theophilus.—An idea is not the thing to be here sought for, it **would rather hinder than help your true knowledge of it.** But perhaps the following similitude may be of some use to you.

The ten commandments, when written by God on tables of stone and given to man, did not then first begin to belong to man, they had their existence in man, were born with him, they lay as a seed and power of goodness, hidden in the form and make of his soul, and altogether inseparable from it, before they were shown to man on tables of stone. And when they were shown to man on tables of stone, they were only an outward imitation of that which was inwardly in man, though not legible, because of that impurity of flesh and blood in which they were drowned and swallowed up. For the earthly nature having overcome the divinity that was in man, it gave commandments of its own to man, and required obedience to all the lusts of the flesh, the lust of the eyes, and the pride of life.

Hence it became necessary that God should give an outward knowledge of such commandments as were become inwardly unknown, unfelt, and, as it were, shut up in death in the soul.

But now, had not all that is in these commandments been really and antecedently in the soul, as its own birth and nature, had they not still lain therein, and, although totally suppressed, yet in such a seed or remains as could be called forth into their first living state, in vain had the tables of stone been given to man; and all outward writing or teaching of the commandments had been as useless as so many instructions given to beasts or stones. If, therefore, you can conceive how all that is good and holy in the commandments lay hid as an unfelt, inactive power or seed of goodness, till called into sensibility and stirring by laws written on tables of stone : this may help your manner of conceiving and believing how Christ, as a seed of life, or power of salvation, lies in the soul, as its **unknown, hidden treasure**, till awakened and called forth into life by the mediatorial office and process of the holy Jesus.

Again, " Thou shalt love the Lord thy God with all thy heart, with all thy soul, and with all thy strength, and thy neighbour as thyself." Now these two precepts given by the written word of God are an absolute demonstration of the first original perfection of man, and also a full and invincible proof that the same original perfection is not quite annihilated, but lies in him, as an **hidden, suppressed seed of goodness**, capable of being raised up to its first perfection. For had not this divine unity, purity, and perfection of love towards God and man been man's first natural state of life, it could have nothing to do with his present state. For had any other nature, or measure, or kind of love began in the first birth of his life, he could only have been called to that.

No creature has, or can have, a call to be above, or act above, its own nature.

Therefore, as sure as man is called to this unity, purity, and perfection of love, so sure is it that it was at first his natural, heavenly state, and still has its seed or remains within him, as his only power and possibility of rising up to it again. And therefore, all that man is called to, every degree of a new and perfect life, every future exaltation and glory he is to have from the mediation of Christ, is a full proof that the same perfection was originally his natural state, and is still in him in such a seed or remains of existence, as to admit of a perfect renewal.

And thus it is that you are to conceive of the holy

Jesus, or the **Word** of God, as the hidden treasure of every human soul, born as a seed of the **Word**, in the birth of the soul immured under flesh and blood, till as a day-star it arises in our hearts, and changes the son of an earthly Adam into a son of God.

And was not the **Word** and **Spirit** of God in us all, antecedent to any dispensation or written word of God, as a real seed of life in the birth of our own life, we could have no more fitness for the gospel redemption, than the animals of this world, which have nothing of heaven in them. And to call us to love God with all our hearts, to put on Christ, to walk according to the Spirit, if these things had not their real **nature** and **root** within us, would be as vain and useless as to make rules and orders how our eyes should smell and taste, or our ears should see.

12. The Witness of Nature to an Inward Life.

Now this mystery of an **inward life hidden** in man, as his most precious treasure, as the ground of all that can be great or good in him, and hidden only since his fall, and which only can be opened and brought forth in its first glory by Him to whom all power in heaven and on earth is given, is a truth to which almost every thing in nature bears full witness. Look where you will, nothing appears or works outwardly in any creature, or in any effect of nature, but what is all done from **its own inward invisible spirit**, not a spirit brought into it, but **its own inward spirit** which is an inward invisible mystery, till made known, or brought forth by outward appearances.

The sun in the firmament gives growth to every

thing that grows in the earth, and life to every thing that lives upon it, not by giving or imparting a life from without, but only by stirring up in every thing its **own growth** and its **own** life, which lay as in a **seed or state** of death, till helped to come out of it by the sun, which, as an emblem of the Redeemer of the spiritual world, helps every earthly thing out of its own death, into its own highest state of life.

That which we call our sensations, as seeing, hearing, feeling, tasting, and smelling, are not things brought into us from without, or given unto us by any external causes, but are only so many **inborn, secret** states of the soul, which lie in their **state of hiddenness,** till they are occasionally awakened and brought forth into sensibility by outward occurrences. And were they not antecedently in the soul, as states and forms of its own life, no outward objects could bring the soul into a sensibility of them. For nothing can have or be in any state of sensation but that which it is, and hath from itself, as its own birth. This is as certain, as that a circle hath only its own roundness.

The stinking gum gives nothing to the soul, nor brings any thing into sensibility, but that which was before in the soul; it has only a fitness to awaken and stir up **that state** of the soul, which lay dormant before, and which, when brought into sensibility, is called the sensation of bad smelling. And the odoriferous gum hath likewise but the same power, viz. a fitness to stir up that state of sensation in the soul, which is called its delightful smelling. But both these sensations are only internal states of the soul, which appear, or disappear, are found, or not found, just as occasions bring them into sensibility.

Again, the greatest artist in music can add no sound
to his instrument, nor make it give forth any other
melody, but that which lieth silently hidden in it, as
its own inward state.

13. The Outward reveals the Inward.

Look now at what you will, whether it be animate
or inanimate, all that it is, or has, or can be, it is and
has in and from itself, as its **own inward state**; and
all outward things can do no more to it than the hand
does to the instrument, make it show forth its own
inward state, either of harmony or discord.

It is strictly thus with ourselves. Not a spark of
joy, of wrath, of envy, of love, or grief, can possibly
enter into us from without, or be caused to be in us
by any outward thing. This is as impossible, as for
the sound of metals to be put into a lump of clay.
And as no metal can possibly give forth any other or
higher sound than that which is enclosed within it,
so we, however struck, can give forth no other or
higher sound, either of loss, hatred, wrath, etc., than
that very degree which lay before shut up within us.

The natural state of our tempers has variety of
covers, under which they lie concealed at times, both
from ourselves and others; but when this or that accident happens to displace such or such a cover, then
that which lay hid under it breaks forth. And then
we vainly think that this or that outward occasion has
not shown us how we are within, but has only infused
or put into us a wrath, or grief, or envy, which is not
our **natural state**, or of our own growth, or has all that
it has from our own inward state.

But this is mere blindness and self-deceit, for it is

as impossible for the mind to have any grief, or wrath, or joy, but what it has all **from its own inward state,** as for the instrument to give forth any other harmony or discord but that which is within and from itself.

Persons, things, and outward occurrences may strike our instrument improperly and variously, but **as we are in ourselves,** such is our outward sound, whatever strikes us.

If our inward state is the renewed life of Christ within us, then every thing and occasion, let it be what it will, only makes the same life to sound forth and show itself; then if one cheek is smitten, we meekly turn the other also. But if nature is alive, and only under a religious cover, then every outward accident that shakes or disturbs this cover gives leave to that bad state, whether of grief, or wrath, or joy, that lay hid within us, to show forth itself.

But nothing at any time makes the least show or sound outwardly, but only that which lay ready within us for an outward birth, as occasion should offer.

What a miserable mistake is it, therefore, to place religious goodness in outward observances, in notions and opinions which good and bad men can equally receive and practise, and to treat the **ready real power and operation of an inward life of God in the birth of our souls** as fanaticism and enthusiasm; when not only the whole letter and spirit of Scripture, but every operation in nature and creature demonstrates that **the kingdom of heaven must be all within us,** or it never can possibly belong to us. Goodness, piety, and holiness can only be ours, **as thinking, willing, and desiring are ours, by being in us, as a power of heaven in the birth and growth of our own life.**

14. The Way of Salvation.

And now, Eusebius, how is the great controversy about religion and salvation shortened.

For since the one only work of Christ as your Redeemer is only this, to take from the earthly life of flesh and blood its usurped power, and to raise the smothered spark of heaven out of its state of death into a powerful governing life of the whole man, your one only work also, under your Redeemer, is fully known. And you have the utmost certainty **what** you are to do, **where** you are to seek, and **in what** you are to find your salvation.

15. What you are to do.

All that you have to do, or can do, is to oppose, resist, and as far as you can to renounce the evil tempers and workings of your own earthly nature. You are under the power of no other enemy, are held in no other captivity, and want no other deliverance, but from the power of your own earthly self. This is the one murderer of the divine life within you. It is your own Cain that murders your own Abel. Now every thing that your earthly nature does is under the influence of self-will, self-love, and self-seeking, whether it carries you to laudable or blameable practices, all is done in the nature and spirit of Cain, and only helps you to such goodness, as when Cain slew his brother. For every action and motion of self has the spirit of Antichrist, and murders the divine life within you.

Judge not therefore of yourself by considering how many of those things you do which divines and moralists call virtue and goodness, nor how much you abstain from those things which they call sin and vice.

But daily and hourly, in every step that you take, see to the spirit that is within you, whether it be heaven or earth that guides you. And judge every thing to be sin and Satan, in which your earthly nature, own love, or self-seeking has any share of life in you; nor think that any goodness is brought to life in you, but so far as it is an actual death to the pride, the vanity, the wrath, and selfish tempers of your fallen, earthly life.

16. Where you are to seek your Salvation.

Again, here you see where and how you are to seek your salvation, not in taking up your travelling staff, or crossing the seas to find out a new Luther or a new Calvin, to clothe yourself with their opinions. No. The oracle is at home that always and only speaks the truth to you, because nothing is your truth but that good and that evil which is yours within you. For salvation or damnation is no outward thing, that is brought into you from without, but is only that which springs up within you as the birth and state of your own life. What you are in yourself, what is doing in yourself, is all that can be either your salvation or damnation.

For all that is our good, and all that is our bad, has no place nor power but within us. Again, nothing that we do is bad, but for this reason, because it resists the power and working of God within us; and nothing that we do can be good but because it conforms to the Spirit of God within us. And therefore, as all that can be good and all that can be evil in us necessarily supposes a God **working within us**, you have the utmost certainty that God, salvation, and the kingdom of heaven are nowhere to be sought or found but within you, and that all outward religion, from the fall of man to this day, is not for itself, but merely for the sake of an **inward and divine** life, which was lost when Adam died his first death in Paradise. And therefore it may well be said that " circumcision is nothing, and uncircumcision is nothing," because nothing is wanted, and therefore nothing can be available, but the **new creature** called out of its captivity, under the death and darkness of flesh and blood, into the light, life, and perfection of its first creation.

17. In what you are to find your Salvation.

And thus also you have the fullest proof in what your salvation precisely consists. Not in any historic faith, or knowledge of any thing absent or distant from you; not in any variety of restraints, rules, and methods of practising virtues; not in any formality of opinion about faith and works, repentance, forgiveness of sins, or justification and sanctification; not in any truth or righteousness that you can have from yourself, from the best of men or books; but **wholly and solely** in the life of God, or Christ of God, quickened, and born again in you, or, in other words, in the restoration and perfect union of the first twofold life in the humanity.

18. The Kingdom of Heaven.

You know we have often spoken of eternal nature, that so sure as there is an eternal God, so sure is it that there is an eternal nature, as universal, as unlimited as God Himself, and everywhere working where God is, and therefore everywhere equally existent, as being His kingdom of heaven, or outward manifestation of the invisible riches, powers, and glories of the Deity.

And this is eternal nature, or the outbirth of the Deity, called the kingdom of heaven, viz. an infinity, or boundless opening of the properties, powers, wonders, and glories of the hidden Deity, and this not once done, but ever doing, ever standing in the same birth, for ever and ever breaking forth and springing up in new forms and openings of the abyssal Deity, in the powers of nature. And out of this ocean of manifested powers of nature, the will of the Deity, created hosts of heavenly beings, full of the heavenly wonders introduced into a participation of the infinity of God, to live in an eternal succession of heavenly sensations, to see and feel, to taste and find new forms of delight in an inexhaustible source of ever-changing and never-ceasing wonders of the divine glory.

Oh, Theogenes! What an eternity is this, out of which and for which thy eternal soul was created! What little crawling things are all that an earthly ambition can set before thee! Bear with patience for a while the rags of thy earthly nature, the veil and darkness of flesh and blood, as the lot of thy inheritance from father Adam, but think nothing worth a thought but that which will bring thee back to thy

first glory, and land thee safe in the region of
eternity.

The Deity is an infinite plenitude, or fulness of
riches and powers, in and from itself; and it is only
want and **desire** that is excluded from it, and can
have no existence in it. And here lies the true
immutable distinction between God and nature, and
shows why neither can ever be changed into the
other; it is, because God is an **universal all**; and
nature, or desire, is an **universal want,** viz. to be
filled with God.

Now, as nature can be nothing but a desire, so
nothing is in or done in any natural way, but as
desire does it; because desire is the all of nature.
And therefore there is no strength or substance, no
power or motion, no cause or effect in nature, but
what is in itself a **desire,** or the working and effect
of it.

For if nature is mere want, and has nothing in it
but a strength of want, generated from the three self-
tormenting properties of a desire; if God is all love,
joy, and happiness, an infinite plenitude of all blessings, then the limits and bounds of good and evil, of
happiness and misery, are made as visibly distinct,
and as certainly to be known, as the difference
between a circle and a straight line.

To live to desire, that is, to nature, is unavoidably
entering into the region of all evil and misery;
because nature has nothing else in it; but, on the
other hand, to die to desire, that is, to turn from
nature to God, is to be united with the infinite source
of all that is good, and blessed, and happy.

SECOND DIALOGUE.

19. Jesus Christ, in all His process, our only Salvation.

Theophilus.

TAKE this matter as it truly is in itself, viz. God is in Himself all love and goodness, therefore can be nothing else but all love and goodness towards fallen man, and that fallen man is subject to no pain or misery, either present or to come, but what is the natural, unavoidable, essential effect of his own evil and disordered nature, impossible to be altered by himself; and that the infinite, never-ceasing love of God has given Jesus Christ, in **all His process,** as the highest and only possible means that heaven and earth can afford to save man from himself, from his own evil, misery, and death, and restore to him his original divine life. When you look at this matter in this true light, then a God, all love, and an atonement for sin by Christ, to bring forth, fulfil, and restore righteousness in the creature that had lost it, has every thing in it that can make the providence of God adorable and the state of man comfortable.

The atonement of Christ is nothing else in itself but the highest, most natural, and efficacious means, through all the possibility of things, that the infinite love and wisdom of God could use to put an end to sin, and death, and hell; and restore to man his first divine state or life. I say, the most natural, efficacious means through all the possibilities of nature; for there is nothing that is supernatural, however mysterious, in the whole system of our redemption; every part of it has its ground in the

4

workings and powers of nature, and all our redemption is only nature set right, or made to be that which it ought to be.

There is nothing that is supernatural but God alone; every thing besides Him is from and subject to the state of nature: it can never rise out of it, or have any thing contrary to it. No creature can have either health or sickness, good or evil, or any state either from God or itself, but strictly according to the capacities, powers, and workings of nature.

The mystery of our redemption, though it comes from the supernatural God, has nothing in it but what is done, and to be done, within the sphere and according to the powers of nature. There is nothing supernatural in it, or belonging to it, but that supernatural love and wisdom which brought it forth, presides over it, and will direct it, till Christ, as a second Adam, has removed and extinguished all that evil which the first Adam brought into the human nature.

And **the whole process of Jesus Christ**, from His being the inspoken word, or bruiser of the serpent, given to Adam, to his birth, death, resurrection, and ascension into heaven, has all its ground and reason in this, because nothing else in all the possibilities of nature, either in heaven or on earth, could **begin, carry on**, and **totally effect** man's deliverance from the evil of his own fallen nature.

Thus is Christ the one full, sufficient atonement for the sin of the whole world, because He is the one **only natural** remedy and possible cure of all the evil that is broke forth in nature, the one **only natural** life and resurrection of all that holiness and happiness that died in Adam. And seeing all **this process of Christ** is given to the world, from the supernatural, antecedent, infinite love of God, therefore is it that the apostle saith, "God was in Christ reconciling the world to Himself." And Christ in God is nothing else in His whole nature but that same certain and natural parent of a redemption to the whole human nature, as fallen Adam was the certain and natural parent of a miserable life to every man that is descended from him. With this only difference, that from fallen Adam we are born in sin, whether we will or no, but we cannot have that new birth which Christ has all power to bring forth in us, unless the will of our heart closes with it.

But as nothing came to us from Adam, but according to the powers of nature, and because he was that which he was, with relation to us; so it is with Christ, and our redemption by Him : all the work is grounded in and proceeds according to the powers of nature, or in a way of natural efficacy or **fitness to produce its** effects; and every thing that is found in the person, character, and condition of Christ is only there as His **true and natural** qualification to do all that He came to do, in us, and for us. That is to say, Christ was made to be that which He was; He was a seed of life in our first fallen father; He lived as a blessing of promise in the patriarchs, prophets, and Israel of God; He was born as a man of a pure virgin; He did all that He did, whether as suffering, dying, conquering, rising, and ascending into heaven, only as so many things, which as **naturally,** and as truly, **according to the nature of things,** qualified Him to be the producer or quickener of a divine life in us, as the state and condition of Adam qualified him to make us the slavish children of earthly, bestial flesh and blood.

This is the comfortable doctrine of our redemption ;
nothing in God but an infinity of love and goodness
towards our fallen condition ; nothing in Christ but
that which had its **necessity** in the nature of things,
to make Him able to give and us to receive our full
salvation from Him.

20. How Christ's Sufferings save us.

All that Christ was, and did, and suffered was
infinitely prized, and highly acceptable to the love of
God, because all that Christ was, and did, and suffered
in His own person was that which gave Him full power
to be a common Father of life to all that died in
Adam.

Had Christ wanted any thing that He was, or did,
or suffered in His own person, He could not have
stood in that relation to all mankind as Adam had
done. Had He not been given to the first fallen man
as a seed of the woman, as a **light** of life, " enlighten-
ing every man that comes into the world," He could
not have had **His seed** in every man, as Adam had, nor
been as universal a Father of life, as Adam was of
death. Had He not in the fitness or fulness of time
become a man, born of a pure virgin, the first seed of
life in every man must have lain only as a seed, and
could not have come to the fulness of the birth of a
new man in Christ Jesus. For the children can have
no other state of life but that which their father first
had. And therefore Christ, as the Father of a re-
generated human race, must first stand in the fulness
of that human state, which was to be derived from
Him into all His children.

This is the absolute necessity of Christ's being all

that He was **before** He became man; a necessity arising from the nature of the thing. Because He could not possibly have had the relation of a Father to all mankind, nor any power to be a quickener of a life of heaven in them, but because He was both God in Himself, and a seed of God in all of them.

Now all that Christ was, and did, and suffered, **after** He became man, is from the same necessity founded in the nature of the thing. He suffered on no other account, but because that which He came to do in and for the human nature was, and could be, nothing else in itself but a work of sufferings and death.

A crooked line cannot become straight but by having all its crookedness given up, or taken from it. And there is but one way possible in nature for a crooked line to lose its crookedness.

Now the sufferings and death of Christ stand in this kind of necessity. He was made man for our salvation, that is, He took upon Him our fallen nature, to bring it out of its evil, **crooked** state, and set it again in that rectitude in which it was created.

Now there was no more two ways of doing this, than there are two ways of making a crooked line to become straight.

If the life of fallen nature, which Christ had taken upon Him, was to be overcome by Him, then every kind of suffering and dying that was **a giving up or departing from the life of fallen nature**, was just as necessary, in the nature of the thing, as that the line to be made straight must give up and part with every kind and degree of its own crookedness.

And therefore the sufferings and death of Christ were, in the nature of the thing, the only possible way of His acting contrary to and overcoming all the evil that was in the fallen state of man.

The apostle saith, "The Captain of our salvation was to be made perfect through sufferings." This was the ground and reason of His sufferings: had He been without them, He could not have been perfect in Himself, as a Son of man, nor the restorer of perfection in all mankind. But why so? Because His perfection as a Son of man, or the Captain of human salvation, could only consist in His acting in and with a spirit suitable to the first created state of perfect man; that is, He must in His spirit be as much above all the good and evil of this fallen world, as the first man was.

But now, He could not show that He was of this spirit, that He was above the world, that He was under no power of fallen nature, but lived in the perfection of the first created man; He could not do this but by showing that **all the good of the earthly life was renounced by Him,** and that all the evil which the world, the malice of men and devils, could bring upon Him, **could not hinder His living wholly and solely to** God, and doing His will on earth with the same fulness as angels do it in heaven.

But had there been any evil in all fallen nature, whether in life, death, or hell, that had not attacked Him with all its force, He could not have been said to have overcome it. And therefore so sure as Christ, as the Son of man, was to overcome the world, death, hell, and Satan, so sure is it that all the evils which they could possibly bring upon Him were to be felt and suffered by Him, as absolutely necessary, in the nature of the thing, to declare His perfection, and prove His superiority over them. Surely, my friend, it is now enough proved to you how a God all love towards fallen man must love, like, desire, and delight in all the sufferings of Christ, which alone could enable Him, as a Son of man, to undo and reverse all that evil which the first man had done to all his posterity.

Eusebius.—Oh, sir, in what an adorable light is this mystery now placed. Christ suffering and dying, as His same victory over death and hell, as when He rose from the dead and ascended into heaven.

Theophilus.—Now you plainly enough see wherein the infinite merits, or the availing efficacy and glorious power of the sufferings and death of Christ consists; since they were **that in and through which Christ Himself came out of the state of fallen nature** and got power to give the same victory to all His brethren of the human race.

Wonder not, therefore, that the Scriptures so frequently ascribe all our salvation to the sufferings and death of Christ, that we are continually referred to them, as the wounds and stripes by which we are healed, as the blood by which we are washed from our sins, as the price (much above gold and precious stones) by which we are bought.

It is because Christ, as suffering and dying, was nothing else but Christ conquering and overcoming all the **false good** and the **hellish evil** of the fallen state of man.

His resurrection from the grave and ascension into heaven, though great in themselves, and necessary parts of our deliverance, were yet but the consequences and genuine effects of His sufferings and death. These were, in themselves, the reality of His conquest; all His great work was done and effected in them and by them, and His resurrection and ascension was only His

entering into the possession of that which His sufferings and death had gained for Him.

Wonder not, then, that all the true followers of
Christ, the saints of every age, have so gloried in the
cross of Christ, have imputed such great things to it,
have desired nothing so much as to be partakers of it,
to live in constant union with it.   It is because His
sufferings, His death, and cross were the fulness of His
victory over all the works of the devil.   Not an evil
in flesh and blood, not a misery of life, not a chain of
death, not a power of hell and darkness, but were all
baffled, broken, and overcome **by the process of a suffering and dying Christ.**   Well, therefore, may the cross
of Christ be the glory of Christians.

21. Of Christ as the Second Adam.

Eusebius.—This matter is so solidly and fully
cleared up, that I am almost ashamed to ask you any
thing further about it.   Yet explain a little more, if
you please, how it is that the sufferings and death of
Christ gave Him power to become a **common Father** of
life to all that died in Adam ?   Or how it is that we,
by virtue of them, have victory over all the evil of our
fallen state ?

Theophilus.—I come now to answer your question,
viz. How it is that the sufferings and death of Christ
gave Him full power to become a **common Father of
life** to all those that died in Adam ?   Or how it is
that we, by virtue of them, are delivered out of all the
evils of our fallen state ?

The fall of all mankind in Adam is no supernatural event or effect, but the natural and necessary
consequence of our relation to him.   Could Adam,

at his fall into this earthly life, have absolutely overcome every power of the world, the flesh, and the devil, in the same spirit as Christ did, he had been his own redeemer, had risen out of his fall, and ascended into Paradise, and been the father of a paradisiacal offspring, just as Christ, when He had overcome them all, rose from the dead, and ascended into heaven. But Adam did not do this, because it was as impossible, in the nature of the thing, as for a beast to raise itself into an angel. If, therefore, man is to come out of his fallen state, there must be something found out that, according to the nature of things, hath power to effect it. For it can no more be done supernaturally by any thing else, than it could by Adam.

Now the matter stood thus, the seed of all mankind was in the loins of fallen Adam. This was unalterable in the nature of the thing, and therefore all mankind must come forth in his fallen state.

Neither can they ever be in any state whatever, whether earthly or heavenly, but by having an earthly man or a heavenly man for their father. For mankind, as such, must of all necessity be born of, and have that nature which it hath, from a man. And this is the true ground and absolute necessity of the one Mediator, the Man Christ Jesus. For seeing mankind, as such, must have that birth and nature which they have from man, seeing they never could have had any relation to Paradise, or any possibility of partaking of it, but because they had a paradisiacal man for their father, never could have had any relation to this earthly world, or any possibility of being born earthly, but because they had an earthly man for their father; and seeing all this must be unalterably so for ever, it

plainly follows that there was an utter impossibility
for the seed of Adam ever to come out of its fallen
state, or ever have another or better life than they had
from Adam, unless such a son of man could be brought
into existence, as had the same relation to all mankind as Adam had, was as much **in them** all as Adam
was, and had as full power, according to the **nature of
things,** to give a heavenly life to all the seed in
Adam's loins, as Adam had to bring them forth in
earthly flesh and blood.

And now, sir, that Christ was this very Son of
man, standing in the **same fulness** of relation to all
mankind as Adam did, having **His seed** as really in
them all as Adam had, and as truly and fully qualified, according to the nature of things, to be a **common**
and universal **Father of life,** as Adam was of death, to
all the human race, shall, in a word or two, be made
as plain and undeniable as that two and two are four.

The doctrine of our redemption absolutely asserts
that the **seed** of Christ was sown into the first fallen
father of mankind, called the **seed of the woman,** the
bruiser of the serpent, the engrafted word of life, called
again in the gospel "that light which lighteth every
man that cometh into the world." Therefore Christ
was in all men, in that same fulness of the relation
of a Father to all mankind, as Adam the first was.
Secondly, Christ was born of Adam's flesh and blood,
took the human nature upon Him, and therefore stood
as an human creature in the **same relation** to mankind
as Adam did. Nothing, therefore, was further wanting in Christ, to make Him as truly a natural Father
of life to all mankind as Adam was at first, but God's
appointment of Him to that end.

For as Adam could not have been the natural father of mankind but because God created and appointed him for that end, so Christ could not have been the natural Regenerator or Redeemer of an heavenly life, that was lost in all mankind, but because God had appointed and brought Him into the world for that end. Now that God did this, that Christ came into the world by divine appointment, to be the Saviour, the resurrection, and life of all mankind, is a truth as evident from Scripture, as that Adam was the first man.

And thus it appears, in the utmost degree of plainness and certainty, that Christ in His single person was, according to the nature of things, as fully qualified to be a common Redeemer as Adam was, in his single person, to be a common father of all mankind. He had His seed in all mankind, as Adam had; He had the human nature, as Adam had; and He had the same divine appointment, as Adam had. But Christ, however qualified to be our Redeemer, could not be actually such till He had gone through and done all that by which our redemption was to be effected.

Adam, however qualified, yet could not be the father of a paradisiacal offspring till he had stood out his trial, and fixed himself victorious over every thing that could make trial of him. In like manner, Christ, however qualified, could not be the Redeemer of all mankind till He had also stood out His trial, had overcome all that by which Adam was overcome, and had fixed Himself triumphantly in that Paradise which Adam had lost.

Now, as Adam's trial was, whether he would keep himself in his paradisiacal state, above and free from

all that was good and evil in this earthly world, so
Christ's trial was, whether as a Son of man, and loaded
with the infirmities of fallen Adam, sacrificed to all
that which the rage and malice of the world, hell, and
devils could possibly do to Him, whether He in the
midst of all these evils could live and die with His
spirit as contrary to them, as much above them, as
unhurt by them, as Adam should have lived in
Paradise?

And then it was that every thing which had overcome Adam was overcome by Christ, and Christ's
victory did, in the nature of the thing, as certainly
and fully open an entrance for Him and all His seed
into Paradise, as Adam's fall cast him and all his seed
into the prison and captivity of this earthly, bestial
world.

Thus is your question fully answered; viz. How
and why the sufferings and death of Christ enabled
Him to be the Author of life to all that died in
Adam? Just as the fall of Adam into this world,
under the power of sin, death, hell, and the devil,
enabled him to be the **common father of death**, that is,
was the natural, unavoidable cause of our being born
under the same captivity; just so that life, and sufferings, and death of Christ, which declared **His breaking
out from them and superiority over them**, must, in the
nature of the thing, as much enable Him to be the
common Author of life, that is, must as certainly be
the **full, natural,** efficacious cause of our inheriting life
from Him. Because, by what Christ was in Himself,
by what He was in us, by His whole state, character,
and the divine appointment, we all had that natural
union with Him, and dependence upon Him, as our

Head in the way of redemption, as we had with Adam as our head in the way of our natural birth. So that as it must be said that, because Adam fell, we must of all necessity be heirs of his fallen state; so, with the same truth, and from the same necessity of the thing, it must be said that, **because Christ our Head is risen victorious out of our fallen state,** we, as His members, and having His seed within us, must be, and are made, heirs of all His glory. Because, in all respects, we are as strictly, as intimately connected with and related to Him as the one Redeemer, as we are to Adam as the one father, of all mankind. So that Christ, by His sufferings and death, become in all of us our wisdom, our righteousness, our justification, and redemption, is the same sober and solid truth, as Adam, by his fall, become in all of us our foolishness, our impurity, our corruption, and death.

And now, my friends, look back upon all that has been said, and then tell me whether it is not sufficiently proved to you that the sufferings and death of Christ are not only consistent with the doctrine of a God all love, but are the fullest and most absolute proof of it?

Eusebius.—Indeed, Theophilus, you have so fully done for us all that we wanted to have done, that we are now ready to take leave of you. As for my part, I want to return home, to enjoy my Bible, and delight myself with reading it in this comfortable light in which you have set the whole ground and nature of our redemption. I am now in full possession of this glorious truth, that God is mere love, the most glorious truth that can possess and edify the heart of man. It drives every evil out of the soul, and gives

life to every spark of goodness that can possibly
be kindled in it. Every thing in religion is made
amiable, by being a service of love to the God of love.

Therefore, dear Theophilus, adieu: God is love, and
he that hath learnt to live in the spirit of love, hath
learnt to live and dwell in God. Love was the
beginner of all the works of God, and from eternity to
eternity, nothing can come from God but a variety
of wonders and works of love over all nature and
creature.

Theophilus.—God prosper, Eusebius, this spark of
heaven in your soul; may it, like the seraphim's coal
taken from the altar, purify your heart from all its
uncleanness. But, before you leave me, I beg one
more conversation, to be on the practical part of the
spirit of love; that so doctrine and practice, hearing
and doing, may go hand in hand.

THE THIRD DIALOGUE.

22. The Great Difference between Knowing and Having.

Eusebius.

YOU have shown great good will towards us,
Theophilus, in desiring another meeting before
we leave you. But yet I seem to myself to have no
need of that which you have proposed by this day's
conversation. For this doctrine of the spirit of love
cannot have more power over me, or be more deeply
rooted in me, than it is already. It has so gained
and got possession of my whole heart, that every thing

else must be under its dominion. I can do nothing else but love; it is my whole nature, I have no taste for any thing else. Can this matter be carried higher in practice?

Theophilus.—No higher, Eusebius. And was this the true state of your heart, you would bid fair to leave the world as Elijah did; or, like Enoch, to have said of you, that you lived wholly to love, and was not. For was there nothing but this divine love alive in you, your fallen flesh and blood would be in danger of being quite burnt up by it. What you have said of yourself, you have spoken in great sincerity, but in a total ignorance of yourself, and the true nature of the spirit of divine love. You are as yet only charmed with the sight, or rather the sound, of it; its real birth is as yet unfelt and unfound in you. Your natural complexion has a great deal of the animal meekness and softness of the lamb and the dove, your blood and spirit are of this turn; and therefore a God all love, and a religion all love, quite transport you; and you are so delighted with it, that you fancy you have nothing in you but this God and religion of love. But, my friend, bear with me, if I tell you that all this is only the good part of the spirit of this bestial world in you, and may be in any unregenerate man that is of your complexion. It is so far from being a genuine fruit of divine love, that, if it be not well looked to, it may prove a real hindrance of it, as it oftentimes does, by its appearing to be that which it is not.

You have quite forgot all that was said in the letter to you on the spirit of love, that it is a birth in the soul, that can only come forth in its proper time

and place, and from its proper causes. Now, **nothing
that is a birth can be taken in or brought into the
soul by any notional conception or delightful apprehension** of it. You may love it as much as you please,
think it the most charming thing in the world, fancy
every thing but dross and dung in comparison of it,
and yet have no more of its birth in you, than the
blind man has of that light of which he has got a
most charming notion. His blindness still continues
the same; he is at the same distance from the light,
because light can only be had by a birth of itself in
seeing eyes. It is thus with the spirit of love; it is
nowhere but where it rises up as a birth.

Eusebius.—But if I am got no farther than this,
what good have I from giving in so heartily to all
that you have said of this doctrine? And to what
end have you taken so much pains to assert and
establish it?

Theophilus.—Your error lies in this: you confound
two things, which are entirely distinct from each other.
You make no difference betwixt the **doctrine** that only
sets forth the nature, excellency, and necessity of the
spirit of love, and the **spirit of love itself;** which yet
are two things so different, that you may be quite
full of the former, and at the same time quite empty
of the latter. I have said every thing that I could
to show you the truth, excellency, and necessity of
the spirit of love: it is of infinite importance to you
to be well established in the belief of this doctrine.
But all that I have said of it is only to induce and
encourage you to buy it at its own price, and to give
all that for it which alone can purchase it. But if
you think (as you plainly do) that you have got it,

because you are so highly pleased with that which you have heard of it, you only embrace the shadow, instead of the substance, of that which you ought to have.

Eusebius.—What is the price that I must give for it?

Theophilus.—You must give up all that you are and all that you have from fallen Adam; for all that you are and have from him, is that life of flesh and blood which cannot enter into the kingdom of God.

Eusebius.—Proceed as you please to lay open all my defects, in the spirit of love; for I am earnestly desirous of being set right in so important a matter.

Theogenes.—Let me first observe to Theophilus, that I am afraid the matter is much worse with me than it is with you. For though this doctrine seems to have got all my heart, as it is a doctrine; yet I am continually thrown out of it in practice, and find myself as daily under the power of my old tempers and passions as I was before I was so full of this doctrine.

23. Two Stages in the Christian Life.

Theophilus.—You are to know, my friends, that every kind of virtue and goodness may be brought into us by two different ways. They may be taught us outwardly by men, by rules and precepts; and they may be inwardly born in us, as the genuine birth of our own renewed spirit. In the former way, as we learn them only from men, by rules and documents of instruction, they at best only change our outward behaviour, and leave our heart in its natural state, and only put our passions under a forced

5

restraint, which will occasionally break forth in spite of the dead letter of precept and doctrine. **Now this way of learning and attaining goodness, though thus imperfect, is yet absolutely necessary in the nature of the thing, and must first have its time, and place, and work in us.** Yet it is only for a time, as the law was a schoolmaster to the gospel. We must first be babes in doctrine, as well as in strength, before we can be men. But of all this outward instruction, whether from good men or the letter of Scripture, it must be said, as the apostle saith of the law, that "it maketh nothing perfect." **And yet is highly necessary in order to perfection.**

The true perfection and profitableness of the holy written word of God is fully set forth by St. Paul to Timothy: "From a child (saith he) thou hast known the Scriptures, which are able to make thee wise unto salvation, which is by faith in Christ Jesus." Now these Scriptures were the law and the prophets, for Timothy had known no other from his youth. And as they, so all other Scriptures since have no other good or benefit in them but as they lead and direct us to a salvation that is not to be had in themselves, but from faith in Christ Jesus. Their teaching is only to teach us where to seek and to find the fountain and source of all light and knowledge.

Of the law, saith the apostle, "it was a schoolmaster to Christ;" of the prophets, he saith the same. "Ye have (says he) a more sure word of prophecy; whereunto you do well that ye take heed, as unto a light that shineth in a dark place, until the day dawn, and the day star ariseth in your hearts." The same thing is to be affirmed of the letter of the New Testament;

it is but our schoolmaster unto Christ, a light like that of prophecy, to which we are to take great heed, until Christ, as the dawning of the day, or the day star, ariseth in our hearts. Nor can the thing possibly be otherwise; no instruction that comes under the form of words can do more for us than sounds and words can do; they can only direct us to something that is better than themselves, that can be the true light, life, spirit, and power of holiness in us.

Eusebius.—I cannot deny what you say, and yet it seems to me to derogate from Scripture.

Theophilus.—Would you then have me to say that the **written word** of God is that word of God which liveth and abideth for ever; that word which is the wisdom and power of God; that word which was with God, which was God, by whom all things were made; that word of God which was made flesh for the redemption of the world; that word of God, of which we must be born again; that word which "lighteth every man that cometh into the world;" that word which in Christ Jesus "is become wisdom, and righteousness, and sanctification in us;" would you have me say that all this is to be understood of the written word of God? But if this cannot possibly be, then all that I have said is granted, namely, that Jesus is alone **that Word** of God that can be the light, life, and salvation of fallen man. Or how is it possible more to exalt the letter of Scripture, than by owning it to be a true, outward, verbal direction to the one only true light and salvation of man?

Suppose you had been a true disciple of John the Baptist, whose only office was to prepare the way to Christ, how could you have more magnified his office,

or declared your fidelity to him, than by going from
his teaching to be taught by that Christ to whom he
directed you ? The Baptist was, indeed, a "burning
and a shining light," and so are the holy Scriptures;
but " he was not that light, but was sent to bear
witness of that light. That was the true light, which
lighteth every man that cometh into the world."

What a folly would it be to say that you had
undervalued the office and character of John the
Baptist, because he was not allowed to be the light
itself, but only a true witness of it, and guide to it !
Now, if you can show that the written word in the
Bible can have any other or higher office or power
than such a ministerial one as the Baptist had, I am
ready to hear you.

Eusebius.—There is no possibility of doing that.

Theophilus.—But if that is not possible to be done,
then you are come to the full proof of this point, viz.
that there are two ways of attaining knowledge, goodness, virtue, etc., the one by the ministry of outward,
verbal instruction, either by men or books, and the
other **by an inward birth** of divine light, goodness,
and virtue in our own renewed spirit; and that the
former is only in order to the latter, and of no
benefit to us, but as it carries us **farther than itself,**
to be united in heart and spirit with the light, and
word, and Spirit of God. Just as the Baptist had
been of no benefit to his disciples, unless he had been
their guide from himself to Christ.

But to come now closer to our subject in hand.

From this twofold light or teaching there necessarily arises a twofold state of virtue and goodness.
For such as the teacher or teaching is, such is the

state and manner of the goodness that can be had from it. Every effect must be according to the cause that produces it. If you learn virtue and goodness only from outward means, from men or books, you may be virtuous and good according to time, and place, and outward forms; you may do works of humility, works of love and benevolence, use times and forms of prayer; all this virtue and goodness is suitable to this kind of teaching, and may very well be had from it. But the spirit of prayer, the spirit of love, and the spirit of humility, or of any other virtue, are only to be attained by the operation of the light and Spirit of God, not outwardly teaching, but inwardly bringing forth a new-born spirit within us.

24. A Personal Application.

And now, let me tell you both that it is much to be feared that you as yet stand only under this outward teaching; your good works are only done under obedience to such rules, precepts, and doctrines as your reason assents to, but are not the fruits of a new-born spirit within you. But till you are thus renewed in the spirit of your minds, your virtues are only taught practices, and grafted upon a corrupt bottom. Every thing you do will be a mixture of good and bad; your humility will help you to pride, your charity to others will give nourishment to your own self-love, and as your prayers increase, so will the opinion of your own sanctity. Because till the heart is purified to the bottom, and has felt the axe at the root of its evil (which cannot be done by out-

ward instruction), every thing that proceeds from it
partakes of its impurity and corruption.

Now, that Theogenes is only under the law, or
outward instruction, is too plain from the complaint
that he made of himself. For, notwithstanding his
progress in the doctrine of love, he finds all the
passions of his corrupt nature still alive in him, and
himself only altered in doctrine and opinion.

The same may be well suspected of you, Eusebius,
who are so mistaken in the spirit of love that you
fancy yourself to be wholly possessed of it, from no
other ground but because you embrace it, as it were,
with open arms, and think of nothing but living
under the power of it. Whereas, if the spirit of love
was really born in you from its own seed, you would
account for its birth and power in you in quite
another manner than you have here done; you would
have known the price that you had paid for it, and
how many deaths you had suffered, before the spirit
of love came to life in you.

Eusebius.—But surely, sir, imperfect as our virtues
are, we may yet, I hope, be truly said to be in a state
of grace; and if so, we are under something more than
mere outward instruction. Besides, you very well
know that it is a principle with both of us to expect
all our goodness from the Spirit of God dwelling and
working in us. We live in faith and hope of the
divine operation; and therefore I must needs say that
your censure upon us seems to be more severe than
just.

Theophilus.—Dear Eusebius, I censure neither of
you, nor have I said one word by way of accusation.
So far from it, that I love and approve the state you

are both in. It is good and happy for Theogenes, that he feels and confesses that his natural tempers are not yet subdued by doctrine and precept. It is good and happy for you also, that you are so highly delighted with the doctrine of love, for by this means each of you have your true preparation for further advancement. And though your state has this difference, yet the same error was common to both of you. You both of you thought you had as much of the spirit of love as you could or ought to have; and therefore Theogenes wondered he had no more benefit from it; and you wondered that I should desire to lead you farther into it. And therefore, to deliver you from this error, I have desired this conference upon the practical ground of the spirit of love, that you may neither of you lose the benefit of that good state in which you stand.

Eusebius.—Pray therefore proceed as you please. For we have nothing so much at heart as to have the truth and purity of this divine love brought forth in us. For as it is the highest perfection that I adore in God, so I can neither wish nor desire any thing for myself, but to be totally governed by it. I could as willingly consent to lose all my being, as to find the power of love lost in my soul. Neither doctrine, nor mystery, nor precept has any delight for me, but as it calls forth the birth, and growth, and exercise of that Spirit, which doth all that it doth, towards God and man, under the one law of love. Whatever, therefore, you can say to me, either to increase the power, manifest the defects, or remove the impediments of divine love in my soul, will be heartily welcome to me.

25. Of the Power of Divine Love.

Theophilus.—I apprehend that you do not yet know what divine love is in itself, nor what is its nature and power in the soul of man. For divine love is perfect peace and joy, it is a freedom from all disquiet, it is all content and mere happiness; and makes every thing to rejoice in itself. Love is the Christ of God; wherever it comes, it comes as the blessing and happiness of every natural life, as the restorer of every lost perfection, a redeemer from all evil, a fulfiller of all righteousness, and a peace of God which passeth all understanding. Through all the universe of things, nothing is uneasy, unsatisfied, or restless, but because it is not governed by love, or because its nature has not reached or attained the full birth of the spirit of love. For when that is done, every hunger is satisfied, and all complaining, murmuring, accusing, resenting, revenging, and striving, are as totally suppressed and overcome, as the coldness, thickness, and horror of darkness are suppressed and overcome, by the breaking forth of the light. If you ask why the spirit of love cannot be displeased, cannot be disappointed, cannot complain, accuse, resent, or murmur, it is because divine love desires nothing but itself; it is its own good, it has all when it has itself, because nothing is good but itself and its own working; for love is God; "and he that dwelleth in God, dwelleth in love:" tell me now, Eusebius, are you thus blessed in the spirit of love?

Eusebius.—Would you have me tell you that I am an angel, and without the infirmities of human flesh and blood?

Theophilus.—No; but I would have you judge of

your state of love by these angelical tempers, and not by any fervour or heat that you find in yourself. For just so much and so far as you are freed from the folly of all earthly affections, from all disquiet, trouble, and complaint about this or that, just so much and so far is the spirit of love come to life in you. For **divine love** is a **new life** and **new nature**, and introduces you into a **new world**; it puts an end to all your former opinions, notions, and tempers; it opens new senses in you, and makes you see high to be low, and low to be high; wisdom to be foolishness, and foolishness wisdom; it makes prosperity and adversity, praise and dispraise, to be equally nothing. "When I was a child (saith the apostle), I thought as a child, I spake as a child; but when I became a man, I put away childish things." Whilst man is under the power of nature, governed only by worldly wisdom, his life (however old he may be) is quite childish; every thing about him only awakens childish thoughts and pursuits in him; all that he sees and hears, all that he desires or fears, likes, or dislikes; that which he gets, and that which he loses; that which he hath, and that which he hath not, serve only to carry him from this fiction of evil to that fiction of good, from one vanity of peace to another vanity of trouble. But when divine love is born in the soul, all childish images of good and evil are done away, and all the sensibility of them is lost, as the stars lose their visibility when the sun is risen.

26. Of Light and Darkness.

Theogenes.—That this is the true power of the spirit of divine love, I am fully convinced from my own uneasiness at finding that my natural tempers are not overcome by it. For whence could I have this trouble, but because that little dawning that I have of the spirit of love in me maketh just demands to be the one light, breath, and power of my life, and to have all that is within me overcome and governed by it. And therefore, I find, I must either silence this small voice of new risen love within me, or have no rest from complaints and self-condemnation, till my whole nature is brought into subjection to it.

Theophilus.—Most rightly judged, Theogenes; and now we are fairly brought to the one great practical point, on which all our proficiency in the spirit of love entirely depends. Namely, that all that we are, and all that we have from Adam, as fallen, must be given up, absolutely denied and resisted, if the birth of divine love is to be brought forth in us. For all that we are by nature is in full contrariety to this divine love, nor can it be otherwise; a death to itself is its only cure, and nothing else can make it subservient to good; just as darkness cannot be altered, or made better in itself, or transmuted into light, it can only be subservient to the light by being lost in it, and swallowed up by it.

Now this was the first state of man; all the natural properties of his creaturely life were hid in God, united in God, and glorified by the life of God manifested in them; just as the nature and qualities of darkness are lost and hid, when enlightened and glorified by the light. But when man fell from or died to the divine life, all the natural properties of his creaturely life, having lost their union in and with God, broke forth in their own natural division, contrariety, and war against one another; just as the darkness, when it has lost the light, must show forth its own coldness, horror, and other uncomfortable qualities.

When God said, " Let there be light, and there was light," no change happened to eternal light itself, nor did any light then begin to be; but the darkness of this world then only began to receive a power or operation of the eternal light upon it, which it had not before; or eternity then began to open some resemblance of its own glory in the dark elements and shadows of time. And thus it is that I assert the priority and glory of light, and put all darkness under its feet, as impossible to be any thing else but its footstool.

The Scripture saith that " God dwelleth in the light, to which no man can approach;" therefore the Scripture teacheth that light in itself is and must be invisible to man; that it cannot be approached or made manifest to him but in and by something that is not light. And this is all that I said, and the very same thing that I said, when I affirmed that light cannot be manifested, or have any visibility to created eyes, but in, and through, and by the darkness.

Light as it is in itself is only in the supernatural Deity; and that is the reason why no man or any created being can approach to it, or have any sensibility of it, as it is in itself. And yet no light can come into this world but that in which God dwelt before any world was created. No light can be in time, but that which was the light of eternity. If therefore the supernatural light is to manifest something of its incomprehensible glory, and make itself, in some degree, sensible and visible to the creature, this supernatural light must enter into nature, it must put on materiality.

Eusebius.—What is it, then, that you understand by the materiality of light ?

Theophilus.—No more than I understand by the materiality of the wisdom, mercy, and goodness of God, when they are made intelligible and credible to me by the materiality of paper and ink, etc. For light is as distinct from, and superior to, all that materiality in and by which it gives forth some visibility of itself; as the wisdom, mercy, and goodness of God are distinct from, and superior to, all that written materiality in and through which they are made, in some degree, intelligible and credible to human minds.

The incomprehensible Deity can make no outward revelation of His will, wisdom, and goodness, but by articulate sounds, voices, or letters written on tables of stone, or such-like materiality. Just so, the invisible, inaccessible, supernatural light can make no outward visibility of itself, but through such darkness of materiality as is capable of receiving its illumination. But as the divine will, wisdom, and goodness, when making outward revelation of themselves by the materiality of things, are not therefore material, so neither is the light material, when it outwardly reveals something of its invisible, incomprehensible splendour and glory by and through the materiality of darkness.

Sight and visibility is but one power of light, but light is all power; it is life, and every joyful sensibility of life is from it. "In Him (says the apostle) was light, and the light was the life of men." Light is all things, and nothing. It is nothing, because it is supernatural; it is all things, because every good power and perfection of every thing is from it. No joy or rejoicing in any creature, but from the power and joy of light. No meekness, benevolence, or goodness, in angel, man, or any creature, but where light is the lord of its life. Life itself begins no sooner, rises no higher, has no other glory, than as the light begins it and leads it on. Sounds have no softness, flowers and gums have no sweetness, plants and fruits have no growth, but as the mystery of light opens itself in them.

Whatever is delightful and ravishing, sublime and glorious, in spirits, minds, or bodies, either in heaven or on earth, is from the power of the supernatural light, opening its endless wonders in them. Hell has no misery, horror, or distraction, but because it has no communication with the supernatural light. And did not the supernatural light stream forth its blessings into this world, through the materiality of the sun, all outward nature would be full of the horror of hell.

And hence are all the mysteries and wonders of light, in this material system, so astonishingly great and unsearchable; it is because the natural light of this world is nothing else but the power and mystery of the supernatural light, breaking forth and opening itself, according to its omnipotence, in all the various forms of elementary darkness which constitute this temporary world.

Theogenes.—I could willingly hear you, Theophilus, on this subject till midnight, though it seems to lead us away from our proposed subject.

Theophilus.—Not so far out of the way, Theogenes, as you may imagine; for darkness and light are the two natures that are in every man, and do all that is done in him.

The Scriptures, you know, make only this division,

the works of darkness are sin, and they who walk in the light are the children of God.   Therefore light and darkness do every thing, whether good or evil, that is done in man.

Theogenes.—What is this darkness in itself, or where is it ?

Theophilus.—It is everywhere, where there is nature and creature.   For all nature, and all that is natural in the creature, is in itself nothing else but darkness, whether it be in soul or body, in heaven or on earth. And therefore, when the angels (though in heaven) had lost the supernatural light, they became imprisoned in the chains of their own natural darkness.   If you ask why nature must be darkness, it is because nature is not God, and therefore can have no light, as it is nature.   For God and light are as inseparable, as God and unity are inseparable.   Every thing, therefore, that is not God, is and can be nothing else in itself but darkness; and can do nothing but in, and under, and according to the nature and powers of darkness.

Theogenes.—What are the powers of darkness ?

Theophilus.—The powers of darkness are the workings of nature or self : for nature, darkness, and self are but three different expressions for one and the same thing.

Now every evil, wicked, wrathful, impure, unjust thought, temper, passion, or imagination, that ever stirred or moved in any creature ; every misery, discontent, distress, rage, horror, and torment that ever plagued the life of fallen man or angel, **are the very things** that you are to understand by the powers or workings of darkness, nature, or self.   For nothing is evil, wicked, or tormenting but that which nature or self doth.

Theogenes.—But if nature is thus the seat and source of all evil, if every thing that is bad is in it and from it, how can such a nature be brought forth by a God who is all goodness?

Theophilus.—Nature has all evil, and no evil, in itself. Nature, as it comes forth from God, is darkness without any evil of darkness in it; for it is not darkness without or separate from light, nor could it ever have been known to have any quality of darkness in it, had it not lost that state of light in which it came forth from God, only as a manifestation of the goodness, virtues, and glories of light. Again, it is nature, viz. a strife and contrariety of properties for this only end, that the supernatural good might thereby come into sensibility, be known, found, and felt, by its taking all the evil of strife and contrariety from them, and becoming the union, peace, and joy of them all. Nor could the evil of strife and contrariety of will ever have had a name in all the universe of nature and creature, had it all continued in that state in which it came forth from God. Lastly, it is self, viz. an own life, that so, through such an own life, the universal, incomprehensible goodness, happiness, and perfections of the Deity might be possessed as properties and qualities of an own life in creaturely finite beings.

And thus, all that is called nature, darkness, or self has not only no evil in it, but is the only true ground of all possible good.

But when the intelligent creature turns from God to self, or nature, he acts unnaturally, he turns from all that which makes nature to be good; he finds nature only as it is in itself, and without God. And then it is that nature, or self, hath all evil in it. Nothing is to be had from it, or found in it, but the work and working of every kind of evil, baseness, misery, and torment, and the utmost contrariety to God and all goodness. And thus, also, you see the plainness and certainty of our assertion, that nature, or self, hath all evil, and no evil, in it.

27. Of the True Nature of Self.

Theogenes.—I plainly enough perceive that nature, or self, without God manifested in it, is all evil and misery. But I would, if I could, more perfectly understand the precise nature of self, or what it is that makes it to be so full of evil and misery.

Theophilus.—Covetousness, envy, pride, and wrath are the four elements of self, or nature, or hell, all of them inseparable from it. And the reason why it must be thus, and cannot be otherwise, is because the natural life of the creature is brought forth for the participation of some high, supernatural good in the Creator. But it could have no fitness or possible capacity to receive such good, unless it was in itself both an extremity of want and an extremity of desire of some high good. When, therefore, this natural life is deprived of or fallen from God, it can be nothing else in itself but an extremity of want continually desiring, and an extremity of desire continually wanting. And hence it is that its whole life can be nothing else but a plague and torment of covetousness, envy, pride, and wrath, all which is precisely nature, self, or hell.

Now covetousness, pride, and envy are not three different things, but only three different names for the restless workings of one and the same will or desire, which, as it differently torments itself, takes these different names, for nothing is in any of them but the working of a restless desire; and all this because the natural life of the creature can do nothing else but work as a desire. And therefore, when fallen from God, its three first births, and which are quite inseparable from it, are covetousness, envy, and pride; it must covet, because it is a desire proceeding from want; it must envy, because it is a desire turned to self; it must assume and arrogate, because it is a desire founded on a real want of exaltation, or a higher state.

Now wrath, which is a fourth birth from these three, can have no existence till some or all of these three are contradicted, or have something done to them that is contrary to their will; and then it is that wrath is necessarily born, and not till then.

And thus you see, in the highest degree of certainty, what nature or self is as to its essential constituent parts. It is the three forementioned, inseparable properties of a desire, thrown into a fourth of wrath that can never cease, because their will can never be gratified. For these four properties generate one another, and therefore generate their own torment. They have no outward cause nor any inward power of altering themselves. And, therefore, all self, or nature, must be in this state till some supernatural good comes into it, or gets a birth in it. And, therefore, every pain or disorder in the mind or body of any intelligent creature is an undeniable proof that it is in a fallen state, and has lost that supernatural good for which it was created. So certain a truth is the fallen state of all mankind. And here lies the absolute, indispensable necessity of the one Christian redemption. Till fallen man is born again from above, till such a supernatural birth is brought forth in him, by the eternal word and Spirit of God, he can have no possible escape or deliverance from these four elements of self or hell.

Whilst man indeed lives amongst the vanities of time, his covetousness, envy, pride, and wrath may be in a tolerable state, may help him to a mixture of peace and trouble; they may have at times their gratifications as well as their torments. But when death has put an end to the vanity of all earthly cheats, the soul that is not born again of the supernatural word and Spirit of God must find itself unavoidably devoured or shut up in its own insatiable, unchangeable, self-tormenting covetousness, envy, pride, and wrath. Oh, Theogenes, that I had power from God to take those dreadful scales from the eyes of every deist, which hinder him from seeing and feeling the infinite importance of this most certain truth!

Theogenes.—God give a blessing, Theophilus, to your good prayer. And then let me tell you that you have quite satisfied my question about the nature of self. I shall never forget it, nor can I ever possibly have any doubt of the truth of it.

I now also see the full truth and certainty of what you said of the nature and power of divine love; viz. "that it is perfect peace and joy, a freedom from all disquiet, making every thing to rejoice in itself. That it is the Christ of God, and wherever it comes, it comes as the blessing and happiness of

every natural life; as the restorer of every lost
perfection; a redeemer from all evil; a fulfiller of
all righteousness; and a peace of God which passes
all understanding." So that I am now a thousand
times more than ever athirst after the spirit of love.
I am willing to sell all, and buy it; its blessing is
so great, and the want of it so dreadful a state, that
I am even afraid of lying down in my bed, till every
working power of my soul is given up to it, wholly
possessed and governed by it.

Theophilus.—You have reason for all that you say,
Theogenes, for were we truly affected with things
as they are our real good, or real evil, we should be
much more afraid of having the **serpents** of covetousness, envy, pride, and wrath well nourished and kept
alive within us, than of being shut up in a pest-house,
or cast into a dungeon of venomous beasts. On the
other hand, we should look upon the lofty eloquence
and proud virtue of a Cicero but as the blessing of
storm and tempest, when compared with the heavenly
tranquillity of that meek and lowly heart to which
our Redeemer has called us.

I said the **serpents** of covetousness, envy, pride, and
wrath, because they are alone the real, dreadful, original
serpents; and all earthly serpents are but transitory,
partial, and weak out-births of them. All evil, earthly
beasts are but short-lived images or creaturely eruptions
of that hellish disorder that is broke out from the fallen
spiritual world; and by their manifold variety, they
show us that multiplicity of evil that lies in the womb
of that abyss of dark rage which (*N.B.*) has no maker,
but the three first properties of nature, fallen from
God and working in their own darkness.

So that all evil, mischievous, ravenous, venomous beasts, though they have no life but what begins in and from this material world, and totally ends at the death of their bodies, yet have they no malignity in their earthly, temporary nature, but from those same wrathful properties of fallen nature, which live and work in our eternal fallen souls. And, therefore, though they are as different from us as time from eternity, yet, wherever we see them, we see so many infallible proofs of the fall of nature and the reality of hell. For, was there no hell broke out in spiritual nature, not only no evil beast, but no bestial life, could ever have come into existence.

But to return. I have, I hope, sufficiently opened unto you the malignant nature of that self which dwells in and makes up the **working life** of every creature that has lost its right state in God—viz. that all the evil that was in the first chaos of darkness, or that still is in hell and devils, all the evil that is in material nature and material creatures, whether animate or inanimate, is nothing else, works in and with nothing else, but those first properties of nature, which drive on the life of fallen man in covetousness, envy, pride, and wrath.

28. Of Deliverance from the Power of Self.

Theogenes.— I could almost say that you have shown me more than enough of this **monster of self,** though I would not be without this knowledge of it for half the world. But now, sir, what must I do **to be saved** from the mouth of this lion, for he is the depth of all subtlety, the satan, that deceiveth the whole world? He can hide himself under all forms of goodness, he can watch and fast, write and instruct, pray much and preach long, give alms to the poor, visit the sick, and yet often gets more life and strength, and a more **unmoveable abode,** in these forms of virtue, than he has in publicans and sinners.

Enjoin me, therefore, whatever you please, all rules, methods, and practices will be welcome to me, if you judge them to be necessary in this matter.

Theophilus.—There is no need of a number of practices or methods in this matter. For to die to self, or to come from under its power, is not, **cannot be done by any active resistance we can** make **to it by the powers of nature.** For nature can no more overcome or suppress itself, than wrath can heal wrath. So long as nature acts, nothing but natural works are brought forth, and therefore the more labour of this kind, the more nature is fed and strengthened with its own food.

But the **one true way of dying to self** is most **simple** and plain; it wants no arts or methods, no cells, monasteries, or pilgrimages; it is equally practicable by every body; it is always at hand; it meets you in every thing; it is free from all deceit; and is never without success.

If you ask what this one, true, simple, plain, immediate, and unerring way is; it is the way of **patience, meekness, humility,** and **resignation to God.** This is the truth and perfection of dying to self; it is nowhere else, **nor** possible to be in any thing else, but in this state of heart.

Theogenes.—The excellency and perfection of these virtues I readily acknowledge; but alas, sir, how will this prove the way of overcoming self to be so **simple,**

plain, immediate, and unerring as you speak of ?   For
is it not the doctrine of almost all men and all books,
and confirmed by our own woeful experience, that
much length of time, and exercise, and variety of
practices and methods are necessary, and scarce sufficient to the attainment of any one of these four
virtues ?

29. Of Faith in Christ as the only way of deliverance from Self.

Theophilus.—When Christ our Saviour was upon
earth, was there anything more simple, plain, immediate,
unerring than the way to Him ?   Did scribes, Pharisees,
publicans, and sinners want any length of time or
exercise of rules and methods before they could have
admission to Him, or have the benefit of faith in Him ?

Theogenes.—I don't understand why you put this
question, nor do I see how it can possibly relate to
the matter before us.

Theophilus.—It not only relates to, but is the very
heart and truth of the matter before us; it is not
appealed to by way of illustration of our subject, but
it is our subject itself, only set in a truer and stronger
light.   For when I refer you to patience, meekness,
humility, and resignation to God as the one simple,
plain, immediate, and unerring way of dying to self, or
being saved from it; I call it so for no other reason but
because you can as easily, and immediately, without
art or method, by the mere turning and faith of
your mind, have all the benefit of these virtues, as
publicans and sinners, by their turning to Christ, could
be helped and saved by Him.

Theogenes.—But, good sir, would you have me then

believe that my turning and giving up myself to these virtues is as certain and immediate a way of my being directly possessed and blessed by their good power, as when sinners turned to Christ to be helped and saved by Him? Surely this is too short a way, and has too much of miracle in it, to be now expected.

Theophilus.—I would have you strictly to believe all this, in the fullest sense of the words. And also to believe that the reasons why you, or any one else, are for a long time vainly endeavouring after, and hardly ever attaining, these first-rate virtues, is because you seek them in the way they are not to be found, in a **multiplicity** of human rules, methods, and contrivances, and not in that **simplicity of faith** in which those who applied to Christ immediately obtained that which they asked of Him.

" Come unto Me, all ye that labour and are heavy laden, and I will refresh you." How short, and simple, and certain a way to peace and comfort, from the misery and burden of sin! What becomes now of your length of time and exercise, your rules and methods and roundabout ways, to be delivered from self, the power of sin, and find the redeeming power and virtue of Christ? Will you say that **turning to Christ in faith** was once indeed the way for Jews and heathens to enter into life, and be delivered from the power of their sins, but that all this happiness was at an end as soon as Pontius Pilate had nailed this good Redeemer to the cross, and so broke off all immediate union and communion between faith and Christ?

What a folly would it be to suppose that Christ, after His having finished His great work, overcome death, ascended into heaven, with all power in heaven and on earth, was become less a Saviour, and gave less certain and immediate helps to those that by faith turn to Him now, than when He was clothed with the infirmity of our flesh and blood upon earth ? Has He less power, after He has conquered, than whilst He was only resisting and fighting with our enemies ? Or has He less good will to assist His Church, His own body, now He is in heaven, than He had to assist publicans, sinners, and heathens, before He was glorified as the Redeemer of the world ? And yet this must be the case, if our **simply turning to Him in faith** and hope is not as sure a way of obtaining immediate assistance from Him now, as when he was upon earth.

Theogenes.—You seem, sir, to me to have stepped aside from the point in question, which was not, whether my turning or giving myself up to Christ, in faith in Him, would not do me as much good as it did to them who turned to Him when He was upon earth ? But whether my turning in faith and desire, to patience, meekness, humility, and resignation to God, would do all that as fully for me now as faith in Christ did for those who became His disciples ?

Theophilus.—I have stuck closely, my friend, to the point before us. Let it be supposed that I had given you a form of prayer in these words : " O Lamb of God, that takest away the sins of the world ; or, O Thou bread that camest down from heaven ; or, Thou that art the resurrection and the life, the light and peace of all holy souls, help me to a living faith in Thee." Would you say that this was not a prayer of faith in and to Christ, because it did not call Him Jesus, or the Son of God ? Answer me plainly.

Theogenes.—What can I answer you, but that this is a most true and good prayer to Jesus, the Son of the living God? For who else but He was the Lamb of God, and the bread that came down?

30. What Faith in the Lamb of God means.

Theophilus.—Well answered, my friend. When, therefore, I exhort you to give up yourself in faith and hope, to **patience, meekness, humility, and resignation to God,** what else do I do but turn you directly to so much faith and hope in the true Lamb of God? For if I ask you **what the Lamb of God is and means,** must you not tell me that **it is and means** the perfection of **patience, meekness, humility, and resignation to God?** Can you say it is either more or less than this? Must you not therefore say that a faith of hunger, and thirst, and desire of these virtues is in spirit and truth the one very same thing as a faith of hunger, and thirst, and desire of salvation through the Lamb of God? And, consequently, that every sincere wish and desire, every inward inclination of your heart, that presses after these virtues, and longs to be governed by them, is an immediate, direct application to Christ, is worshipping and falling down before Him, is **giving up yourself** unto Him, and the **very perfection** of faith in Him.

If you distrust my words, hear the words of Christ Himself: "Learn of Me (says He), for I am meek and lowly of heart; and ye shall find rest unto your souls." Here you have the plain truth of our two points fully asserted—*first*, that to be given up to, or stand in a desire of patience, meekness, humility,

and resignation to God, is strictly the same thing as
to learn of Christ, or to have faith in Him. *Secondly*,
that this is the one simple, short, and infallible way
to overcome or be delivered from all the malignity
and burden of self expressed in these words, "and
ye shall find rest unto your souls."

And all this, because this simple tendency or
inward inclination of your heart to sink down into
patience, meekness, humility, and resignation to God,
is truly giving up all that you are and all that you
have from fallen Adam; it is perfectly leaving all
that you have, to follow and be with Christ; it is
your highest act of faith in Him, and love of Him,
the most ardent and earnest declaration of your
cleaving to Him with all your heart, and seeking for
no salvation but in Him and from Him. And,
therefore, all the good and blessing, pardon and
deliverance from sin, that ever happened to any one
from any kind or degree of faith and hope, and
application to Christ, is sure to be had from this
state of heart, which stands **continually turned to
Him in a hunger and desire of being led and governed
by His spirit of patience, meekness, humility, and
resignation to God.** Oh, Theogenes, could I help you
to perceive or feel what a good there is in this state
of heart, you would desire it with more eagerness
than the thirsty hart desireth the water-brooks, you
would think of nothing, desire nothing, but constantly
to live in it. It is a security from all evil and all
delusion; no difficulty or trial, either of body or
mind, no temptation, either within you or without you,
but what has its full remedy in this state of heart.
You have no questions to ask of any body, no new

way that you need inquire after; no oracle that you need to consult, for whilst you shut up yourself, in patience, meekness, humility, and resignation to God, you are in the very arms of Christ, your whole heart is His dwelling-place, and He lives and works in you, as certainly as He lived in and governed that body and soul which He took from the Virgin Mary.

31. Christ is only to be found in the Virtues of His Character.

Learn whatever else you will from men and books, or even from Christ Himself, besides or without these virtues, and you are only a poor wanderer in a barren wilderness, where no water of life is to be found. For Christ is nowhere but in these virtues; and where they are, there is He in His own kingdom. From morning to night let this be the Christ that you follow, and then you will fully escape all the religious delusions that are in the world, and what is more, all the delusions of your own selfish heart.

For to seek to be saved by patience, meekness, humility of heart, and resignation to God, is truly coming to God through Christ; and when these tempers live and abide in you, as the spirit and aim of your life, then Christ is in you of a truth, and the life that you then lead is not yours, but Christ that liveth in you. For this is following Christ with all your power; you cannot possibly make more haste after Him, you have no other way of walking as He walked, no other way of being like Him, of truly believing in Him, of showing your trust in Him and dependence upon Him, but by **wholly giving up your-**

self to that which He was, viz. to patience, meekness, humility, and resignation to God.

Tell me now, have I enough proved to you the short, simple, and certain way of destroying that body of self which lives and works in the four elements of covetousness, envy, pride, and wrath?

32. Of Covetousness.

Theogenes.— Enough of all reason. But as to covetousness, I thank God I cannot charge myself with it, it has no power over me—nay, I naturally abhor it. And I also now clearly see why I have been so long struggling in vain against other selfish tempers.

Theophilus.—Permit me, my friend, to remove your mistake. Had covetousness no power over you, you could have no other selfish tempers to struggle against. They are all dead as soon as covetousness has done working in you. You take covetousness to relate only to the wealth of this world. But this is but one single branch of it, its nature is as large as desire, and wherever selfish desire is, there is all the evil nature of covetousness.

Now envy, pride, hatred, or wrath can have no possibility of existence in you, but because there is some selfish desire alive in you that is not satisfied, not gratified, but resisted or disappointed. And therefore so long as selfish tempers, whether of envy, uneasiness, complaint, pride, or wrath, are alive in you, you have the fullest proof that all these tempers are born and bred in and from your own covetousness; that is, from that same selfish bad desire which, when it is turned to the wealth of this world, is called covetousness. For all these four elements of self, or fallen nature, are tied together in one inseparable band; they mutually generate, and are generated from one another; they have but one common life, and **must all of them live, or all die together.** This may show you again the absolute necessity of our one simple and certain way of dying to self, and the absolute insufficiency of all human means whatever to effect it.

33. Of the total Despair of Self.

For, consider only this, that to be angry at our own anger, to be **ashamed** of our own pride, and **strongly** resolve not to be weak, is the upshot of all human endeavours; and yet all this is **rather the life** than the death of self. There is no help but from a total despair of all human help. When a man is brought to such an inward full **conviction,** as to have no more hope from all human means, than he hopes to see with his hands or hear with his feet, then it is that he is truly prepared to die to self; that is, to give up all thoughts of having or doing any thing that is good in any other way but that of a meek, humble, patient, total resignation of himself to God. All that we do before **this conviction** is in great ignorance of ourselves, and full of weakness and impurity. Let our zeal be ever so wonderful, yet if it begins sooner, or proceeds farther, or to any other matter, or in any other way than as it is led and guided by **this conviction,** it is full of delusion. No repentance, however long or laborious, is conversion to God till it falls into this state. **God must do all, or all is nothing.** But God cannot do all till all is ex-

pected from Him. And all is not expected from Him
till, by a true and good despair of every human help,
we have no hope, or trust, or longing after any thing
but a patient, meek, humble, total resignation to God.

And now, my dear friends, I have brought you to the
very place for which I desired this day's conversation;
which was to set your feet upon sure ground with
regard to the spirit of love. For all that variety of
matters through which we have passed has been only
a variety of proofs that the spirit of divine love can
have no place or possibility of birth in any fallen
creature till it wills and chooses to be dead to all self,
in a patient, meek, humble resignation to the good
power and mercy of God.

And from this state of heart also it is that the
spirit of prayer is borne, which is the desire of the soul
turned to God. Stand, therefore, steadfastly in this
will, let nothing else enter into your mind, have no
other contrivance, but every where, and in every thing,
to nourish and keep up this state of heart, and then
your house is built upon a rock; you are safe from
all danger; the light of heaven and the love of God
will begin their work in you, will bless and sanctify
every power of your fallen soul. You will be in a
readiness for every kind of virtue and good work, and
will know what it is to be led by the Spirit of God.

34. Of True Resignation to God apart from Feeling.

Theogenes.—But, dear Theophilus, though I am so
delighted with what you say that I am loth to stop
you, yet permit me to mention a fear that rises up in
me. Suppose I should find myself so overcome with

my own darkness and selfish tempers as not to be able to sink from them into a sensibility of this meek, humble, patient, full resignation to God ; what must I then do, or how shall I have the benefit of what you have taught me ?

Theophilus.—You are then at **the very time and place of receiving the fullest benefit from it,** and practising it with the greatest advantage to yourself. For though this patient, meek resignation is to be exercised with regard to all outward things and occurrences of life, yet it chiefly respects our own inward state, the troubles, perplexities, weaknesses, and disorders of our own fallen souls. And to stand turned to a patient, meek, humble resignation to God, when your own impatience, wrath, pride, and irresignation attacks yourself, is a higher and more beneficial performance of this duty, than when you stand turned to meekness and patience when attacked by the pride, or wrath, or disorderly passions of other people. I say, **stand turned** to this patient, humble resignation, for this is your true performance of this duty at that time; and though you may have no comfortable **sensibility** of your performing it, yet in this state you may always have **one full proof** of the truth and reality of it; and that is, when you seek for help no other way, nor in any thing else, neither from men nor books, but **wholly leave and give up yourself to be helped by the mercy of God.** And thus, be your state what it will, you may always have the full benefit of this short and sure way of resigning up yourself to God. And the greater the perplexity of your distress is, the nearer you are to the greatest and best relief, provided you have but **patience to expect it all from God.**

Nothing brings you so near to divine relief as the extremity of distress.

For the goodness of God hath no other name or nature, but the helper of all that wants to be helped; and nothing can possibly hinder your finding this goodness of God, and every other gift and grace that you stand in need of; nothing can hinder or delay it but your turning from the only fountain of life and living water, to some cracked cistern of your own making; to this or that method, opinion, division, or subdivision, amongst Christians, carnally expecting some mighty things, either from Samaria or Jerusalem, Paul or Apollos, which are only and solely to be had by worshipping the Father in spirit and truth; which is then only done when your whole heart, and soul, and spirit trusts **wholly and solely to the operation of that God within you,** in whom we live, move, and have our being. And be assured of this, as a most certain truth, that we have neither more nor less of the divine operation within us, because of this or that outward form or manner of our life, but just and strictly in that degree, as our faith, and hope, and trust, and dependence upon God is more or less in us.

What a folly, then, to be so often perplexed about the way to God! **Nothing is the way to God, but our heart.** God is nowhere else to be found, and the heart itself cannot find Him, or be helped by any thing else to find Him, but by its own love of Him, faith in Him, dependence upon Him, resignation to Him, and expectation of all from Him.

These are short, but full articles of true religion, which carry salvation along with them, which make **a true and full offering and oblation of our whole nature** to the divine operation, and also a true and full confession of the Holy Trinity in unity. For as they look wholly to the Father, as blessing us with the operation of His own word and Spirit, so they truly confess and worship the Holy Trinity of God. And as they ascribe all to, and expect all from, this Deity alone, so they make the truest and best of all confessions, that there is no God but one.

Your foundation standeth sure, whilst you look for all your salvation through the Father, working life in your soul by His own Word and Spirit, which dwell in Him, and are one life, both in Him and you.

35. The Blessedness of total Resignation to God.

Theogenes.—I can never enough thank you, Theophilus, for this good and comfortable answer to my scrupulous fear. It seems now as if I could always know how to find full relief in this humble, meek, patient, total resignation of myself to God. It is, as you said, a remedy that is always at hand, equally practicable at all times, and never in greater reality than when my own tempers are making war against it in my own heart.

You have quite carried your point with me; the God of patience, meekness, and love is the one God of my heart. It is now the whole bent and desire of my soul to seek for all my salvation in and through the merits and mediation of the meek, humble, patient, resigned, suffering Lamb of God, **who alone hath power to bring forth the blessed birth of these heavenly virtues in my soul.** He is the bread of God that came

7

down from heaven, of which the soul must eat, or
perish and pine in everlasting hunger.

He is the eternal love and meekness, that left the
bosom of His Father, **to be Himself the** resurrection of
meekness and love in all the darkened, wrathful souls
of fallen men.

What a comfort is it to think that this Lamb of
God, Son of the Father, Light of the world, who is the
glory of heaven and the joy of angels, **is as near to us,**
as truly in the midst of us, as He is in the midst of
heaven. And that not a thought, look, and desire of
our heart, that presses towards Him, longing to catch,
as it were, one small spark of His heavenly nature,
but is **in as sure a way of finding Him, touching Him,**
and drawing virtue from Him, as the woman who was
healed by longing to touch the border of His garment.

This doctrine also makes me quite weary and
ashamed of all my own natural tempers, as so many
marks of the beast upon me; every whisper of my
soul that stirs up impatience, uneasiness, resentment,
pride, and wrath within me, shall be rejected with a
" Get thee behind me, Satan," for it is his, and has its
whole nature from him. To rejoice in a resentment
gratified, appears now to me to be quite frightful.
For what is it in reality but rejoicing that my own
serpent of self has new life and strength given to it,
and that the precious Lamb of God is denied entrance
into my soul? For this is the strict truth of the
matter. For to give in to resentment, and go willingly
to gratify it, is calling up the courage of your own
serpent, and truly helping it to be more stout and
valiant, and successful in you. On the other hand, to
give up all resentment of every kind, and on every

occasion, however artfully, beautifully, outwardly
coloured, and to sink down into the humility of meekness under all contrariety, contradiction, and injustice,
always turning the other cheek to the smiter, however
haughty, is the best of all prayers, the surest of all
means, to have nothing but Christ living and working
in you, as the Lamb of God, that taketh away every
sin that ever had power over your soul.

What a blindness was it in me to think that I had
no covetousness, because the love of pelf was not felt
by me! For to covet is to desire; and what can it
signify whether I desire this or that? If I desire
any thing but that which God would have me to be
and do, I stick in the mire of covetousness, and must
have all that evil and disquiet living and working in
me which robs misers of their peace both with God
and man.

Oh, **sweet resignation of myself to God**, happy death
of every selfish desire, blessed unction of a holy life,
the only driver of all evil out of my soul, be thou my
guide and governor wherever I go! Nothing but thee
can take me from myself, nothing but thee can lead
me to God; hell has no power where thou art; nor
can heaven hide itself from thee. Oh, may I never
indulge a thought, bring forth a word, or do any thing
for myself or others, but under the influence of thy
blessed inspiration.

Forgive, dear Theophilus, this transport of my soul!
I could not stop it. The sight, though distant, of this
heavenly Canaan, this Sabbath of the soul, freed from
the miserable labour of self, to rest in meekness,
humility, patience, and resignation under the Spirit of
God, is like the joyful voice of the Bridegroom to my

soul, and leaves no wish in me but to be at the marriage feast of the Lamb.

36. The Absolute Necessity of the Death of Self.

Theophilus.—Thither, Theogenes, you must certainly come, if you keep to the path of meekness, humility, and patience, under a full resignation to God. But if you go aside from it, let the occasion seem ever so glorious, or the effects ever so wonderful to you, it is only preparing for yourself a harder death. **For die you must**, to all and every thing that you have worked or done under any other spirit but that of meekness, humility, and true resignation to God. Every thing else, be it what it will, hath its rise from the fire of nature, it belongs to nothing else, and must of all necessity be given up, lost, and taken from you again by fire, either here or hereafter.

For these virtues are the only wedding garment; they are the lamps and vessels well furnished with oil.

There is nothing that will do in the stead of them; they must have their own full and perfect work in you, if not before, yet certainly after the death of the body, or the soul can never be delivered from its fallen, wrathful state. And all this is no more than is implied in this Scripture doctrine, viz. that there is no possibility of salvation but in and by **the birth of the meek, humble, patient, resigned Lamb of God in our souls.** And when this Lamb of God has brought forth a real birth of His own meekness, humility, and full resignation to God in our souls, then are our lamps trimmed, and our virgin hearts made ready for the marriage feast.

This marriage feast signifies the entrance into the highest state of union that can be between God and the soul in this life. Or, in other words, it is the **birthday of the spirit of love in our souls,** which, whenever we attain, will feast our souls with such peace and joy in God as will blot out the remembrance of every thing that we called peace or joy before.

As sure as the light of God is absolutely necessary to make nature to be a heavenly kingdom of light and love, so sure and certain is it that the creaturely life, that is fallen from God, can have no deliverance, cannot have a birth of heavenly light and love, by any other possible way but that of **dying to self,** by meekness, humility, patience, and full resignation to God.

And the reason is this. It is because the **will is** the leader of the creaturely life, and it can have nothing but that to which its will is turned. And therefore it cannot be saved from, or raised out of, the wrath of nature, till **its will turns** from nature, and wills to be no longer driven by it. But it cannot turn from nature, or show a will to come from under its power, any other way than by turning and giving up itself to that meekness, humility, patience, and resignation to God, which, so far as it goes, is a leaving, rejecting, and **dying to all the guidance of nature.**

37. The One Infallible Way to God.

And thus you see that this one simple way is, according to the immutable nature of things, the one only possible and absolutely necessary way to God. It is as possible to go two contrary ways at once, as to go to God any other way than this. But what is best of all, this **way is absolutely infallible;** nothing

can defeat it.   And all this infallibility is fully
grounded in the twofold character of our Saviour—
(1) As He is the Lamb of God, **a principle and source
of all meekness and humility in the soul**.   And (2)
as He is the **light of eternity**, that blesses eternal
nature, and turns it into a kingdom of heaven.

For, in this twofold respect, He has a power of
redeeming us, which nothing can hinder ; but, sooner
or later, He must see all His and our enemies under
His feet, and all that is fallen in Adam into death
must rise and return into a unity of an eternal life in
God.

For as the Lamb of God He has all **power to bring
forth in us a sensibility** and a **weariness** of our own
wrathful state, and a **willingness** to fall from it into
meekness, humility, patience, and resignation to that
mercy of God which alone can help us.   And when
we are thus **weary** and heavy laden, and **willing** to
get rest to our souls in meek, humble, patient resignation to God, then it is that **He, as the light of God** and
heaven, **joyfully breaks in upon us**, turns our darkness
into light, our sorrow into joy, and begins that kingdom
of God and divine love within us, which will never
have an end.

Need I say any more, Theogenes, to show you how
to come out of the wrath of your evil, earthly nature,
into the sweet peace and joy of the spirit of love ?
Neither notions, nor speculations, nor heat, nor fervour,
nor rules, nor methods, can bring it forth.   It is the
child of light, and cannot possibly have any birth in
you but **only and solely from the light of God rising in
your own soul,** as it rises in heavenly beings.   But
the light of God cannot arise, or be found in you, by

any art or contrivance of your own, but only and solely in the way of that meekness, humility, and patience, which waits, trusts, resigns to, and **expects all from the inward, living, life-giving operation of the triune God within you;** creating, quickening, and reviving in your fallen soul that birth, and image, and likeness of the Holy Trinity, in which the first father of mankind was created.

Theogenes. — You need say no more, Theophilus; you have not only removed that difficulty which brought us hither, but have, by a variety of things, fixed and confirmed us in a full belief of that great truth elsewhere asserted, namely, That there is but one salvation for all mankind, and that is the life of God in the soul. And also, that there is but one possible way for man to attain this life of God.

God is one, human nature is one, salvation is one, and the way to it is one, and that is **the desire of the soul turned to God.**

Therefore, dear Theophilus, adieu. If we seek you no more in this life, you have sufficiently taught us how to seek and find every kind of goodness, blessing, and happiness in

GOD ALONE.

THE SPIRIT OF PRAYER

THE SPIRIT OF PRAYER

CHAPTER I.

TREATING OF SOME MATTERS PREPARATORY TO THE SPIRIT OF PRAYER.

1. The Vanity of Time, and the Riches of Eternity.

THE greatest part of mankind, nay, of Christians, may be said to be asleep; and that particular way of life which takes up each man's mind, thoughts, and affections, may very well be called his particular dream. This degree of vanity is equally visible in every form and order of life. The learned and the ignorant, the rich and the poor, are all in the same state of slumber; only passing away a short life in a different kind of dream. But why so?

It is because man has an eternity within him, is born into this world, not for the sake of living here, not for any thing this world can give him, but only to have time and place to become either an eternal partaker of a divine life with God, or to have a hellish eternity amongst fallen angels; and, therefore, every man who has not his eyes, his heart, and his hands continually governed by this twofold eternity, may be justly said to be fast asleep—to have no awakened sensibility of himself. And a life devoted to the interests and enjoyments of this world, spent and wasted in the slavery of earthly desires, may be truly called a dream, as having all the shortness, vanity, and delusion of a dream; only with this great difference—that when a dream is over, nothing is lost but fictions and fancies; but when the dream of life is ended only by death, all that eternity is lost for which we were brought into being. Now, there is no misery in this world, nothing that makes either the life or death of man to be full of calamity, but this blindness and insensibility of his state into which he so willingly, nay, obstinately, plunges himself. Every thing that has the nature of evil and distress in it takes its rise from hence. Do but suppose a man to know himself; that he comes into this world on no other errand **but to rise out of the vanity of time into the riches of eternity**: do but suppose him to govern his inward thoughts and outward actions by this view of himself, and then to him every day has lost all its evil; prosperity and adversity have no difference, because he receives and uses them both in the same spirit; life and death are equally welcome, because equally parts of his way to eternity.

2. The Spirit of Prayer.

For poor and miserable as this life is, we have all of us free access to all that is great, and good, and happy, and carry within ourselves a key to all the treasures that Heaven has to bestow upon us. **We starve in** the midst of plenty, groan under infirmities, with the remedy in our own hands.

We live and die without knowing and feeling any thing of the **one only good**, whilst we have it in our power to know and enjoy it in as great a reality as we know and feel the power of this world over us: for heaven is as near to our souls as this earth is to our bodies; and we are created, we are redeemed, to have our conversation in it. God, the only good of all intelligent natures, is not an absent or distant God, but is more present in and to our souls than our own bodies; and we are strangers to heaven, and without God in the world, for this only reason—because we are void of that Spirit of Prayer, which alone can, and never fails to unite us with the one only good, and to open heaven and the kingdom of God within us.

A root set in the finest soil, in the best climate, and blessed with all that sun and air and rain can do for it, is not in so sure a way of its **growth to perfection,** as every man may be, whose spirit aspires after all that which God is ready and infinitely desirous to give him.

For the sun meets not the springing bud that stretches towards him, with half that certainty, as God, the Source of all good, communicates Himself to the soul that longs to partake of Him.

3. Of the Creation of Man in the Image of God.

We are all of us, by birth, the offspring of God, more nearly related to Him than we are to one another; for " in Him we live, and move, and have our being."

The first man that was brought forth from God, had
the Breath and Spirit of Father, Son, and Holy Ghost
breathed into him, and so he became a living soul.
Thus was our first father born of God, descended from
Him, and stood in Paradise in the image and likeness
of God. He was the image and likeness of God, not
with any regard to his outward shape or form, for no
shape has any likeness to God; but he was in the
image and likeness of God, because the Holy Trinity
had breathed Their own Nature and Spirit into him.
And as the Deity, Father, Son, and Holy Spirit, **are
always in heaven, and make heaven to be everywhere;**
so this Spirit, breathed by Them into man, brought
heaven into man along with it; and so man was in
heaven as well as on earth—that is, in Paradise, which
signifies a heavenly state, or Birth of Life.

4. Man in Paradise.

Adam had all that divine nature, both as to a
heavenly spirit, and heavenly body, which the angels
have; but as he was brought forth to be a lord and
ruler of a new world, created out of the chaos or ruins
of the kingdom of fallen angels; so it was necessary
that he should also have the nature of this new-created
world in himself, both as to its spirit and materiality.
Hence it was that he had a body taken from this new-
created earth, not such dead earth as we now make
bricks of, but the blessed earth of Paradise, that had
the powers of heaven in it, out of which the Tree of
Life itself could grow. Into the nostrils of this outward body was the breath or spirit of this world
breathed; and in this spirit and body of this world,
did the inward celestial spirit and body of Adam dwell;

it was the medium or means through which he was
to have commerce with this world, become visible to
its creatures, and rule over it and them.   Thus stood
our first father; an angel both as to body and spirit
(as he will be again after the resurrection), yet dwelling in a body and spirit taken from this new-created
world; which, however, was as inferior to him, as
subject to him, as the earth and all its creatures were.
It was no more alive in him, no more brought forth
its nature within him, than Satan and the serpent
were alive in him at his first creation.   He was to
have no share of its life and nature, no feeling of good
or evil from it; but to act in it as an heavenly artist,
that had power and skill to open the wonders of God
in every power of outward nature.

And herein lay the ground of Adam's ignorance of
good and evil; it was because his outward body, and
the outward world (in which alone was good and evil),
could not discover their own nature, or open their own
life within him, but were kept inactive by the power
and life of the celestial man within it.   And this was
man's first and great TRIAL; a trial, not imposed upon
him by the mere will of God, or by way of experiment;
but a trial necessarily implied in the nature of his
state; he was created an angel, both as to body and
spirit; and this angel stood in an outward body, of the
nature of the outward world; and therefore, by the
nature of his state, he had his trial, or power of
choosing, whether he would live as an angel, using
only his outward body as a means of opening the
wonders of the outward world to the glory of his
Creator; or whether he would turn his desire to the
opening of the bestial life of the outward world in

himself, for the sake of knowing the good and evil
that was in it. The fact is certain, that he lusted
after the knowledge of this good and evil, and made
use of the means to obtain it. No sooner had he got
this knowledge, by the opening of the bestial life and
sensibility within him, but in that day, nay, in that
instant, he died; that is, his heavenly spirit, with its
heavenly body, were both extinguished in him; but his
soul, an immortal fire that could not die, became a poor
slave in a prison of bestial flesh and blood.

5. Of the Nature of Redemption.

See here the nature and necessity of our redemption;
it is to redeem the first angelic nature that departed
from Adam; it is to make that heavenly spirit and
body which Adam lost, to be alive again in all the
human nature; and this is called regeneration.

See also the true reason why only the Son, or
Eternal Word of God, could be our Redeemer; it is
because He alone, by whom all things were at first
made, could be able to bring to life again that celestial
spirit and body which had departed from Adam.

The necessity of our regaining our first heavenly
body, is the necessity of our eating the Body and Blood
of Christ. The necessity of having again our first
heavenly spirit, is declared, by the necessity of our
being baptized by the Holy Ghost. Our fall is nothing
else but the falling of our soul from this celestial body
and spirit, into a bestial body and spirit of this world.
Our rising out of our fallen state, or Redemption, is
nothing else but the regaining our first angelic spirit
and body, which in Scripture is called our inward, or
"new man, created again in Christ Jesus."

See here, lastly, the true ground of all the mortifications of flesh and blood required in the gospel; it
is because this bestial life of this outward world should
not have been opened in man; it is his separation
from God, and death to the kingdom of heaven; and
therefore all its **workings, appetites,** and **desires** are to
be restrained and kept under, that the first heavenly
life to which Adam died, may have room to rise up in us.

6. Of the Entrance of Evil into this World.

It is plain that the command of God, not to lust
after, and eat of the forbidden tree, was not an arbi-
trary command of God, given at pleasure, or as a mere
trial of man's obedience; but was a most kind and
loving information given by the God of Love to His
new-born offspring, concerning the state he was in
with regard to the outer world; warning him to with-
draw all desire of entering into a sensibility of its
good and evil; because such sensibility could not be
had without his immediate dying to that divine and
heavenly life which he then enjoyed. " Eat not,"
says the God of Love, " of the tree of knowledge of
good and evil, for in the day thou eatest thereof, thou
wilt surely die."

As if it had been said, " I have brought thee into
this Paradise, with such a nature as the angels have
in heaven. By the order and dignity of thy creation,
every thing that lives and moves in this world, is
made subject to thee as to their ruler. I have made
thee in thy outward body of this world, to be for a
time a little lower than the angels, till thou hast
brought forth a numerous offspring, fit for that kingdom which they have lost."

7. Of the Fall of the Angels.

" The world around thee, and the life which is newly
awakened in it, is much lower˚ than thou art; of a
nature quite inferior to thine. It is a gross, corruptible state of things, that cannot stand long before Me;
but must for a while bear the marks of those creatures
which first made evil to be known in the creation.

" The angels that first inhabited this region, where
thou art to bring forth a new order of beings, were
great and powerful spirits, highly endowed with the
riches and powers of their Creator;—whilst they stood
(as the order of creation requires) in meekness and
resignation, under their Creator, nothing was impossible to them; there was no end of their glorious
powers throughout their whole kingdom; perpetual
scenes of light, and glory, and beauty were rising and
changing through all the height and depth of their Glassy
Sea, merely at their will and pleasure; but, finding what
wonders of light and glory they could perpetually
bring forth; how all the Powers of eternity, treasured
up in their Glassy Sea, unfolded themselves, and broke
forth in ravishing forms of wonder and delight, merely
in obedience to their call; they began to admire and
even adore themselves, and to fancy that there was
some infinity of power hidden in themselves, which
they supposed was kept under, and suppressed, by
that meekness and subjection to God under which they
acted. Fired and intoxicated with this proud imagination, they boldly resolved, with all their eternal energy
and strength, to take their kingdom, with all its glories,
to themselves, by eternally abjuring all meekness and
submission to God. No sooner did their eternal,

potent desires fly in this direction of a revolt from God, but in-the swiftness of a thought heaven was lost; and they found themselves dark spirits, stripped of all their light and glory: instead of rising up above God (as they hoped), by breaking off from Him, there was no end to their eternal sinking into new depths of slavery, under their own self-tormenting natures.

"As a wheel going down a mountain that has no bottom, must continually keep on its turning, so are they whirled down by the impetuosity of their own wrong-turned wills in a continual descent from the fountain of all glory, into the bottomless depths of their own dark, fiery, working powers. In no hell, but what their own natural strength had awakened; bound in no chains but their own unbending, hardened spirits; made such, by their renouncing, with all their eternal strength, all meekness and subjection to God. In that moment the beautiful materiality of their kingdom, their Glassy Sea in which they dwelt, was, by the wrathful, rebellious workings of those apostate spirits, broke all into pieces, and became a black lake, a horrible chaos of fire and wrath, thickness and darkness, a height and depth of the confused, divided, fighting properties of nature."

8. Of Chaos and the Creation of this World.

"My created fiat stopped the workings of these rebellious spirits, by dividing the ruins of their wasted kingdom into an earth, sun, planets, and separated elements. Had not this revolt of angels brought forth that disordered chaos, no such materiality as this outward world is made of had ever been known.

Gross compacted earth, stones, rocks, wrathful fire here, dead water there, fighting elements, with all their gross vegetables and animals, are things not known in Eternity, and will be only seen in Time, till the great designs are finished, for which thou art brought forth in Paradise; and then as a fire awakened by the rebel creature, began all the disorders of nature, and turned that Glassy Sea into a chaos; so a last fire, kindled at My word, shall thoroughly purge the floor of this world. In those purifying flames, the sun, the planets, the air, the earth, and water, shall part with all their dross, deadness, and division, and all become again that first, heavenly materiality, a Glassy Sea of everlasting light and glory, in which thou and thy offspring shall sing hallelujahs to all eternity. Look not, therefore, thou child of Paradise, thou son of eternity! look not, with a longing eye, after any thing in this outward world; there are the remains of the fallen angels in it; thou hast nothing to do in it, but as a ruler over it. It stands before thee, as a mystery big with wonders; and thou, whilst an angel in Paradise, hast power to open and display them all. It stands not in thy sphere of existence; it is, as it were, but a picture, and transitory figure of things; for all that is not eternal, is but as an image in a glass, that seems to have a reality which it hath not. The life which springs up in this figure of a world, in such an infinite variety of kinds and degrees, is but as a shadow; it is a life of such days and years, as in eternity have no distinction from a moment. It is a life of such animals and insects, as are without any divine sense, capacity, or feeling. Their natures have nothing in them, but what I commanded this new modelled chaos, this order of planets and fighting elements, to bring forth.

"In heaven, all births and growths, all figures and spiritual forms of life, though infinite in variety, are yet all of a heavenly kind; and only so many manifestations of the goodness, wisdom, beauty, and riches of the divine nature. But in this new modelled chaos, where the disorders that were raised by Lucifer are not wholly removed, but evil and good must stand in strife, till the last purifying fire, here every kind and degree of life, like the world from whence it springs, is a mixture of good and evil in its birth.

"Therefore, My son, be content with thy angelic nature; be content, as an angel in Paradise, to eat angels' food, and to rule over this mixed, imperfect, and perishing world, without partaking of its corruptible, impure, and perishing nature. Lust not to know how the animals feel the evil and good which this life affords them: for if thou couldest feel what they feel, thou must be as they are; thou canst not have their sensibility unless thou hast their nature: thou canst not at once be an angel and an earthly animal. If the bestial life is raised up in thee, the same instant the heavenly birth of thy nature must die in thee. Therefore, turn away thy lust and imagination from a tree that can only help thee to the knowledge of such good or evil, as belongs only to the animals of this outward world, for nothing but the bestial nature can receive good or evil from the stars and elements: they have no power but over that life which proceeds from them. Eat, therefore, only the food of Paradise; be content with angels' bread; for if thou eatest of this tree, it will unavoidably awaken and open the bestial

life within thee; and in that moment all that is
heavenly must die, and cease to have any power in
thee. And thou must fall into a slavery for life,
under the divided, fighting powers of stars and
elements; stripped of thy angelic garment, that hid
thy outward body under its glory, thou wilt become
more naked than any beast upon earth, be forced to
seek from beasts a covering, to hide thee from the
sight of thine own eyes. A shameful, fearful, sickly,
wanting, suffering, and distressed heir of the same
speedy death in the dust of the earth, as the poor
beasts, whom thou wilt thus have made to be thy
brethren."

9. Of Love as the Nature of God.

God, considered in Himself, is as infinitely separate
from all possibility of doing hurt, or willing pain to
any creature, as He is from a possibility of suffering
pain or hurt from the hand of a man; and this, for
this plain reason, because He is in Himself, in His
Holy Trinity, nothing else but the boundless Abyss
of all that is good, and sweet, and amiable; and therefore stands in the utmost contrariety to every thing
that is not a blessing; in an eternal impossibility of
willing and intending a moment's pain or hurt to any
creature; for, from this unbounded Source of goodness and perfection, nothing but infinite streams of
blessing are perpetually flowing forth upon all nature
and creature, in a more incessant plenty than rays
of light stream from the sun. And as the sun has
but one nature, and can give forth nothing but the
blessings of light; so the Holy Triune God has but
one nature and intent towards all the creation, which

is, to pour forth the richness and sweetness of His divine perfections upon every thing that is capable of them, and according to its capacity to receive them.

The goodness of God breaking forth into a desire to communicate good, was the cause and the beginning of the creation. Hence it follows, that to all eternity God can have no thought or intent towards the creature, but to **communicate good**; because He made the creature for this sole end, to receive good. The first motive towards the creature is unchangeable; it takes its rise from God's desire to **communicate good**, and it is an eternal impossibility that any thing can ever come from God, as His will and purpose towards the creature, but **that same love and goodness** which first created it. He must always will that to it, which He willed at the creation of it. This is the amiable nature of God. He is **the Good**, the unchangeable, overflowing Fountain of good, that sends forth nothing but good to all eternity. He is **the Love** itself, the unmixed, unmeasurable Love, doing nothing but from love, giving nothing but gifts of love, to every thing that He has made; requiring nothing of all His creatures, but the spirit and fruits of that love, which brought them into being.

Oh, how sweet is this contemplation of the height and depth of the riches of divine Love! With what attraction must it draw every thoughtful man to return love for love to this overflowing Fountain of boundless goodness! What charms has that religion, which discovers to us our existence in, relation to, and dependence upon this Ocean of divine Love! View every part of our redemption from Adam's first sin, to the resurrection of the dead, and you will find nothing but successive mysteries of that first love which

created angels and men.   All the mysteries of the gospel
are only so many marks and proofs of God's desiring to
make His Love triumph, in the removal of sin and
disorder from all nature and creature.[1]

10. The Need of the New Birth.

But to return, and consider further the nature of
Adam's fall.

See here the deep ground and absolute necessity of
that new birth of the Word, Son, and Spirit of God,
which the Scripture speaks so much of.   It is because
our soul, as fallen, is quite **dead** to and separate from
the kingdom of heaven, by having lost the Light and
Spirit of God in itself; and therefore is, and must be,
incapable of entering into heaven, till by this new
birth, the soul gets again its first heavenly nature.

If thou hast nothing of this birth when thy body
dies, then thou hast only that root of life in thee which
the devils have ; thou art as far from heaven, and as
incapable of it, as they are ; thy nature is their nature,
and therefore their habitation must be thine.   For
nothing can possibly hinder thy union with fallen
angels, when thou diest, but a birth of that in thy
soul, which the fallen angels have lost.

Now, that the soul, as fallen, is in this **real state of
death,** is a doctrine not only plain from the whole
tenor of Scripture, but affirmed in all systems of
divinity.   For all hold and teach, that man, unredeemed, must, at the death of his body, have fallen
into a state of misery, like that of the fallen angels :
but how can this be true, unless it be true that the
life of heaven was extinguished in the soul ? and that

[1] *Spirit of Love*, Part the Second.

man had really lost that Light and Spirit of God, which alone can make any being capable of living in heaven? All, therefore, that I have here and elsewhere said, concerning the death of the soul by its fall, and its wanting a real new birth of the Son and Holy Spirit of God in it, in order to its salvation, cannot be denied, but by giving up this great, fundamental doctrine, namely, **That man in his fallen state, and unredeemed, must have been eternally lost.** For it cannot be true, that the fall of man unredeemed, would have kept him for ever out of heaven, but because his fall had absolutely put an end to the life of heaven in his soul.

On the other hand, it cannot be true that Jesus Christ is his Redeemer, and does deliver him from his fallen state, unless it be true that Jesus Christ helps him to a new birth of that Light and Spirit of God, which was extinguished by his fall. For nothing could possibly be the redemption, or recovery of man, but regeneration alone. His misery was his having lost the Life and Light of heaven from his soul, and therefore nothing in all the universe of nature, but **a new birth** of that which he had lost, could be his deliverance from his fallen state.

And therefore, if angels after angels had come down from heaven, to assure him that God had no anger at him, he would still have been in the same helpless state; nay, had they told him that God had pity and compassion towards him, he had yet been unhelped, because in the nature of the thing nothing could make so much as a beginning of his deliverance, but that which made a **beginning of a new** birth in him, and nothing could fully effect his recovery, but which

perfectly finished the new birth of all that heavenly
life which he had lost.

11. How Man again becomes Partaker of the Divine Nature.

One would wonder how any persons, who believe
the great Mystery of our redemption, who adore the
depths of the divine goodness, in that the Son of God,
the second Person in the Trinity, became a man Himself, in order to make it possible for man by a birth
from Him, to enter again into the kingdom of God,
should yet seek to, and contend for, not a real, but
a figurative sense of a new birth in Jesus Christ.   Is
there any thing more inconsistent than this ?   Or can
any thing strike more directly at the heart of the whole
nature of our redemption ?   God became man, took
upon Him a birth from the fallen nature.   But why
was this done ? Or wherein lies the adorable depth of
this Mystery ?   How does all this manifest the infinity
of the divine Love towards man ?   It is because
nothing less than this mysterious incarnation (which
astonishes angels) could open a way, or begin a possibility, for fallen man to be born again from above, and
made again a partaker of the divine nature.   It was
because man was become so dead to the kingdom of
heaven, that there was no help for him through all
nature ; no powers, no abilities of the highest order of
creatures, could kindle the least spark of life in him,
or help him to the least glimpse of that heavenly
light which he had lost.   Now, when all nature and
creature stood round about Adam, as unable to help
him as he was to help himself, and all of them unable
to help him for this reason, because that which he had

lost was the life and **light of heaven**; how glorious, how adorable, is that Mystery, which enables us to say, that when man lay thus, incapable of any relief from all the powers and possibilities of nature, that then the Son, the Word of God, entered by a birth into this fallen nature, that by this mysterious incarnation, all the fallen nature might be **born again** of Him, according to the Spirit, in the same reality as they were born of Adam according to the flesh. Look at this Mystery in this true light, in this plain sense of Scripture, and then you must be forced to fall down before it, in adoration of it. For all that is great and astonishing in the goodness of God, all that is glorious and happy with regard to man, is manifestly contained in it.

For this new birth is not a part, but **the whole** of our salvation. Every thing in religion, from the beginning to the end of time, is only for the sake of it. Nothing does us any good, but either as it helps forward our regeneration, or as it is a true fruit, or effect of it.

All the glad tidings of the gospel, all the benefits of our Saviour, however variously expressed in Scripture, all centre in this one point, that He is become our Light, our Life, our Resurrection, our Holiness, and Salvation; that we are in Him new creatures, **created again** unto righteousness, born again of Him from above, of the Spirit of God. Every thing in the gospel is for the sake of this new creature, this new man in Christ Jesus, and nothing is regarded without it.

12. Of Union to Christ.

"I am the vine, ye are the branches." Here Christ, our second Adam, uses this similitude to teach us that the new birth that we are to have from Him is real, in the most strict and literal sense of the words, and that there is the same nearness of relation betwixt Him and His true disciples, that there is betwixt the vine and its branches; that He does all that in us, and for us, which the vine does to its branches. Now, the life of the vine must be really derived into the branches,—they cannot be branches till the birth of the vine is brought forth in them. And therefore, as sure as the birth of the vine must be brought forth in the branches, so sure is it that we must be born again of our second Adam. And that unless the Life of the holy Jesus be in us by a birth from Him, we are as dead to Him and the kingdom of God, as the branch is dead to the vine from which it is broken off.

Again, our blessed Saviour saith, "Without Me ye can do nothing." The question is, when, or how a man may be said to be without Christ? Consider again the vine and its branches. A branch can, then, only be said to be without its vine when the vegetable life of the vine is no longer in it. This is the only sense in which we can be said to be without Christ; when He is no longer in us, as a Principle of a heavenly life, we are then without Him, and so can do nothing—that is, nothing that is good or holy.

A Christ not in us is the same thing as a Christ not ours. If we are only so far with Christ as to own and receive the history of His birth, person, and character, if this is all that we have of Him, we are as much without Him, as much left to ourselves, as little helped by Him, as those evil spirits which cried out, "We know Thee, who Thou art, the Holy One of God." For those evil spirits, and all the fallen angels, are totally without Christ, have no benefit from Him, for this one and only reason, because Christ is not in them; nothing of the Son of God is generated or born in them. Therefore every son of Adam that has not something of the Son of God generated or born within him, is as much without Christ, as destitute of all help from Him, as those evil spirits who could only make an outward confession of Him.

13. Of Christ within Us.

It is the language of Scripture that **Christ in us is** our hope of glory; that Christ formed in us—living, growing, and raising His own Life and Spirit in us— is our only salvation. And, indeed, all this is plain from the nature of the thing, for since the serpent, sin, death, and hell are all essentially **within us**, the very **growth** of our nature,—must not our redemption be equally **inward**, an inward **essential death** to this state of our souls, and an inward growth of a contrary life within us? If Adam was only **an outward person,** if his whole nature was not **our nature**, born in us, and derived from him unto us, it would be nonsense to say that his fall is our fall. So, in like manner, if Christ our second Adam was only an **outward person**, if He entered not as deeply into our nature as the first Adam does, if we have not as **really** from

Him a new inward, spiritual man, as we have outward
flesh and blood from Adam, what ground could there
be to say that our righteousness is from Him as our
sin is from Adam ?

Let no one here think to charge me with disregard
to the holy Jesus, who was born of the Virgin Mary,
or of setting up an inward Saviour in opposition to
that outward Christ whose history is recorded in the
gospel.   No ; it is with the utmost fulness of faith
and assurance, that I ascribe all our redemption to
that blessed and mysterious Person that was then
born of the Virgin Mary ; and will assert no inward
redemption but what wholly proceeds from, and is
effected by, that life-giving Redeemer who died on
the Cross for our redemption.

Was I to say that a plant, or vegetable, must
have the sun within it, must have the life, light, and
virtues of the sun incorporated in it, that it has no
benefit from the sun till the sun is thus inwardly
forming, generating, quickening, and raising up a
life of the sun's virtues in it, would this be setting
up an inward sun in opposition to the outward one ?
Could any thing be more ridiculous than such a
charge ?   For is not all that is here said of an
inward sun in the vegetable, so much said of a
power and virtue derived from the sun in the firmament ?   So, in like manner, all that is said of an
inward Christ, inwardly formed and generated in the
root of the soul, is only so much said of an inward
life, brought forth by the power and efficacy of that
blessed Christ who was born of the Virgin Mary.

CHAPTER II.

DISCOVERING THE TRUE WAY OF TURNING TO GOD, AND OF FINDING THE KINGDOM OF HEAVEN, THE RICHES OF ETERNITY, IN OUR SOULS.

14. Of the Life of Christ in the Soul.

THOU hast seen, dear reader, the nature and necessity of regeneration. Be persuaded, therefore, fully to believe, and firmly to settle in thy mind, this most certain Truth, that all our salvation consists in the **manifestation of the Nature, Life, and Spirit of Jesus Christ in our inward new man.** This alone is Christian redemption, this alone delivers from the guilt and power of sin, this alone redeems, renews, and regains the first Life of God in the soul of man.

Every thing besides this is self, is fiction, is **propriety, is own will,** and, however coloured, is only thy "old man with all his deeds." Enter, therefore, with all thy heart into this Truth, let thine eye be always upon it, do every thing in view of it, try every thing by the truth of it, love nothing but for the sake of it. Wherever thou goest, whatever thou doest, at home or abroad, in the field or at church, do all **in a desire of union with Christ, in imitation of His tempers and inclinations,** and look upon all as nothing but that which exercises and increases the **Spirit and Life of Christ in thy soul.** From morning to night keep Jesus in thy heart, long for nothing, desire nothing, hope for nothing, but to have all that is within thee changed into **the spirit and temper**

of the holy Jesus. Let this be thy Christianity, thy
Church, and thy religion.

For this new birth in Christ thus firmly believed,
and continually desired, will do every thing that thou
wantest to have done in thee; it will dry up all the
springs of vice, stop all the workings of evil in thy
nature; it will bring all that is good into thee; it will
open all the gospel within thee, and thou wilt know
what it is to be taught of God. This longing desire of
thy heart to be **one with Christ,** will soon put a stop
to all the vanity of thy life, and nothing will be ad-
mitted to enter into thy heart, or proceed from it, but
what comes from God and returns to God: thou wilt
soon be, as it were, tied and bound in the chains of all
holy affections and desires; thy mouth will have a
watch set upon it, thine ears would willingly hear
nothing that does not tend to God, nor thine eyes be
open but to see and find occasions of doing good.

In a word, when this faith has got both thy head
and thy heart, it will then be with thee as it was
with the merchant who found a Pearl of great price,
it will make thee gladly to **sell all thou hast,** and buy
It. For all that had seized and possessed the heart of
any man, whatever the merchant of this world had
got together, whether of riches, power, honour, learning,
or reputation, loses all its value, is counted but as
dung, and willingly parted with as soon as this
glorious Pearl, the new birth in Christ Jesus, is discovered and found by him.

15. Of the Way to the New Birth.

But thou wilt perhaps say, How shall this great
work, the birth of Christ, be effected in me? It

might rather be said, Since Christ has an infinite power and also an infinite desire to save mankind, how can any one miss of this salvation but through his own unwillingness to be saved by Him? Consider, how was it that the lame and blind, the lunatic and leper, the publican and sinner, found Christ to be their Saviour, and to do all that for them, which they wanted to be done to them? It was because they had a **real desire** of having that which they asked for, and therefore, in true faith and prayer, applied to Christ, that His Spirit and Power might enter into them, and heal that which they wanted and desired to be healed in them. Every one of these said in **faith and desire,** " Lord, if Thou wilt, Thou canst make me whole." And the answer was always this, " According to thy faith, so be it done unto thee." This is Christ's answer now, and thus it is done to every one of us at this day, as our faith is, so is it done unto us. And here lies the whole reason of our falling short of the salvation of Christ, it is because we have no will to it.

16. Wherein the Salvation of Christ consists.

But you will say, Do not all Christians desire to have Christ to be their Saviour? Yes; but here is the deceit: all would have Christ to be their Saviour in the next world, and to help them into heaven when they die, by His Power and Merits with God. But this is not willing Christ to be thy Saviour; for His salvation, if it is had, must be had in this world; if He saves thee, it must be done in this life, by changing and altering all that is within thee, by helping thee to a new heart, as He helped the blind to see,

9

the lame to walk, and the dumb to speak. For to
have salvation from Christ, is nothing else but to be
made like unto Him; it is to have His humility and
meekness, His mortification and self-denial, His renunciation of the spirit, wisdom, and honours of this
world, His love of God, His desire of doing God's will,
and seeking only His honour. To have these tempers
formed and begotten in thy heart, is to have salvation
from Christ; but if thou willest not to have these
tempers brought forth in thee, if thy faith and desire
does not seek and cry to Christ for them in the same
reality as the lame asked to walk, and the blind to
see, then thou must be said to be unwilling to have
Christ to be thy Saviour.

Again, consider how it was that the carnal Jew,
the deep-read Scribe, the learned Rabbi, the religious
Pharisee, not only did not receive, but crucified their
Saviour. It was because they willed and desired no
such Saviour as He was, no such inward salvation as
He offered to them; they desired no change of their
own nature, no inward destruction of their own
natural tempers, no deliverance from the love of
themselves, and the enjoyments of their passions;
they liked their state, the gratifications of their old
man, their long robes, their broad phylacteries, and
greetings in the markets. They wanted not to have
their pride and self-love dethroned, their covetousness
and sensuality to be subdued, by a new nature from
heaven derived into them. Their only desire was the
success of Judaism, to have an outward Saviour, a
temporal Prince, that should establish their law and
ceremonies over all the earth; and therefore they
crucified their dear Redeemer, and would have none

of His salvation, because it all consisted in a change
of their nature, in a new birth from above, and a
kingdom of heaven to be opened **within** them by the
Spirit of God.

Oh, Christendom! look not only at the old Jews,
but see thyself in this glass. For at this day (Oh,
sad truth to be told!) **a Christ within us,** an **inward**
Saviour raising a birth of His own Nature, Life, and
Spirit within us, is rejected as gross enthusiasm, the
learned Rabbis take counsel against it. The propagation of Popery, the propagation of Protestantism,
the success of some particular Church, is the salvation
which priests and people are chiefly concerned about.

17. How the Birth of Christ is to be effected in Us.

But to return: It is manifest that no one can fail
of the benefit of Christ's salvation, but through an
unwillingness to have it, and from the same spirit
and temper which made the Jews unwilling to receive
it. But if thou wouldst still further know **how** this
great work, **the birth of Christ, is to be effected in thee,**
then let this joyful truth be told thee, that this great
work is already begun in every one of us. For this
holy Jesus, that is to be formed in thee, that is to be
the Saviour and new Life of thy soul, that is to raise
thee out of the darkness of death into the Light of
Life, and give thee power to become a son of God,
is already within thee, living, stirring, calling, knock-
ing at the door of thy heart, and wanting nothing but
thy own faith and good-will, to have as real a birth
and form in thee as He had in the Virgin Mary.

For the eternal Word, or Son of God, did not then

first begin to be the Saviour of the world when He
was born in Bethlehem of Judea; but that Word
which became man in the Virgin Mary, did, from the
beginning of the world, enter as a Word of life, a Seed
of salvation, into the first father of mankind,—was
inspoken into him, as an ingrafted Word, under the
name and character of the "Bruiser of the serpent's
head."

Hence it is that Christ said to His disciples, "The
kingdom of God is within you;" that is, the divine
nature is within you, given unto your first father, into
the light of his life; and from him, rising up in the
life of every son of Adam.

Hence, also, the holy Jesus is said to be the "Light
which lighteth every man that cometh into the world."
Not as He was born at Bethlehem, not as He had a
human form upon earth; in these respects He could
not be said to have been the Light of every man that
cometh into the world.   But as He was that Eternal
Word, by which all things were created, which was
the Life and Light of all things, and which had as
a second Creator entered again into fallen man, as
a Bruiser of the serpent, in this respect it was truly
said of our Lord, when on earth, that "He was that
Light which lighteth every man that cometh into the
world."   For He was really and truly all this, as He
was the Immanuel, the God with us, given unto Adam,
and in him to all his offspring.

When our blessed Lord conversed with the woman
at Jacob's well, He said unto her, "If thou knewest
the gift of God, and who it is that talketh with thee,
thou wouldst have asked of Him, and He would have
given thee living water."   How happy (may any one

well say) was this woman of Samaria, to stand so near
this Gift of God, from whom she might have had living
water, had she but vouchsafed to have asked for it!
But, dear Christian, this happiness is thine; for this
holy Jesus, "the Gift of God," first given into Adam,
and in him to all that are descended from him, is the
Gift of God to thee, as sure as thou art born of
Adam; nay, hast thou never yet owned Him, art thou
wandered from Him, as far as the prodigal son from
his father's house, yet is He still with thee, He is the
Gift of God to thee, and if thou wilt turn to Him, and
ask of Him, He has living water for thee.

18. Of turning to the Heart to find Christ there.

Poor sinner! consider the treasure thou hast within
thee: the Saviour of the world, the eternal Word of
God, lies hid in thee, as a spark of the divine nature,
which is to overcome sin, and death, and hell, within
thee, and generate the life of heaven again in thy soul.
Turn to thy heart, and thy heart will find its Saviour,
its God, within itself. Thou seest, hearest, and feelest
nothing of God, because thou seekest for Him **abroad**
with thine outward eyes; thou seekest for Him in
books, in controversies, in the church, and outward
exercises, but there thou wilt not find Him, till thou
hast **first** found Him in thy heart. Seek for Him in thy
heart, and thou wilt never seek in vain; for there He
dwelleth, there is the seat of His Light and Holy Spirit.

For this turning to the Light and Spirit of God
within thee, is thine **only true** turning unto God;
there is **no other way of finding Him,** but in that place
where He dwelleth in thee. For though God be

everywhere present, yet He is only present to thee in
the deepest and most central part of thy soul. Thy
natural senses cannot possess God, or unite thee to
Him; nay, thine inward faculties of **understanding,
will, and memory** can only reach after God, but cannot
be the **place of His habitation in thee.** But there is a
root or **depth** in thee, from whence all these faculties
come forth, as lines from a centre, or as branches from
the body of the tree. This depth is called the **centre,**
the fund or **bottom,** of the soul. This depth is the
unity, the **eternity,** I had almost said the **infinity** of
thy soul, for it is so infinite that nothing can satisfy
it, or give it any rest, but the infinity of God.

In this depth of the soul the Holy Trinity brought
forth its own living image in the first created man,
bearing in himself a living representation of Father,
Son, and Holy Ghost, and this was his dwelling in
God and God in him. This was the kingdom of God
within him, and made Paradise without him. But the
day that Adam did eat of the forbidden earthly tree,
in that day he absolutely died to this kingdom of
God **within him.** This **depth** or **centre** of his soul,
having lost its God, was shut up in death and darkness, and became a prisoner in an earthly animal, that
only excelled its brethren, the beasts, in an upright
form, and serpentine subtlety. Thus ended the fall of
man. But from that moment that the God of mercy
inspoke into Adam the Bruiser of the serpent, from
that moment all the riches and treasures of the divine
nature came again into man, as a Seed of salvation
sown into the **centre** of the soul, and only lieth hidden
there in every man, till he desires to rise from his
fallen state, and to be born again from above.

Awake, then, thou that sleepest, and CHRIST, who from all eternity hath been espoused to thy soul, shall give thee Light. Begin to search and dig in thine own field for this Pearl of eternity, that lieth hidden in it; it cannot cost thee too much, nor canst thou buy it too dear, for it is all, and when thou hast found it, thou wilt know that all which thou hast sold or given away for it is as a mere nothing, as a bubble upon the water.

19. The Pearl of Eternity is the Light and Spirit of God within thee.

But I will now show a little more distinctly what this Pearl of eternity is. First, It is the Light and Spirit of God within thee, which has hitherto done thee but little good, because all the desire of thy heart has been after the light and spirit of this world. Thy reason and senses, thy heart and passions, have turned all their attention to the poor concerns of this life, and therefore thou art a stranger to this Principle of heaven, this riches of eternity, within thee. For as God is not, cannot be, truly found by any worshippers but those who worship Him in spirit and in truth, so this Light and Spirit, though always within us, is not, cannot be, found, felt, or enjoyed but by those whose whole spirit is turned to it.

When man first came into being, and stood before God, as His own image and likeness, this Light and Spirit of God was as natural to him, as truly the light of his nature, as the light and air of this world is natural to the creatures that have their birth in it. But when man, not content with the food of eternity, did eat of the earthly tree, this Light and Spirit of heaven was no more natural to him, no more rose up as a birth of his nature, but instead thereof, he was left solely to the light and spirit of this world. And this is that death, which God told Adam he should surely die, in the day that he should eat of the forbidden tree.

But the goodness of God would not leave man in this condition; a redemption from it was immediately granted, and the Bruiser of the serpent brought the Light and Spirit of heaven once more into the human nature. Not as it was in its first state, when man was in Paradise, but as a **treasure hidden** in the centre of our souls, which should discover, and open itself by degrees, in such proportion as the faith and desires of our hearts were turned to it.

This Light and Spirit of God thus freely restored again to the soul, and lying in it as a secret source of heaven, is called grace, free grace, or the supernatural gift, or power of God in the soul, because it was something that the natural powers of the soul could no more obtain.

Hence it is, that in the greatest truth, and highest reality, every stirring of the soul, every tendency of the heart towards God and goodness, is justly and necessarily ascribed to the Holy Spirit, or the grace of God.

It is because this first Seed of life, which is sown into the soul, as the gift or grace of God to fallen man, is itself the Light and Spirit of God; and therefore every stirring or opening of this Seed of Life, every awakened thought or desire that arises from it, must be called the moving, or the quickening of the Spirit of God; and therefore that new man which arises from it, must of all necessity be said to be solely the work and operation of God.

Hence also we have an easy and plain declaration of the true meaning, solid sense, and certain truth of all those scriptures which speak of the inspiration of God, the operation of the Holy Spirit, the power of the divine Light, as the sole and necessary agents in the renewal and sanctification of our souls, and also as being things common to all men. It is because this Seed of life, or Bruiser of the serpent, is common to all men, and has in all men a degree of life, which is in itself so much of the inspiration or Life of God, the Spirit of God, the Light of God, which is in every soul, and is its power of becoming born again of God.

Hence also it is, that all men are exhorted not to quench, or resist, or grieve the Spirit; that is, this Seed of the Spirit and Light of God that is in all men, as the only source of good. Again, "the flesh lusteth against the Spirit, and the Spirit against the flesh." By the flesh, and its lustings, are meant the mere human nature, or the natural man, as he is by the fall; by the Spirit is meant the Bruiser of the serpent, that Seed of the Light and Spirit of God, which lieth as a treasure hid in the soul, in order to bring forth the life that was lost in Adam. Now, as the flesh hath its life, its lustings, whence all sorts of evil are truly said to be inspired, quickened, and stirred up in us; so the Spirit, being a living principle **within us,** has its inspiration, its breathing, its moving, its quickening, from which alone the divine life, or the angel that died in Adam, can be born in us.

See here, in short, the state of man as redeemed. He has a spark of the Light and Spirit of God, as a

supernatural gift of God given into the birth of his
soul, to bring forth by degrees a new birth of that
life which was lost in Paradise.

This holy Spark of the divine nature within him
has a natural, strong, and almost infinite tendency, or
reaching, after that eternal Light and Spirit of God,
from whence it came forth.   It came forth from God,
it came out of God, it partaketh of the divine nature,
and therefore it is always in a state of tendency and
return to God.   And all this is called the breathing,
the moving, the quickening, of the Holy Spirit within
us, which are so many operations of this Spark of life
tending towards God.

On the other hand, the Deity, as considered in
Itself and without the soul of man, has an infinite,
unchangeable tendency of love and desire towards the
soul of man, to unite, and communicate its own riches
and glories to it, just as the spirit of the air **without**
man, unites and communicates its riches and virtues
to the spirit of the air that is **within** man; this love
or desire of God towardsthe soul of man is so great,
that He gave His only-begotten Son, the brightness of
His glory, to take the human nature upon Him, in its
fallen state, that by this mysterious union of God and
man, all the enemies of the soul of man might be overcome, and every human creature might have a power
of being born again, according to that image of God in
which he was first created.   The gospel is the history
of this love of God to man.   **Inwardly,** he has a Seed
of the divine Life given into the birth of his soul, a
Seed that has all the riches of eternity in it, and is
always wanting to come to the birth in him, and be
alive in God.   **Outwardly,** he has Jesus Christ, who, as

a Sun of righteousness, is always casting forth His enlivening beams on this inward Seed, to kindle and call It forth to the birth, doing that to this Seed of heaven in man, which the sun in the firmament is always doing to the vegetable seeds in the earth.

Consider this matter in the following similitude. A grain of wheat has the air and light of this world enclosed, or incorporated in it : this is the mystery of its life, this is its power of growing. By this it has a strong continual tendency of **uniting** again with that ocean of light and air from whence it came forth, and so it helps to kindle its own vegetable life.

On the other hand, that great ocean of light and air having its own offspring hidden in the heart of the grain, has a perpetual strong tendency to **unite**, and communicate with it again. From this desire of union on **both sides**, the vegetable life arises, and all the virtues and powers contained in it.

But here let it be well observed, that this desire on both sides cannot have its effect till the **husk** and gross part of the grain falls into a state of corruption and **death** ; till this begins, the mystery of life hidden in it cannot come forth. The application may here be left to the reader. I shall only observe, that we may here see the true ground and absolute necessity of that dying to ourselves, and to the world, to which our blessed Lord so constantly calls all His followers. An universal self-denial, a perpetual mortification of the lust of the flesh, the lust of the eyes, and the pride of life, is not a thing imposed upon us by the mere will of God, is not required as a punishment, is not an invention of dull and monkish spirits, but has its ground and reason in the nature of the thing, and

is as absolutely necessary to make way for the new
birth, as the death of the husk and gross part of the
grain is necessary to make way for its vegetable life.

20. The Pearl of Eternity is the Wisdom and Love of God within thee.

But, secondly, this **Pearl of eternity** is the **Wisdom
and Love** of God within thee. In this Pearl of thy
serpent Bruiser, all the holy nature, spirit, tempers,
and inclinations of Christ lie as in a seed in the centre
of thy soul, and divine wisdom and heavenly love will
grow up in thee, if thou givest but true attention to
God present in thy soul. On the other hand, there
is hidden also in the depth of thy nature, the root or
possibility of all the hellish nature, spirit, and tempers
of the fallen angels. For heaven and hell have each
of them their foundation within us; they come not
into us from **without**, but spring up in us, according as
our **will** and **heart** is turned either to the Light of God,
or the kingdom of darkness. But when this life, which
is in the midst of these two eternities, is at an end,
either an angel or a devil will be found to have a
birth in us.

Thou needest not, therefore, run here, or there, saying, "Where is Christ?" Thou needest not say, "Who
shall ascend into heaven, that is, to bring Christ down
from above? or who shall descend into the deep, to
bring Christ up from the dead?" for behold the Word,
which is the Wisdom of God, is in thy heart; it is
there as a Bruiser of thy serpent, as a light unto thy
feet, and lantern unto thy paths. It is there as a
speaking Word of God in thy soul; and as soon as
thou art ready to hear, this eternal speaking Word

will speak wisdom and love in thy inward parts, and
bring forth the birth of Christ, with all His holy
nature, spirit, and tempers, within thee.

Hence it is, that in the Christian Church there
have been in all ages, amongst the most illiterate,
both men and women, who have attained to a deep
understanding of the mysteries of the wisdom and
love of God in Christ Jesus.   And what wonder ?
Since it is not art or science, or skill in grammar or
logic, but the opening of the divine Life in the soul,
that can give true understanding of the things of God.
This Life of God in the soul, which for its smallness
at first, and capacity for great growth, is by our Lord
compared to a grain of mustard-seed, may be, and too
generally is, suppressed and kept under, either by
worldly cares, or pleasures, by vain learning, sensuality,
or ambition.

On the other hand, wherever this Seed of heaven
is suffered to take root, to get life and breath in the
soul, whether it be in man or woman, young or old,
there this new-born inward man is justly said to be
inspired, enlightened, and moved by the Spirit of God,
because his whole birth and life is a birth from above,
of the Light and Spirit of God, and therefore all that
is in him hath the nature, spirit, and tempers of
heaven in it.   As this regenerate life grows up in
any man, so there grows up a true and real knowledge
of the whole mystery of godliness in himself.   All
that the gospel teaches of sin and grace, of life and
death, of heaven and hell, of the new and old man, of
the Light and Spirit of God, are things not got by
hearsay, but inwardly known, felt, and experienced in
the growth of his own new-born life.   He has then

an unction from above which teacheth him all things,
a spirit that "knoweth what it ought to pray for;"
a spirit that "prays without ceasing," that is risen
with Christ from the dead, and has all its conversation in heaven; a spirit that hath "groans and sighs
that cannot be uttered;" that travaileth and groaneth
with the whole creation to be delivered from vanity,
and have its glorious liberty in that God from whom
it came forth.

21. The Pearl of Eternity is the Temple of God within thee.

Again, thirdly, this **Pearl of eternity is the Church,
or temple of God** within thee, the consecrated place of
divine worship, where alone thou canst worship God
" in spirit and in truth."   In **spirit,** because thy spirit
is that alone in thee, which can unite and cleave unto
God, and receive the workings of His divine Spirit
upon thee.   In **truth,** because this adoration in spirit
is that truth and reality, of which all outward forms
and rites, though instituted by God, are only the
figure for a time; but this worship is eternal.

**Accustom thyself to the holy service of this inward
temple;** in the midst of it is the Fountain of living
water, of which thou mayest drink, and live for ever.
There the mysteries of thy redemption are celebrated,
or rather, opened in life and power.   **There** the supper
of the Lamb is kept; the " Bread that came down from
heaven, that giveth life to the world," is thy true
nourishment: all is done, and known in real experience, in a living sensibility of the work of God on
the soul.   **There** the birth, the life, the sufferings,
the death, the resurrection, and ascension of Christ,

are not merely remembered, but inwardly found and
enjoyed as the real states of thy soul, which has
followed Christ in the regeneration. When once thou
art well grounded in this inward worship, thou wilt
have learnt to live unto God above time and place;
for every day will be Sunday to thee, and wherever
thou goest, thou wilt have a priest, a church, and an
altar, along with thee. For when God has all that
He should have of thy heart, when renouncing the
will, judgment, tempers, and inclinations of thy old
man, thou art wholly given up to the obedience of
the Light and Spirit of God within thee, to will only
in His Will, to love only in His Love, to be wise only
in His Wisdom; then it is that every thing thou dost
is as a song of praise, and the common business of thy
life is a conforming to God's will on earth, as angels
do in heaven.

22. The Pearl of Eternity is the Peace and Joy of God within thee.

Fourthly, and lastly, this Pearl of eternity is the
Peace and Joy of God within thee; but can only be
found by the manifestation of the Life and Power of
Jesus Christ in thy soul. But Christ cannot be thy
Power and thy Life, till, in obedience to His call, thou
deniest thyself, takest up thy daily cross, and followest
Him, in the regeneration. This is peremptory; it
admits of no reserve or evasion, it is the one way to
Christ and eternal life. But be where thou wilt, either
here, or at Rome, or Geneva, if self is undenied, if
thou livest to thine own will, to the pleasures of thy
natural lust and appetites, senses and passions, and in
conformity to the vain customs and spirit of this world,

thou art dead whilst thou livest, the seed of the woman
is crucified within thee, CHRIST can profit thee
nothing, thou art a stranger to all that is holy and
heavenly within thee, and utterly incapable of finding
the Peace and Joy of God in thy soul: and thus thou
art poor, and blind, and naked, and empty, and livest
a miserable life in the vanity of time; whilst all the
riches of eternity, the Light and Spirit, the Wisdom
and Love, the Peace and Joy of God, are **within thee.**
And thus it will always be with thee, there is no
remedy: go where thou wilt, do what thou wilt, all
is shut up, there is no open door of salvation, no awaken-
ing out of the sleep of sin, no deliverance from the
power of thy corrupt nature, no overcoming of the
world, no revelation of Jesus Christ, no joy of the new
birth from above, till, **dying to thyself and the world,**
thou turnest to the Light, and Spirit, and Power of
God in thy soul. All is fruitless and insignificant,
all the means of thy redemption are at a stand, all
outward forms are but a dead formality, till this
Fountain of Living Water is found within thee.

23. Of the Way to Possess this Pearl of Eternity.

But thou wilt perhaps say, How shall I discover this
Riches of eternity, this Light, and Spirit, and Wisdom,
and Peace of God, treasured up within me? Thy **first
thought** of repentance, or **desire** of turning to God, is
thy first discovery of this Light and Spirit of God
within thee; it is the voice and language of the **Word**
of God within thee, though thou knowest it not. It is
the Bruiser of thy serpent's head, thy dear Immanuel,
who is beginning to preach **within thee,** that same which

He first preached in public, saying, "Repent, for the kingdom of heaven is at hand." When, therefore, but the smallest instinct or desire of thy heart calleth thee towards God, and a newness of life, give it time and leave to speak ; and take care thou refuse not Him that speaketh. For it is not an angel from heaven that speaketh to thee, but it is the eternal **speaking Word** of God in thy heart, that Word which at first created thee, is thus beginning to create thee a second time unto righteousness, that a new man may be formed again in thee in the image and likeness of God. But above all things, beware of taking this desire of repentance to be the effect of thy own natural sense and reason, for in so doing thou losest the key of all the heavenly treasure that is in thee, thou shuttest the door against God, turnest away from Him, and thy repentance (if thou hast any) will be only a vain, unprofitable work of thy own hands, that will do thee no more good than a well that is without water. But if thou takest this **awakened desire** of turning to God to be, as in truth it is, the **coming of Christ** in thy soul, the working, redeeming power of the Light and Spirit of the holy Jesus within thee, if thou dost reverence and adhere to it as such, this faith will save thee, will make thee whole ; and by thus believing in Christ, though thou wert dead, yet shalt thou live.

Now, all dependeth upon thy right submission and obedience to this speaking of God in thy soul. Stop, therefore, all self-activity, listen not to the suggestions of thy own reason, run not on in thy own will; but be **retired, silent, passive, and humbly attentive** to this new-risen Light within thee. Open thy heart, thine eyes, and ears, to all its impressions. Let it enlighten, teach, frighten, torment, judge, and condemn thee as it pleaseth, turn not away from it, hear all it saith, seek for no relief out of it, consult not with flesh and blood, but, **with a heart full of faith and resignation to God**, pray only this prayer, that God's Kingdom may come, and His Will be done in thy soul. Stand faithfully in this state of preparation, thus given up to the Spirit of God, and then the work of thy repentance will be wrought in God, and thou wilt soon find that He that is in thee is much greater than all that are against thee.

24. Of Dependence on God's Spirit.

But that thou mayest do all this the better, and be more firmly assured that this **resignation** to, and **dependence** upon, the working of God's Spirit within thee is right and sound, I shall lay before thee two great, and infallible, and fundamental truths, which will be as a rock for thy faith to stand upon.

First. That through all the whole nature of things, nothing can do, or be a **real good** to thy soul, but the **operation of God** upon it. Secondly. That all the dispensations of God to mankind, from the fall of Adam to the preaching of the gospel, were only for this one end, to fit, prepare, and dispose the soul for the **operation** of the Spirit of God upon it. These two great truths, well and deeply apprehended, put the soul in its right state, in a continual dependence upon God, in a readiness to receive all good from Him, and will be a continual source of light in thy mind. They will keep thee safe from all errors, and false zeal in things and forms of religion,—from a sectarian spirit, from bigotry and superstition; they will teach

thee the true difference between the **means** and the
end of religion, and the regard thou showest to the
shell will be only so far as the **kernel** is to be found
in it.

25. Of Nature and Grace.

Man, by his fall, had broke off from his true centre,
his proper place in God, and therefore the Life and
operation of God was no more in him. He was
fallen from a life in God, into a life of self, into an
animal life of self-love, self-esteem, and self-seeking
in the poor perishing enjoyments of this world. This
was the natural state of man by the fall. He was
an apostate from God, and His natural life was all
idolatry, where self was the great idol that was
worshipped instead of God. See here the whole truth
in short. All sin, death, damnation, and hell is
nothing else but this kingdom of **self,** or the various
operations of self-love, self-esteem, and self-seeking,
which separate the soul from God, and end in eternal
death and hell.

On the other hand, all that is grace, redemption,
salvation, sanctification, spiritual life, and the new
birth, is nothing else but so much of the Life and
operation of God found again in the soul. It is man
come back again into his **centre** or place in God, from
whence he had broke off. The beginning again of the
Life of God in the soul was then first made, when the
mercy of God inspoke into Adam a Seed of the divine
Life, which should bruise the head of the serpent,
which had wrought itself into the human nature.
Here the Kingdom of God was again with us, though
only as a Seed; yet, small as it was, it was yet a

degree of the divine Life, which, if rightly cultivated, would overcome all the evil that was in us, and make of every fallen man a new-born son of God.

26. Of the Old and New Testament.

All the sacrifices and institutions of the ancient patriarchs, the Law of Moses, with all its types and rites and ceremonies, had this only end: they were the methods of divine Wisdom for a time, to keep the hearts of men from the wanderings of idolatry, in a state of **holy expectation** upon God,—they were to keep the first Seed of life in a state of growth, and make way for the **further operation** of God upon the soul; or, as the apostle speaks, to be as a schoolmaster [leading us] unto Christ. That is, till the birth, the death, the resurrection, and ascension of Christ, should conquer death and hell, open a new Dispensation of God, and baptize mankind afresh with the Holy Ghost and fire of heaven. Then, that is, on the day of Pentecost, a new Dispensation of God came forth, which, on God's part, was **the operation of the Holy Spirit** in gifts and graces upon the whole Church. And on man's part, it was the adoration of God in " spirit and in truth." Thus, all that was done by God, from the Bruiser of the serpent given to Adam, to Christ's sitting down on the right hand of God, was all for this end, to remove all that stood between God and man, and to make way for the **immediate** and **continual** operation of God upon the soul. And that man, baptized with the Holy Spirit, and born again from above, should absolutely renounce self, and wholly give up his soul to the operation of God's Spirit, to know, to love, to will, to pray, to worship, to preach, to exhort, to use all the faculties of his mind, and all the outward things of this world, as **enlightened, inspired, moved, and guided by the Holy Ghost;** who by this last dispensation of God was given to be a Comforter, a Teacher, and Guide to the Church, who should abide with it for ever.

27. Of the Kingdom of God.

This is Christianity, a Spiritual Society, not because it has no worldly concerns, but because all its members, as such, are born of the Spirit, kept alive, animated, and governed by the Spirit of God. It is constantly called by our Lord **the kingdom of God,** or heaven, because all its **ministry** and **service,** all that is done in it, is done in obedience and subjection to **that Spirit** by which angels live and are governed in heaven.[1] Hence our blessed Lord taught His disciples to pray, that His Kingdom might come, that so God's will might be done on earth, as it is in heaven; which could not be, but by that same Spirit by which it is done in heaven. The short is this: the kingdom of **self** is the fall of man, or the great apostasy from the Life of God in the soul, and every one, wherever he be, that liveth unto **self,** is still under the fall and great apostasy from God. The Kingdom of Christ is the Spirit and Power of God, dwelling and manifesting itself in the birth of a new inward man; and no one **is** a member of this kingdom, but so far as a true birth of the Spirit is brought forth in him. These two kingdoms take in all mankind: he that is not of one is certainly in the other; dying to one, is living to the other.

[1] *Way to Divine Knowledge,* etc.

28. Of Subjection to the Spirit of God.

Hence we may gather these following truths:
First. Here is shown the true ground and reason of
what was said above, namely, that when the call of
God to repentance first ariseth in thy soul, thou art
to be **retired, silent, passive,** and humbly attentive to
this new-risen Light within thee, by wholly stopping,
or disregarding the workings of **thy own will, reason,
and judgment.** It is because all these are false counsellors, the sworn servants, bribed slaves of thy fallen
nature, they are all **born and bred in the kingdom
of self;** and therefore if a new kingdom is to be set
up in thee, if the operation of God is to have its effect
in thee, all **these natural powers** of **self** are to be
silenced and suppressed, till **they have learned obedience and subjection to the Spirit of God.** Now, this
is not requiring thee to become a fool, or to give up
thy claim to sense and reason, but is the shortest way
to have thy sense and reason delivered from folly,
and thy whole rational nature strengthened, enlightened, and guided by that Light, which is Wisdom
itself.

A child that obediently denies his own will and
own reason to be guided by the will and reason of a
truly wise and understanding tutor, cannot be said to
make himself a fool, and give up the benefit of his
rational nature, but to have taken the shortest way
to have his own will and reason made truly a blessing
to him.

29. The Need of Mortifying Self.

Secondly. Hence is to be seen the true ground
and necessity of that universal mortification and self-

denial with regard to all our senses, appetites, tempers, passions, and judgments. **It is because all our whole nature, as fallen from the Life of God, is in a state of contrariety to the order and end of our creation, a continual source of disorderly appetites, corrupt tempers, and false judgments.** And therefore **every motion of it is to be mortified,** changed, and purified from its natural state, before we can enter into the Kingdom of God.

Thus, when our Lord saith, " Except a man hateth his father and mother, yea, and his own life, he cannot be My disciple," it is because our best tempers are yet **carnal,** and full of the imperfections of our fallen nature. The doctrine is just and good ; not as if father and mother were to be hated ; but **that love,** which an unregenerate person, or **natural man,** hath towards them, is to be hated ; as being a blind **self-love,** full of all the weakness and partiality with which fallen man loves, honours, esteems, and cleaves to himself. This love, born from corrupt flesh and blood, and polluted with self, is to be hated and parted with, that we may love them with a love born of God, with such a love, and on such a motive, as Christ hath loved us. And then the disciple of Christ far exceeds all others in the love of parents.

Again, our **own life** is to be **hated ;** and the reason is plain, it is because there is nothing lovely in it. It is a legion of evil, a monstrous birth of the serpent, the world, and the flesh ; it is an apostasy from the Life and Power of God in the soul ; a life that is death to heaven, that is pure unmixed idolatry, that lives wholly to self, and not to God, and therefore all **this own life** is to be absolutely hated, all this self is to be **denied and mortified;** the nature, spirit, tempers, and inclinations of Christ are to be brought to life in us. For it is as impossible to live to both these lives at once, as for a body to move two contrary ways at the same time. And therefore all these mortifications and self-denials have an absolute necessity in the nature of the thing itself.

30. Of forsaking All.

Thus, when our Lord further saith, unless a man forsake " all that he hath, he cannot be My disciple," the reason is plain, and the necessity absolute; it is because **all** that the natural man hath, is in the possession of **self-love,** and therefore this possession is to be absolutely forsaken and parted with. **All that he hath is to be put into other hands,** to be given to divine Love, or this natural man cannot be changed into a disciple of Christ. For **self-love, in all that it hath,** is earthly, sensual, and devilish, and therefore must have **all** taken away from it; and then to the natural man **all** is lost; he hath nothing left, all is laid down at the feet of Jesus. And then all things are common, as soon as **self-love** has lost the possession of them. And then the disciple of Christ, " though having nothing, yet possesseth all things," all that the natural man hath forsaken, is restored to the disciple of Christ an hundred-fold. For **self-love,** the greatest of all thieves, being now cast out, and all that he had stolen and hidden thus taken from him, and **put into the hands of divine Love,** every mite becometh a large treasure, and Mammon openeth the door into everlasting habitations. This was the spirit of the first draught of a Christian Church at Jerusalem, a

Church made truly after the pattern of heaven, where
the love that reigns in heaven reigned in it, where
divine Love broke down all the selfish fences, the locks
and bolts of **me, mine, my own,** etc., and laid all things
common to the members of this new Kingdom of God
on earth.

Now, though many years did not pass after the age
of the apostles, before Satan and self got footing in
the Church, and set up merchandise in the House of
God, yet this **one Heart,** and **one Spirit,** which then
first appeared in the Jerusalem Church, is that **one
Heart** and **Spirit** of divine Love, to which all are called,
who would be true disciples of Christ. And though
the practice of it is lost as to the Church in general,
yet it ought not to have been lost; and therefore
every Christian ought to make it his great care and
prayer, to have it restored in himself; and then,
though born in the dregs of time, or living in Babylon,
he will as truly be a member of the first heavenly
Church at Jerusalem, as if he had lived in it in the
days of the apostles. This **Spirit of Love, born of that
celestial Fire** with which Christ baptizes His true
disciples, is alone that Spirit which can enter into
heaven, and therefore is that Spirit which is to be born
in us whilst we are on earth.

For no one can enter into heaven till he is made
heavenly, till the Spirit of heaven is entered into him.
And therefore all that our Lord hath said of denying and **dying to self,** and of his parting with all that
he hath, are practices absolutely necessary from the
nature of the thing.

31. Of the Love of our Neighbour in and for God.

Because all turning to self is so far turning **from God,** and so much as we have of self-love, so much we have of a hellish, earthly weight, that must be taken off, or there can be no ascension into heaven.   But thou wilt perhaps say, if all self-love is to be renounced, then all love of our neighbour is renounced along with it, because the commandment is only " to love our neighbour as ourselves."   The answer here is easy, and yet no quarter given to self-love.   There is but one only love in **heaven,** and yet the angels of God love one another in the same manner as they love themselves.   The matter is thus : the one supreme, unchangeable rule of love, which is a law to all intelligent beings of all worlds, and will be a law to all eternity, is this—viz. that God alone is to be loved **for Himself,** and **all other beings only in Him and for Him**.   Whatever intelligent creature lives not under this rule of love, is so far fallen from the order of his creation, and is, till he returns to this eternal Law of Love, an apostate from God, and incapable of the Kingdom of heaven.

Now, if God alone is to be loved for Himself, then no creature is to be loved for itself ; and so all **self-love** in every creature is absolutely condemned.

And if all created beings are only to be loved in and for God, then my neighbour is to be loved as I love myself, and I am only to love myself as I love my neighbour, or any other created being,—that is, only **in and for God**.   And thus the command of loving our neighbours as ourselves stands firm, and yet all self-love is plucked up by the roots. But what is loving any creature only in, and for God? It is when we love it only as it is God's **work, image, and delight**, when we love it merely as it is God's, and belongs to Him; this is loving it in God: and when all that we wish, intend, or do to it, is done from a love of God, for the honour of God, and in conformity to the Will of God; this is loving it for God. This is the **one love** that is, and must be, the spirit of all creatures that live united to God. Now, this is no speculative refinement or fine-spun fiction of the brain, but the simple truth, a first law of nature, and a necessary bond of union between God and the creature. The creature is not in God, is a stranger to Him, has lost the Life of God in itself, whenever its love does not thus **begin and end in God**.

32. The Necessity of Self-Denial.

The loss of this love was the fall of man, as it opened in him a kingdom of self, in which Satan, the world, and the flesh could all of them bring forth their own works.[1] If, therefore, man is to rise from his fall, and return to his life in God, there is an absolute necessity that self, with all his brood of gross affections, be deposed, that his first love, in and for which he was created, may be born again in him. Christ came into the world to save sinners, to destroy the works of the devil. Now, **self** is not only the seat and habitation, but the **very life** of sin: the works of the devil are all wrought in **self**; it is his peculiar workhouse: and therefore Christ is not come as a Saviour from sin, as a destroyer of the works of the

[1] *Spirit of Prayer*, Part the Second.

devil in any of us, but so far as self is beaten down, and overcome in us. It is literally true what our Lord said, that "His kingdom was not of this world;" then it is a truth of the same certainty, that no one is a member of this kingdom, but he that, in the literal sense of the words, renounces the spirit of this world. Christians might as well part with half the articles of their creed, or but half believe them, as to really refuse, or but by halves enter into these self-denials.

For all that is in the creed, is only to bring forth this dying and death to all and every part of the old man, that the Life and Spirit of Christ may be formed in us.

Our redemption is this **new birth;** if this is not done, or doing in us, we are still unredeemed. And though the Saviour of the world is come, He is not come in us, He is not received by us, is a stranger to us, is not ours, if His Life is not within us. His Life is not, cannot be, within us, but so far as the spirit of the world, self-love, self-esteem, and self-seeking are renounced and driven out of us.

33. The True Nature and Worth of Self-Denial.

Thirdly. Hence we may also learn the true nature and worth of all self-denials and mortifications. As to their nature, considered in themselves, they have nothing of goodness or holiness, nor are any real parts of our sanctification; they are not the true food or nourishment of the divine Life in our souls, they have **no quickening, sanctifying power** in them; their only worth consists in this, that they remove the impediments of holiness, break down that which stands between God and us, and **make way** for the **quickening, sanctifying Spirit of God to operate** on our souls: which operation of God is the one only thing that can raise the divine Life in the soul, or help it to the smallest degree of real holiness, or spiritual life. As in our creation we had only that degree of a divine Life which the power of God derived into us; as then all that we had, and were, was the **sole operation** of God, in the creation of us, so in our redemption, or regaining that first perfection which we have lost, all must be again the **operation of God.** Every degree of the divine Life restored in us, be it ever so small, must and can be nothing else but so much of the Life and operation of God found again in the soul. All the activity of man in the works of self-denial, has no good in itself, but is only to open an entrance for the **one only good,** the Light of God, to operate upon us.

34. Of the Danger of Trusting in our Self-Denial, and the only Way to avoid this.

Hence, also, we may learn the reason why many people not only lose the benefit, but are even the worse for all their mortifications. It is because they mistake the whole nature and worth of them. They practise them for their own sakes, as things good in themselves; they think them to be **real** parts of holiness, and so **rest** in them, and look no farther, but grow full of self-esteem and self-admiration for their own progress in them. This makes them self-sufficient, morose, severe judges of all those that fall short of their mortifications.

And thus their self-denials do only that for them which indulgences do for other people; they withstand

and hinder the operation of God upon their souls, and instead of being really self-denials, they strengthen and keep up the kingdom of self.

There is no avoiding this fatal error, but by deeply entering into this great truth, that all our own activity and working has no good in it, can do no good to us, but as it leads and turns us in the best manner to the Light and Spirit of God, which alone brings life and salvation into the soul. "Stretch forth thy hand," said our Lord to the "man that had a withered hand;" he did so, and "it was immediately made whole as the other."

Now, had this man any ground for pride, or a high opinion of himself, for the share he had in the restoring of his hand? Yet just such is our share in the raising up of the spiritual life within us. All that we can do by our own activity, is only like this man's stretching out his hand; the rest is the work of Christ, the only Giver of life to the withered hand, or the dead soul. We can only, then, do living works, when we are so far born again as to be able to say with the apostle, "Yet not I, but Christ that liveth in me."

35. Of our Absolute Dependence upon God.

But to return, and further show how the soul that feels the call of God to repentance, is to behave under it, that this stirring of the divine Power in the soul may have its full effect, and bring forth the birth of the new man in Christ Jesus. We are to consider it (as in truth it is) as the Seed of the divine nature within us, that can only grow by its own strength and union with God. It is a divine Life, and therefore can grow from nothing but divine Power. When the

Virgin Mary conceived the birth of the holy Jesus, all that she did towards it herself was only this single act of faith and resignation to God: "Behold the handmaid of the Lord, be it unto me according to Thy word." This is all that we can do towards the conception of that new man that is to be born in ourselves. Now, this truth is easily consented to, and a man thinks he believes it, because he consents to it, or rather, does not deny it. But that is not enough: it is to be apprehended in a deep, full, and practical assurance, in such a manner as a man knows and believes that he did not create the stars, or cause life to rise up in himself. Then it is a belief that puts the soul into a right state, that makes room for the operation of God upon it. His Light then enters with full power into the soul, and His Holy Spirit moves and directs all that is done in it, and so man lives again in God as a new creature.

36. Of the Effects of this Absolute Dependence upon God.

This truth, thus firmly believed, will have these two most excellent effects:

First. It will keep the soul fixed, and continually turned towards God, in faith, prayer, desire, confidence, and resignation to Him, for all that it wants to have done in it, and to it; which will be a continual source of all divine virtues and graces. The soul thus turned to God, must be always receiving from Him. It stands at the true door of all divine communications, and the Light of God as freely enters into it as the light of the sun enters into the air.

Secondly. It will fix and ground the soul in a true

and lasting self-denial. For by thus knowing and owning our own nothingness and inability, that we have no other capacity for good but that of receiving it from God alone, **self** is wholly denied, its kingdom is destroyed; no room is left for spiritual pride and self-esteem; we are saved from a pharisaical holiness, from wrong opinions of our own works and good deeds, and from a multitude of errors, the most dangerous to our souls, all which arise from the something that we take ourselves to be either in nature or grace. But when we once apprehend but in some good degree, the **All of God** and the **nothingness of ourselves**, we have got a Truth, whose usefulness and benefit no words can express. When our religion is founded on this Rock, it has the firmness of a rock, and its height reaches unto heaven. The world, the flesh, and the devil can do no hurt to it; all enemies are known, and all disarmed by this great Truth, dwelling in our souls.

It is the knowledge of the **All of God** that makes Cherubims and Seraphims to be flames of divine Love. Where this **All of God** is truly known and felt in any creature, there its whole breath and spirit is a fire of love; nothing but a pure, disinterested love can rise up in it, or come from it,—a love that begins and ends in God. Where this love is born in any creature, there a seraphic life is born along with it. This pure love introduces the creature into the **All of God**,—all that is in God is opened in the creature; it is united with God, and hath the Life of God manifested in it.

There is but one **salvation** for all mankind, and that is the **Life of God** in the soul. God has but **one design** or intent towards all mankind, and that is to introduce

or generate **His own Life**, Light, and Spirit in them,
that all may be as so many images, temples, and
habitations of the Holy Trinity.

37. Of the one Salvation, and the Way to it.

Now, there is but one possible way for man to
attain this salvation, or Life of God in the soul.
God is One, human nature is one, salvation is one,
and the Way to it is one; and that is, **the desire of
the soul turned to God.** When this desire is alive,
and breaks forth in any creature under heaven, then
the lost sheep is found, and the Shepherd hath it upon
His shoulders.   Through **this desire** the poor prodigal
son leaveth his husks and swine, and hasteth to his
Father; it is because of **this desire** that the Father
seeth the son while yet afar off, that He runs out to
meet him, falleth on his neck, and kisseth him.   See
here how plainly we are taught that no sooner is **this
desire** arisen and in motion towards God, but the
operation of God's Spirit answers to it, cherishes and
welcomes its first beginnings, signified by the Father's
seeing and having compassion on His son, whilst yet
afar off,—that is, in the first beginnings of his desire.
Thus does **this desire** do all; it brings the soul to God,
and God into the soul; it unites with God, it co-
operates with God, and is one life with God.

Oh my God, just and good, how great is Thy love
and mercy to mankind, that heaven is thus everywhere open, and Christ thus the common Saviour to
all that turn the desire of their hearts to Thee!   Oh
sweet Power of the Bruiser of the serpent, born in
every son of man, that stirs and works in every man,

11

and gives every man a power, and desire, to find his
happiness in God! Oh holy Jesus, heavenly " Light,
that lighteth every man that cometh into the world,"
that redeemeth every soul that followeth Thy light,
which is **always within him**! Oh Holy Trinity,
immense Ocean of divine Love, in which all mankind
live, and move, and have their being! None are
separated from Thee, none live out of Thy love, but
all are embraced in the arms of Thy mercy, all are
partakers of Thy divine Life, the operation of Thy
Holy Spirit, as soon as their heart is turned to Thee!

Oh plain, and easy, and simple way of salvation!
wanting no subtleties of art or science, no borrowed
learning, no refinements of reason, but all done by the
simple natural motion of every heart, that truly longs
after God. For no sooner is the finite desire of the
creature in motion towards God, but the infinite
desire of God is united with it, co-operates with it.
And in this united desire of God, and the creature, is
the salvation and life of the soul brought forth. For
the soul is shut out of God, and imprisoned in its own
dark workings of flesh and blood, merely and solely
because it desires to live to the vanity of this world.
This desire is its darkness, its death, its imprisonment,
and separation from God.

When, therefore, the first spark of **a desire after God**
arises in thy soul, **cherish it with all thy care**, give all
thy heart into it; it is nothing less than a touch of
the divine Loadstone that is to draw thee out of the
vanity of time into the riches of eternity. Get up,
therefore, and follow it as gladly as the wise men of
the east followed the star from heaven that appeared
to them. It will do for thee, as the star did for them;

it will lead thee to the birth of Jesus, not in a stable at Bethlenem in Judea, but to the birth of Jesus in the **dark centre** of thine own fallen soul.

I shall conclude this First Part with the words of the heavenly illuminated and blessed man Jacob Behmen:

" It is much to be lamented that we are so blindly led, and the truth withheld from us through imaginary conceptions; for if the divine Power in the inward ground of the soul was manifest, and working with its lustre in us, then is the whole Triune God present in the life and will of the soul; and the heaven, wherein God dwelleth, is opened in the soul; **and there, in the soul, is the place where the Father begetteth His Son, and where the Holy Ghost proceedeth from the Father and the Son.**

" Christ saith, ' I am the Light of the world; he that followeth Me walketh not in darkness.' He directs us only to Himself. He is the Morning Star, and is generated and riseth in us, and shineth in the darkness of our nature. **Oh how great a triumph is there in the soul when He ariseth in it!** then a man knows, as he never knew before, that he is a stranger in a foreign land."

A SERIOUS CALL TO A DEVOUT
AND HOLY LIFE

A SERIOUS CALL TO A DEVOUT
AND HOLY LIFE

CHAPTER I.

CONCERNING THE NATURE AND EXTENT OF CHRISTIAN DEVOTION.

(True Devotion does not consist in the performance of certain Religious Duties at set times, but in the Spirit in which the Ordinary Duties of common life are performed.)

DEVOTION is neither private nor public prayer; but prayers, whether private or public, are particular parts or instances of devotion. Devotion signifies a life given, or devoted, to God.

He therefore is the devout man, who lives no longer to his own will, or the way and spirit of the world, but to the sole will of God; who considers God in every thing, who serves God in every thing, who makes all the parts of his common life parts of piety, by doing every thing in the name of God, and under such rules as are comformable to His glory.

We readily acknowledge that God alone is to be the rule and measure of our prayers; that in them we are to look wholly unto Him, and act wholly for Him; that we are only to pray in such a manner, for such things, and such ends, as are suitable to His glory.

Now let any one but find out the reason why he is to be thus strictly pious in his prayers, and he will find the same as strong a reason to be as strictly pious in all the other parts of his life. For there is not the least shadow of a reason why we should make God the rule and measure of our prayers; why we should then look **wholly unto Him,** and pray according to His will; but what equally proves it necessary for us to look **wholly unto God,** and make Him the rule and measure of all the other actions of our life. For any ways of life, any employment of our talents, whether of our parts, our time, or money, that is not strictly **according to the will of God,** that is not for such ends as are **suitable to His glory,** are as great absurdities and failings, as prayers that are not **according to the will of God.** For there is no other reason why our prayers should be according to the will of God, why they should have nothing in them but what is wise, and holy, and heavenly; there is no other reason for this, but that our lives may be of the same nature, full of the same wisdom, holiness, and heavenly tempers, that we may live unto God in the same spirit that we pray unto Him. . . .

As sure, therefore, as there is any wisdom in praying for the Spirit of God, so sure is it that we are to make that Spirit the rule of all our actions; as sure as it is our duty to look wholly unto God in our prayers, so sure is it that it is our duty to live wholly unto

God in our lives. But we can no more be said to live unto God, unless we live unto Him in all the ordinary actions of our life, unless He be the rule and measure of all our ways, than we can be said to pray unto God, unless our prayers look wholly unto Him. . . .

It is for want of knowing, or at least considering this, that we see such a mixture of ridicule in the lives of many people. You see them strict as to some times and places of devotion, but when the service of the church is over, they are but like those that seldom or never come there. In their way of life, their manner of spending their time and money, in their cares and fears, in their pleasures and indulgences, in their labour and diversions, they are like the rest of the world. . . . This is the reason why they are the jest and scorn of careless and worldly people; not because they are really devoted to God, but because they appear to have no other devotion but that of occasional prayers. . . .

And indeed there cannot any thing be imagined more absurd in itself, than wise, and sublime, and heavenly prayers, added to a life of vanity and folly, where neither labour nor diversions, neither time nor money, are under the direction of the wisdom and heavenly tempers of our prayers. . . . And to allow ourselves in any ways of life that neither are, nor can be offered to God, is the same irreligion, as to neglect our prayers, or use them in such a manner as make them an offering unworthy of God.

The short of the matter is this; either reason and religion prescribe **rules and ends to all the ordinary actions** of our life, or they do not: if they do, then it is as necessary to govern all our actions by those rules, as it is necessary to worship God. For if religion teaches us any thing concerning eating and drinking, or spending our time and money; if it teaches us how we are to use and contemn the world; if it tells us **what tempers we are to have in common life,** how we are to be disposed towards all people; how we are to behave towards the sick, the poor, the old, the destitute; if it tells us whom we are to treat with a particular love, whom we are to regard with a particular esteem; if it tells us how we are to treat our enemies, and how we are to mortify and deny ourselves; he must be very weak that can think these parts of religion are not to be observed with as much exactness, as any doctrines that relate to prayers.

It is very observable, that there is not one command in all the gospel for public worship; and perhaps it is a duty that is least insisted upon in Scripture of any other. The frequent attendance at it is never so much as mentioned in all the New Testament. Whereas that religion or devotion which is to govern the ordinary actions of our life, is to be found in almost every verse of Scripture. Our blessed Saviour and His apostles are wholly taken up in doctrines that relate to common life. They call us to renounce the world, and differ in every temper and way of life, from the spirit and the way of the world: to renounce all its goods, to fear none of its evils, to reject its joys, and have no value for its happiness: to be as new-born babes, that are born into a new state of things: to live as pilgrims in spiritual watching, in holy fear, and heavenly aspiring after another life: to take up our daily cross, to deny ourselves, to profess the blessedness of mourning, to seek the blessedness of poverty of spirit : to forsake the pride and vanity of riches, to take no thought for the morrow, to live in the profoundest state of humility, to rejoice in worldly sufferings : to reject the lust of the flesh, the lust of the eyes, and the pride of life : to bear injuries, to forgive and bless our enemies, and to love mankind as God loveth them : to give up our whole hearts and affections to God, and strive to enter through the strait gate into a life of eternal glory.

This is the common devotion which our blessed Saviour taught, in order to make it **the common life** of all Christians. Is it not therefore exceeding strange, that people should place so much piety in the attendance upon public worship, concerning which there is not one precept of our Lord's to be found, and yet neglect these **common duties of our ordinary life,** which are commanded in every page of the gospel ?

If contempt of the world and heavenly affection is a necessary temper of Christians, it is necessary that this temper appear in **the whole course of their lives,** in their manner of using the world, because it can have no place anywhere else. If self-denial be a condition of salvation, all that would be saved must make it a part of their **ordinary life.** If humility be a Christian duty, then the **common** life of a Christian is to be a constant course of humility in all its kinds. If poverty of spirit be necessary, it must be the spirit and temper of **every day** of our lives. If we are to relieve the naked, the sick, and the prisoner, it must be the common charity **of our lives,** as far as we can render ourselves able to perform it. If we are to love our enemies, we must make **our common life** a visible exercise and demonstration of that love. If content and thankfulness, if the patient bearing of evil be duties to God, they are the duties of every day, and in every circumstance of our life. If we are to be wise and holy as the new-born sons of God, we can no otherwise be so, but by renouncing every thing that is foolish and vain in every part of our common life. If we are to be in Christ new creatures, we must show that we are so, by having new ways of living in the world. If we are to follow Christ, it must be in our common way of spending every day.

Thus it is in all the virtues and holy tempers of Christianity; they are not ours unless they be the virtues and tempers of our ordinary life. So that Christianity is so far from leaving us to live in the common ways of life, conforming to the folly of customs, and gratifying the passions and tempers which the spirit of the world delights in, it is so far from indulging us in any of these things, that all its virtues which it makes necessary to salvation are only so many ways of living above and contrary to the world, in all the common actions of our life. If our common life is not a common course of humility, of self-denial, renunciation of the world, poverty of spirit, and heavenly affection, we do not live the lives of Christians. . . .

Now to have right notions and tempers with relation to this world, is as essential to religion as to have right notions of God. And it is as possible for a man to worship a crocodile, and yet be a pious man, as to have his affections set upon this world, and yet be a good Christian. . . .

But it is notorious that Christians are now not only

like other men in their frailties and infirmities, this might be in some degree excusable, but the complaint is, they are like heathens in all the main and chief articles of their lives. They enjoy the world, and live every day in the same tempers, and the same designs, and the same indulgences, as they did who knew not God, nor of any happiness in another life. You may see them different from other people, so far as to times and places of prayer, but generally like the rest of the world in all the other parts of their lives: that is, adding Christian devotion to a heathen life. I have the authority of our blessed Saviour for this remark, where He says, "Take no thought, saying, What shall we eat? or, What shall we drink? or, Wherewithal shall we be clothed? for after all these things do the Gentiles seek."[1] But if to be thus affected even with the necessary things of this life, shows that we are not yet of a Christian spirit, but are like the heathens, surely to enjoy the vanity and folly of the world as they did, to be like them in the main chief tempers of our lives, in self-love and indulgence, in sensual pleasures and diversions, in the vanity of dress, the love of show and greatness, or any other gaudy distinctions of fortune, is a much greater sign of an heathen temper. And, consequently, they who add devotion to such a life, must be said to **pray as Christians,** but **live as heathens.**

[1] Matt. vi. 31, 32.

CHAPTER II.

AN INQUIRY INTO THE REASON, WHY THE GENERALITY OF
CHRISTIANS FALL SO FAR SHORT OF THE HOLINESS
AND DEVOTION OF CHRISTIANITY.

(**The first and most Fundamental Principle of
Christianity is an intention to please God
in all our actions. It is because the
generality of Christians have no such
intention, that they so fall short of True
Devotion.**)

IT may now be reasonably inquired, how it comes to
pass, that the lives even of the better sort of
people are thus strangely contrary to the principles
of Christianity? But before I give a direct answer to
this, I desire it may also be inquired, how it comes
to pass that swearing is so common a vice among
Christians? . . . Now I ask, how comes it that men
are guilty of so gross and profane a sin as this is?
There is neither ignorance nor human infirmity to
plead for it; it is against an express commandment,
and the most plain doctrines of our blessed Saviour.

Do but now find the reason why the generality of
men live in this notorious vice, and then you will have
found the reason why the generality even of the better
sort of people live so contrary to Christianity.

Now the reason of common swearing is this; it is
because men have not so much as the intention to
please God in all their actions. For let a man but
have so much piety as to intend to please God in all
the actions of his life, as the happiest and best thing
in the world, and then he will never swear more.

It seems but a small and necessary part of piety

to have such a sincere intention as this; and that he has no reason to look upon himself as a disciple of Christ who is not thus far advanced in piety. And yet it is purely for want of this degree of piety, that you see such a mixture of sin and folly in the lives even of the better sort of people. . . .

It was this general intention, that made the primitive Christians such eminent instances of piety, and made the goodly fellowship of the saints, and all the glorious army of martyrs and confessors. And if you will here stop, and ask yourselves, why you are not as pious as the primitive Christians were, your own heart will tell you, that it is neither through ignorance, nor inability, but purely because you **never thoroughly intended it.** You observe the same Sunday worship that they did; and you are strict in it, because it is your full intention to be so. And when you as fully intend to be like them in their ordinary common life, when you intend to please God in all your actions, you will find it as possible, as to be strictly exact in the service of the Church. And when you have this intention **to please God in all your actions,** as the happiest and best thing in the world, you will find in you as great an aversion to every thing that is vain and impertinent in common life, whether of business or pleasure, as you now have to any thing that is profane. You will be as fearful of living in any foolish way, either of spending your time, or your fortune, as you are now fearful of neglecting the public worship. . . .

Let a tradesman but have this intention, and it will make him a saint in his shop; his everyday business will be a course of wise and reasonable actions, made holy to God, by being done in obedience to His will and pleasure. He will buy and sell, and labour and travel, because by so doing he can do some good to himself and others. But then, as nothing can please God but what is wise, and reasonable, and holy, so he will neither buy nor sell, nor labour in any other manner, nor to any other end, but such as may be shown to be wise, and reasonable, and holy. He will therefore consider, not what arts, or methods, or application, will soonest make him richer and greater than his brethren, or remove him from a shop to a life of state and pleasure; but he will consider what arts, what methods, what application, can make worldly business most acceptable to God, and make a life of trade a life of holiness, devotion, and piety. This will be the temper and spirit of every tradesman; he cannot stop short of these degrees of piety, whenever it is **his intention to please God in all his actions, as the best and happiest thing in the world.** And, on the other hand, whoever is not of this spirit and temper in his trade and profession, and does not carry it on only so far as is best subservient to a wise, and holy, and heavenly life, it is certain that he has not this intention; and yet without it, who can be shown to be a follower of Jesus Christ?

Again, let the gentleman of birth and fortune but have this intention, and you will see how it will carry him from every appearance of evil, to every instance of piety and goodness. He cannot live by chance, or as humour and fancy carry him, because he knows that nothing can please God but a wise and regular course of life. . . . As he thus removes from all appearance of evil, so he hastens and aspires after every instance of goodness. He does not ask what is allowable and pardonable, but what is commendable and praiseworthy. He does not ask whether God will forgive the folly of our lives, the madness of our pleasures, the vanity of our expenses, the richness of our equipage, and the careless consumption of our time ; but he asks, whether God is pleased with these things, or whether these are the appointed ways of gaining His favour ? He does not inquire, whether it be pardonable to hoard up money, to adorn ourselves with diamonds, and gild our chariots, whilst the widow and the orphan, the sick and the prisoner, want to be relieved ; but he asks, whether God has required these things at our hands ? whether we shall be called to account at the last day for the neglect of them ? because it is not his intent to live in such ways as, for aught we know, God may perhaps pardon ; but to be diligent in such ways as we know that God will infallibly reward.

He will not therefore look at the lives of Christians, to learn how he ought to spend his estate, but he will look into the Scriptures, and make every doctrine, parable, precept, or instruction, that relates to rich men, a law to himself in the use of his estate.

He will have nothing to do with costly apparel, because the rich man in the Gospel was clothed with purple and fine linen. He denies himself the pleasures and indulgences which his estate could procure, because our blessed Saviour saith, "Woe unto you that are rich ! for ye have received your consolation." [1] He will have but one rule for charity, and that will be, to spend all that he can that way, because the Judge of quick and dead hath said, that all that is so given, is given to Him.

[1] Luke vi. 24.

12

He will have no hospitable table for the rich and
wealthy to come and feast with him, in good eating
and drinking; because our blessed Lord saith, "When
thou makest a dinner, call not thy friends, nor thy
brethren, neither thy kinsmen, nor thy rich neighbours;
lest they also bid thee again, and a recompense be
made thee.   But when thou makest a feast, call the
poor, the maimed, the lame, the blind : and thou shalt
be blessed; for they cannot recompense thee: for thou
shalt be recompensed at the resurrection of the just." [1]

Let not any one look upon this as an imaginary
description of charity, that looks fine in the notion,
but cannot be put in practice.   For it is so far from
being an imaginary, impracticable form of life, that it
has been practised by great numbers of Christians in
former ages, who were glad to turn their whole estates
into a constant course of charity.   And it is so far
from being impossible now, that if we can find any
Christians that sincerely intend to please God in all
their actions, as the best and happiest thing in the
world, whether they be young or old, single or married,
men or women, if they have but this intention, it will
be impossible for them to do otherwise.   This one
principle will infallibly carry them to this height of
charity, and they will find themselves unable to stop
short of it. . . .

I have chosen to explain this matter, by appealing
to this intention, because it makes the case so plain,
and because every one that has a mind may see it in
the clearest light, and feel it in the strongest manner,
only by looking into his own heart.   For it is as easy
for every person to know whether he intends to please

[1] Luke xiv. 12, 13, 14.

God in all his actions, as for any servant to know whether this be his intention towards his master. Every one also can as easily tell how he lays out his money, and whether he considers how to please God in it, as he can tell where his estate is, and whether it be in money or land. So that here is no plea left for ignorance or frailty as to this matter; everybody is in the light, and everybody has power. And no one can fail, but he that is not so much a Christian, as to intend to please God in the use of his estate.

Here, therefore, let us judge ourselves sincerely; let us not vainly content ourselves with the common disorders of our lives, the vanity of our expenses, the folly of our diversions, the pride of our habits, the idleness of our lives, and the wasting of our time, fancying that these are such imperfections as we fall into through the unavoidable weakness and frailty of our natures; but let us be assured that these disorders of our common life are owing to this, that we have not so much Christianity, as **to intend to please God in all the actions of our life, as the best and happiest thing in the world.** So that we must not look upon ourselves in a state of common and pardonable imperfection, but in such a state as wants **the first and most fundamental principle** of Christianity, viz. **an intention to please God in all our actions.** . . .

So that the fault does not lie here, that we desire to be good and perfect, but through the weakness of our nature fall short of it; but it is, because we have not piety enough to intend to be as good as we can, or to please God in all the actions of our life. This we see is plainly the case of him that spends his time in sports when he should be at church; it is not his want of power, but his want of intention, or desire to be there. . . .

This doctrine does not suppose that we have no need of Divine grace, or that it is in our own power to make ourselves perfect. It only supposes that, through the want of a sincere intention of pleasing God in all our actions, we fall into such irregularities of life as by the ordinary means of grace we should have power to avoid; and that we have not that perfection which our present state of grace makes us capable of, because we do not so much as intend to have it. It only teaches us that the reason why you see no real mortification or self-denial, no eminent charity, no profound humility, no heavenly affection, no true contempt of the world, no Christian meekness, no sincere zeal, no eminent piety in the common lives of Christians, is this, because they do not so much as intend to be exact and exemplary in these virtues.

CHAPTER III.

OF THE GREAT DANGER AND FOLLY OF NOT INTENDING TO BE AS EMINENT AND EXEMPLARY AS WE CAN, IN THE PRACTICE OF ALL CHRISTIAN VIRTUES.

(The want of True Devotion, arising from the want of any intention to serve God to the very best of our powers, will leave us without excuse.)

ALTHOUGH the goodness of God, and His rich mercies in Christ Jesus, are a sufficient assurance to us that He will be merciful to our unavoidable weaknesses and infirmities, that is, to such failings as are the effects of ignorance or surprise; yet we have no reason to expect the same mercy towards those sins which we have lived in, through a want of intention to avoid them.

For instance; the case of a common swearer, who dies in that guilt, seems to have no title to the Divine mercy; for this reason, because he can no more plead any weakness or infirmity in his excuse, than the man that hid his talent in the earth could plead his want of strength to keep it out of the earth.

But now if this be right reasoning in the case of a common swearer, that his sin is not to be reckoned a pardonable frailty, because he has no weakness to plead in its excuse, why then do we not carry this way of reasoning to its true extent? why do not we as much condemn every other error of life, that has no more weakness to plead in its excuse than common swearing?

For if this be so bad a thing, because it might be avoided, if we did but **sincerely intend it**, must not then all other erroneous ways of life be very guilty, if we live in them, not through weakness and inability, but because we **never sincerely intended to avoid them**?

For instance; you perhaps have made no progress in the most important Christian virtues, you have scarce gone half way in humility and charity; now, if your failure in these duties is purely owing to **your want of intention** of performing them in any true degree, have you not then as little to plead for yourself, and are you not **as much without all excuse, as the common swearer**? . . .

You, it may be, are as far from Christian perfection,

as the common swearer is from keeping the third commandment; are you not therefore as much condemned by the doctrines of the gospel as the swearer is by the third commandment?

You perhaps will say, that all people fall short of the perfection of the gospel, and therefore you are content with your failings. But this is saying nothing to the purpose. For the question is not, whether gospel perfection can be fully attained, but whether **you come as near it as a sincere intention and careful diligence can carry you.** Whether you are not in a much lower state than you might be, if you sincerely intended, and carefully laboured, to advance yourself in all Christian virtues? . . .

The sum of this matter is this: From many passages of Scripture, it seems plain, that our salvation depends upon the sincerity and perfection of our endeavours to obtain it.

Weak and imperfect men shall, notwithstanding their frailties and defects, be received, as having pleased God, if they have done their utmost to please Him.

The rewards of charity, piety, and humility will be given to those whose lives have been a careful labour to exercise these virtues in as high a degree as they could.

We cannot offer to God the service of angels; we cannot obey Him as man in a state of perfection could; but fallen men can do their best, and this is the perfection that is required of us; it is only the **perfection of our best endeavours,** a careful labour to be **as perfect as we can.**

But if we stop short of this, for aught we know, we stop short of the mercy of God, and leave ourselves nothing to plead from the terms of the gospel. For

God has there made no promises of mercy to the sloth-ful and negligent. His mercy is only offered to our frail and imperfect, but best endeavours, to practise all manner of righteousness.

CHAPTER IV.

WE CAN PLEASE GOD IN NO STATE, OR EMPLOYMENT OF LIFE, BUT BY INTENDING AND DEVOTING IT ALL TO HIS HONOUR AND GLORY.

(True Devotion implies a life devoted to God everywhere, and in every thing, and must be seen in every calling in life.)

HAVING in the first chapter stated the general nature of devotion, and shown that it implies not any form of prayer, but a certain form of life, that is offered to God, not at any particular times or places, but everywhere, and in every thing; I shall now descend to some particulars, and show how we are to devote our labour and employment unto God.

As a good Christian should consider every place as holy, because God is there, so he should look upon every part of his life as a matter of holiness, because it is to be offered unto God.

The profession of a clergyman is an holy profession, because it is a ministration in holy things, an attend-ance at the altar. But worldly business is to be made holy unto the Lord, by being done as a service to Him, and in conformity to His Divine will.

For as all men, and all things in the world, as truly

belong unto God, as any places, things, or persons, that are devoted to Divine service, so **all things** are to be used, and **all persons** are to act in their several states and employments, **for the glory of God.**

Men of worldly business, therefore, must not look upon themselves as at liberty to live to themselves, to sacrifice to their own humours and tempers, because their employment is of a worldly nature. But they must consider that, as the world and all worldly professions as truly **belong to God,** as persons and things that are devoted to the altar, so it is as much the duty of men in worldly business to live **wholly unto God,** as it is the duty of those who are devoted to Divine service.

As the whole world is God's, so the whole world is **to act for God.** As all men have the same relation to God, as all men have all their powers and faculties from God, so all men are obliged **to act for God, with all their powers and faculties.**

As all things are God's, so **all things** are to be used and regarded **as the things of God.** For men to abuse things on earth, and **live to themselves,** is the same rebellion against God, as for angels to abuse things in heaven; because God is just the same Lord of all on earth, as He is the Lord of all in heaven.

Things may, and must differ in their use, but yet they are all to be used according to the will of God.

Men may, and must differ in their employments, but yet they must all act for the same ends, as dutiful servants of God, in the right and pious performance of their several callings.

Clergymen must live **wholly unto God** in one particular way, that is, in the exercise of holy offices, in the ministration of prayers and sacraments, and a zealous distribution of spiritual goods.

But men of other employments are, in their particular ways, as much obliged to act as the servants of God, and live **wholly unto Him** in their several callings.

This is the only difference between clergymen and people of other callings. . . .

As there is but one God and Father of us all, whose glory gives light and life to every thing that lives, whose presence fills all places, whose power supports all beings, whose providence ruleth all events; so every thing that lives, whether in heaven or earth, whether they be thrones or principalities, men or angels, they must all, with one spirit, live **wholly to the praise and glory of this one God and Father of them all.** . . .

It is therefore absolutely necessary for all Christians, whether men or women, to consider themselves as persons **that are devoted to holiness,** and so order their common ways of life, by such rules of reason and piety, as may turn it into continual service unto Almighty God. . . .

For **vain and earthly desires are no more allowable in our employments, than in our alms and devotions.** For these tempers of worldly pride, and vain-glory, are not only evil, when they mix with our good works, but they have the same evil nature, and make us odious to God, when they enter into the common business of our employment. If it were allowable to indulge covetous or vain passions in our worldly employments, it would then be allowable to be vainglorious in our devotions. But as our alms and

devotions are not an acceptable service, but when they
proceed from a heart truly devoted to God, so our
common employment cannot be reckoned a service to
Him, but when it is performed with the same temper
and piety of heart.

Most of the employments of life are in their own
nature lawful; and all those that are so may be made
a substantial part of our duty to God, if we engage in
them only so far, and for such ends, as are suitable to
beings that are to live above the world, all the time
that they live in the world.   This is the only measure
of our application to any worldly business: let it be
what it will, or where it will, it must have no more of
our hands, our hearts, or our time, than is consistent
with a hearty, daily, careful preparation of ourselves
for another life.   For as all Christians, as such, have
renounced this world, to prepare themselves, by daily
devotion and universal holiness, for an eternal state of
quite another nature, they must look upon worldly
employments, as upon worldly wants, and bodily infirmities; things not to be desired, but only to be endured
and suffered, till death and the resurrection have carried
us to an eternal state of real happiness. . . .

If, therefore, a man will so live, as to show that he
feels and believes the most fundamental doctrines of
Christianity, he must live above the world; this is the
temper that must enable him to do the business of life,
and yet live wholly unto God, and to go through some
worldly employment with a heavenly mind.   And it
is as necessary that people live in their employments
with this temper, as it is necessary that their employment itself be lawful. . . .

Now the only way to do this, is for people to con-

sider their trade as something that they are obliged
to devote to the glory of God, something that they are
to do only in such a manner as that they may make
it a duty to Him. Nothing can be right in business,
that is not under these rules.—The apostle commands
servants to be obedient to their masters " in singleness
of heart, as unto Christ. Not with eye-service, as
men-pleasers; but as the servants of Christ, doing the
will of God from the heart; with good will doing
service, as unto the Lord, and not to men." [1]

This passage sufficiently shows that all Christians
are to live wholly unto God in every state and condition,
doing the work of their common calling in such a
manner, and for such ends, as to make it a part of
their devotion or service to God. For certainly if
poor slaves are not to comply with their business as
men-pleasers, if they are to look wholly unto God in
all their actions, and serve in singleness of heart, as
unto the Lord, surely men of other employments and
conditions must be as much obliged to go through
their business with the same singleness of heart; not
as pleasing the vanity of their own minds, not as
gratifying their own selfish worldly passions, but as
the servants of God in all that they have to do. For
surely no one will say that a slave is to devote his
state of life unto God, and make the will of God the
sole rule and end of his service, but that a tradesman
need not act with the same spirit of devotion in his
business. For this is as absurd, as to make it
necessary for one man to be more just or faithful
than another.

It is therefore absolutely certain that no Christian

[1] Eph. vi. 5; Col. iii. 22, 23.

is to enter any farther into business, nor for any other
ends, than such as he can in singleness of heart offer
unto God, as a reasonable service.   For the Son of
God has redeemed us for this only end, that we should,
by a life of reason and piety, live to the glory of God;
this is the only rule and measure for every order and
state of life.   Without this rule, the most lawful
employment becomes a sinful state of life. . . .

If, therefore, we desire to live unto God, it is
necessary to bring our whole life under this law, to
make His glory the sole rule and measure of our acting
in every employment of life.   For there is no other
true devotion, but this of living devoted to God in the
common business of our lives. . . .

All this only shows us the great necessity of such
a regular and uniform piety, as extends itself to all
the actions of our common life.—

That we must eat and drink, and dress and discourse,
according to the sobriety of the Christian spirit, engage
in no employments but such as we can truly devote
unto God, nor pursue them any farther than so far as
conduces to the reasonable ends of a holy devout life;
—That we must be honest, not only on particular
occasions, and in such instances as are applauded in
the world, easy to be performed, and free from danger,
or loss, but from such a living principle of justice, as
makes us love truth and integrity in all its instances,
follow it through all dangers, and against all opposition;
as knowing that the more we pay for any truth, the
better is our bargain, and that then our integrity
becomes a pearl, when we have parted with all to
keep it;—That we must be humble, not only in such
instances as are expected in the world, or suitable to

our tempers, or confined to particular occasions; but in such a humility of spirit as renders us meek and lowly in the whole course of our lives, as shows itself in our dress, our person, our conversation, our enjoyment of the world, the tranquillity of our minds, patience under injuries, submission to superiors, and condescensions to those that are below us, and in all the outward actions of our lives. That we must devote, not only times and places to prayer, but be everywhere in the spirit of devotion; with hearts always set towards heaven, looking up to God in all our actions, and doing every thing as His servants; living in the world as in a holy temple of God, and always worshipping Him, though not with our lips, yet with the thankfulness of our hearts, the holiness of our actions, and the pious and charitable use of all His gifts;—That we must not only send up petitions and thoughts now and then to heaven, but must go through all our worldly business with a heavenly spirit, as members of Christ's mystical body; that, with new hearts and new minds, we may turn an earthly life into a preparation for a life of greatness and glory in the Kingdom of heaven. Now the only way to arrive at this piety of spirit, is to bring all your actions to the same rule as your devotions and alms.

CHAPTER V.

PERSONS THAT ARE FREE FROM THE NECESSITY OF
    LABOUR AND EMPLOYMENTS ARE TO CONSIDER THEM-
    SELVES AS DEVOTED TO GOD IN A HIGHER DEGREE.

**(Those who have their time at their own
disposal, have a special calling to devote
it entirely to God's service.)**

GREAT part of the world are free from the necessities of labour and employments, and have their
time and fortunes in their own disposal.

But as no one is to live in his employment according
to his own humour, or for such ends as please his own
fancy, but is to do all his business in such a manner
as to make it a service unto God; so those who have
no particular employment are so far from being left at
greater liberty to live to themselves, to pursue their
own humours, and spend their time and fortunes as
they please, that they are under greater obligations of
living **wholly unto God** in all their actions.

The freedom of their state lays them under a greater
necessity of always choosing, and doing, the best things.

They are those, of whom much will be required,
because much is given unto them.

A slave can only live unto God in one particular
way, that is, by religious patience and submission in
his state of slavery.

**But all ways of holy living, all instances, and all
kinds of virtue, lie open to those who are masters of
themselves, their time, and their fortune.**

It is as much the duty, therefore, of such persons,
to make a wise use of their liberty, to devote themselves

to all kinds of virtue, to aspire after every thing that is holy and pious, to endeavour to be eminent in all good works, and **to please God in the highest and most perfect manner**; it is as much their duty to be thus wise in the conduct of themselves, and thus extensive in their endeavours after holiness, as it is the duty of a slave to be **resigned unto God** in his state of slavery.

You are no labourer, or tradesman, you are neither merchant nor soldier; consider yourself, therefore, as placed in a state in some degree like that of good angels who are sent into the world as ministering spirits, for the general good of mankind, to assist, protect, and minister for them who shall be heirs of salvation.

For the more you are free from the common necessities of men, the more you are to imitate the higher perfections of angels.

Had you, Serena, been obliged, by the necessities of life, to wash clothes for your maintenance, or to wait upon some mistress that demanded all your labour, it would then be your duty to serve and **glorify God,** by such humility, obedience, and faithfulness, as might adorn that state of life. It would then be recommended to your care, to improve that one talent to its greatest height. That when the time came, that mankind were to be rewarded for their labours by the great Judge of quick and dead, you might be received with a " Well done, good and faithful servant, enter thou into the joy of thy Lord." [1]

But as God has given you five talents, as He has placed you above the necessities of life, as He has left you in the hands of yourself, in the happy liberty of

[1] Matt. xxv. 21.

choosing the most exalted ways of virtue; as He has enriched you with many gifts of fortune, and left you nothing to do, but to make the best use of variety of blessings, to make the most of a short life, to study your own perfection, the honour of God, and the good of your neighbour; so it is now your duty to imitate the greatest servants of God, to inquire how the most eminent saints have lived, **to study all the arts and methods of perfection,** and to set no bounds to your love and gratitude to the bountiful Author of so many blessings. . . .

This, Serena, is your profession. For as sure as God is **one God,** so sure it is that He has **but one command** to all mankind, whether they be bond or free, rich or poor; and that is, to act up to the excellency of that nature which He has given them, to live by reason, to walk in the light of religion, to use every thing as wisdom directs, **to glorify God in all His gifts,** and dedicate every condition of life to His service.

This is the one common command of God to all mankind. If you have an employment, you are to be thus reasonable, and pious, and holy in the exercise of it; if you have time and a fortune in your own power, you are obliged to be thus reasonable, and holy, and pious in the use of all your time, and all your fortune.

The right religious use of every thing and every talent is the indispensable duty of every being that is capable of knowing right and wrong.

For the reason why we are to do **any thing** as unto God, and with regard to our duty and relation to Him, is the same reason why we are to do **every thing as unto God,** and with regard to our duty and relation to Him.

That which is a reason for our being wise and holy in the discharge of all our business, is the same reason for our being wise and holy in the use of all our money.

As we have **always** the same natures, and are **every- where** the servants of the same God, as **every** place is **equally** full of His presence, and **every** thing is **equally** His gift, so we must **always** act according to the reason of our nature; we must do **every thing** as the servants of God; we must live in **every place** as in His pre- sence; we must use **every thing** as that ought to be used which **belongs to God.**

Either this piety, and wisdom, and devotion is to go through **every way of life,** and to extend to the use of **every thing,** or it is to go through no part of life. . . .

If it is our glory and happiness to have a rational nature, that is endued with wisdom and reason, that is capable of imitating the Divine nature, then it must be our glory and happiness to improve our reason and wisdom, to act up to the excellency of our rational nature, and to imitate God in all our actions, to the utmost of our power. They therefore who confine religion to times and places, and some little rules of retirement, who think that it is being too strict and rigid **to introduce religion into common life,** and make it **give laws to all their actions and ways of living,** they who think thus, not only mistake, but they mistake the whole nature of religion. **For surely they mistake the whole nature of religion, who can think any part of their life is made more easy, for being free from it. They may well be said to mistake the whole nature of wisdom, who do not think it desirable to be always wise.** He has not learnt the nature of piety, who

13

thinks it too much to be pious in all his actions. He does not sufficiently understand what reason is, who does not earnestly desire to live in every thing according to it. . . .

Farther, as God is one and the same Being, always acting like Himself and suitably to His own nature, so it is the duty of every being that He has created, to live according to the nature that He has given it, and always to act like Himself.

It is therefore an immutable law of God, that all rational beings should act reasonably in all their actions; not at this time, or in that place, or upon this occasion, or in the use of some particular thing, but at all times, in all places, on all occasions, and in the use of all things. This is a law that is as unchangeable as God, and can no more cease to be, than God can cease to be a God of wisdom and order. . . .

The infirmities of human life make such food and raiment necessary for us, as angels do not want; but then it is no more allowable for us to turn these necessities into follies, and indulge ourselves in the luxury of food, or the vanities of dress, than it is allowable for angels to act below the dignity of their proper state. For a reasonable life, and a wise use of our proper condition, is as much the duty of all men, as it is the duty of all angels and intelligent beings. Our blessed Saviour has plainly turned our thoughts this way, by making this petition a constant part of all our prayers, " Thy will be done on earth, as it is in heaven." A plain proof, that the obedience of men is to imitate the obedience of angels, and that rational beings on earth are to live unto God, as rational beings in heaven live unto Him.

CHAPTER VI.

CONTAINING THE GREAT OBLIGATIONS, AND THE GREAT
ADVANTAGES OF MAKING A WISE AND RELIGIOUS
USE OF OUR ESTATES AND FORTUNES.

(True Devotion will make us religiously exact in the use of our money and worldly goods.)

AS the holiness of Christianity consecrates all states and employments of life unto God, as it requires us to aspire after an universal obedience, doing and using every thing as the servants of God, so are we more especially obliged to observe this religious exactness in the use of our **estates and fortunes.**

The reason of this would appear very plain, if we were only to consider that our estate is as much the gift of God as our eyes or our hands, and is no more to be buried or thrown away at pleasure, than we are to put out our eyes, or throw away our limbs as we please.

But, besides this consideration, there are several other great and important reasons why we should be religiously exact in the use of our estates.

First, Because the manner of using our money or spending our estate enters so far into the business of every day, and makes so great a part of our common life, that our common life must be much of the same nature as our common way of spending our estate. If reason and religion govern us in this, then reason and religion hath got great hold of us; but if humour, pride, and fancy are the measures of our spending our estate, then humour, pride, and fancy will have the direction of the greatest part of our life.

Secondly, Another great reason for devoting all our estate to right uses, is this: because it is capable of being used to the most excellent purposes, and is so great a means of doing good. If we waste it we do not waste a trifle, that signifies little, but we waste that which might be made as eyes to the blind, as a husband to the widow, as a father to the orphan; we waste that which not only enables us to minister worldly comforts to those that are in distress, but that which might purchase for ourselves everlasting treasures in heaven. So that if we part with our money in foolish ways, we part with a great power of comforting our fellow-creatures, and of making ourselves for ever blessed.

If there be nothing so glorious as doing good, if there is nothing that makes us so like to God, then nothing can be so glorious in the use of our money, as to use it all in works of love and goodness, making ourselves friends, and fathers, and benefactors, to all our fellow-creatures, imitating the Divine love, and turning all our power into acts of generosity, care, and kindness to such as are in need of it.

If a man had eyes, and hands, and feet, that he could give to those that wanted them; if he should either lock them up in a chest, or please himself with some needless or ridiculous use of them, instead of giving them to his brethren that were blind and lame, should we not justly reckon him an unhuman wretch? If he should rather choose to amuse himself with furnishing his house with those things, than to entitle himself to an eternal reward, by giving them to those that wanted eyes and hands, might we not justly reckon him mad ?

Now money has very much the nature of eyes and feet ; if we either lock it up in chests, or waste it in needless and ridiculous expenses upon ourselves, whilst the poor and the distressed want it for their necessary uses ; if we consume it in the ridiculous ornaments of apparel, whilst others are starving in nakedness ; we are not far from the cruelty of him that chooses rather to adorn his house with the hands and eyes than to give them to those that want them. . . .

Thirdly, If we waste our money, we are not only guilty of wasting a talent which God has given us, we are not only guilty of making that useless, which is so powerful a means of doing good, but we do ourselves this further harm, that we turn this useful talent into a powerful means of corrupting ourselves ; because so far as it is spent wrong, so far it is spent in the support of some wrong temper, in gratifying some vain and unreasonable desires, in conforming to those fashions, and pride of the world, which, as Christians and reasonable men, we are obliged to renounce. . . .

For so much as is spent in the vanity of dress, may be reckoned so much laid out to fix vanity in our minds. So much as is laid out for idleness and indulgence, may be reckoned so much given to render our hearts dull and sensual. So much as is spent in state and equipage, may be reckoned so much spent to dazzle your own eyes, and render you the idol of your own imagination.' And so in every thing, when you go from reasonable wants, you only support some unreasonable temper, some turn of mind, which every good Christian is called upon to renounce.

Every exhortation in Scripture to be wise and
reasonable, satisfying only such wants as God would
have satisfied; every exhortation to be spiritual and
heavenly, pressing after a glorious change of our
nature; every exhortation to love our neighbour as
ourselves, to love all mankind as God has loved them,
is a command to be strictly religious in the use of our
money.

These tempers, and this use of our worldly goods,
is so much the doctrine of all the New Testament,
that you cannot read a chapter without being taught
something of it.   I shall only produce one remarkable
passage of Scripture, which is sufficient to justify all
that I have said concerning this religious use of all
our fortune.

" When the Son of Man shall come in His glory,
and all the holy angels with Him, then shall He sit
upon the throne of His glory : and before Him shall be
gathered all nations : and He shall separate them one
from another, as a shepherd divideth his sheep from
the goats : and He shall set the sheep on His right
hand, but the goats on the left.   Then shall the King
say unto them on His right hand, Come, ye blessed of
My Father, inherit the kingdom prepared for you from
the foundation of the world : for I was an hungred,
and ye gave Me meat : I was thirsty, and ye gave Me
drink : I was a stranger, and ye took Me in : naked,
and ye clothed Me : I was sick, and ye visited Me : I
was in prison, and ye came unto Me.—Then shall He
say unto them on the left hand, Depart from Me, ye
cursed, into everlasting fire, prepared for the devil and
his angels : for I was an hungred, and ye gave Me no
meat : I was thirsty, and ye gave Me no drink : I was

a stranger, and ye took Me not in: naked, and ye clothed Me not: sick, and in prison, and ye visited Me not. These shall go away into everlasting punishment: but the righteous into life eternal." [1]

I have quoted this passage at length, because if one looks at the way of the world, one would hardly think that Christians had ever read this part of Scripture. For what is there in the lives of Christians, that looks as if their salvation depended upon these good works? And yet the necessity of them is here asserted in the highest manner, and pressed upon us by a lively description of the glory and terrors of the day of judgment. . . .

You own, that you have no title to salvation, if you have neglected these good works; because such persons as have neglected them are, at the last day, to be placed on the left hand, and banished with a " Depart, ye cursed." There is, therefore, no salvation but in the performance of these good works. Who is it, therefore, that may be said to have performed these good works? Is it he that has sometime assisted a prisoner, or relieved the poor or sick? This would be as absurd as to say, that he had performed the duties of devotion, who had some time said his prayers. Is it, therefore, he that has several times done these works of charity? This can no more be said, than he can be said to be the truly just man, who had done acts of justice several times. What is the rule, therefore, or measure of performing these good works? How shall a man trust that he performs them as he ought?

Now the rule is very plain and easy, and such as

[1] Matt. xxv. 31-46.

is common to every other virtue, or good temper, as
well as to charity. Who is the humble, or meek, or
devout, or just, or faithful man ? Is it he that has
several times done acts of humility, meekness, devotion, justice, or fidelity ? No; but it is he that
lives in the habitual exercise of these virtues. In
like manner, he only can be said to have performed
these works of charity, who lives in the habitual
exercise of them to the utmost of his power. He
only has performed the duty of Divine love, who loves
God with all his heart, and with all his mind, and
with all his strength. And he only has performed
the duty of these good works, who has done them with
all his heart, and with all his mind, and with all his
strength. For there is no other measure of our doing
good, than our power of doing it.

The Apostle St. Peter puts this question to our
blessed Saviour : " Lord, how oft shall my brother sin
against me, and I forgive him ? till seven times ?
Jesus saith unto him, I say not unto thee, Until
seven times, but, Until seventy times seven." [1] Not
as if after this number of offences a man might then
cease to forgive ; but the expression of seventy times
seven, is to show us that we are not to bound our
forgiveness by any number of offences, but are to
continue forgiving the most repeated offences against
us. . . .

Now the rule of forgiving is also the rule of giving :
you are not to give, or do good to seven, but to seventy
times seven. You are not to cease from giving,
because you have given often to the same person, or
to other persons ; but must look upon yourself as much

[1] Matt. xviii. 21, 22.

obliged to continue relieving those that continue in want, as you were obliged to relieve them once or twice. Had it not been in your power, you had been excused from relieving any person once ; but if it is in your power to relieve people often, it is as much your duty to do it often, as it is the duty of others to do it but seldom, because they are but seldom able. He that is not ready to forgive every brother, as often as he wants to be forgiven, does not forgive like a disciple of Christ. And he that is not ready to give to every brother that wants to have something given him, does not give like a disciple of Christ. For it is as necessary to give to seventy times seven, to live in the continual exercise of all good works to the utmost of our power, as it is necessary to forgive until seventy times seven, and live in the habitual exercise of this forgiving temper, towards all that want it.

And the reason of all this is very plain, because there is the same goodness, the same excellency, and the same necessity of being thus charitable at one time as at another. It is as much the best use of our money, to be always doing good with it, as it is the best use of it at any particular time ; so that that which is a reason for a charitable action, is as good a reason for a charitable life. That which is a reason for forgiving one offence, is the same reason for forgiving all offences. For such charity has nothing to recommend it to-day, but what will be the same recommendation of it to-morrow ; and you cannot neglect it at one time, without being guilty of the same sin, as if you neglected it at another time.

As sure, therefore, as these works of charity are necessary to salvation, so sure is it that we are to do

them **to the utmost of our power;** not to-day, or
to-morrow, but through the whole course of our life.
If, therefore, it be our duty at any time to deny ourselves any needless expenses, to be moderate and
frugal, that we may have to give to those that want,
it is as much our duty to do so at all times, that we
may be farther able to do more good. For if it is at
any time a sin to prefer needless vain expense to
works of charity, it is so at all times; because charity
as much excels all needless and vain expenses at
one time as at another. So that if it is ever necessary
to our salvation, to take care of these works of
charity, and to see that we make ourselves in some
degree capable of doing them, it is as necessary to our
salvation, to take care to make ourselves as capable as we
can be, of performing them in all the parts of our life.

Either, therefore, you must so far renounce your
Christianity, as to say that you need never perform
any of these good works; or you must own that you
are to perform them **all your life in as high a degree
as you are** able. There is no middle way to be taken,
any more than there is a middle way betwixt pride
and humility, or temperance and intemperance. If you
do not strive to fulfil all charitable works, if you
neglect any of them that are in your power, and deny
assistance to those that want what you can give, let it
be when it will, or where it will, you number yourself
amongst those that want Christian charity. Because it
is as much your duty to do good with all that you
have, and to live in the continual exercise of good
works, as it is your duty to be temperate in all that
you eat and drink.

CHAPTER VII.

HOW THE IMPRUDENT USE OF AN ESTATE CORRUPTS
ALL THE TEMPERS OF THE MIND, AND FILLS THE
HEART WITH POOR AND RIDICULOUS PASSIONS,
THROUGH THE WHOLE COURSE OF LIFE; REPRE-
SENTED IN THE CHARACTER OF FLAVIA.

(The reason that so many people make no progress in religion, is from the want of religious exactness in the use of their money.)

IT has already been observed, that a prudent and religious care is to be used in the manner of spending our money or estate, because the manner of spending our estates makes so great a part of our common life, and is so much the business of every day, that according as we are wise, or imprudent, in this respect, the whole course of our lives will be rendered either very wise or very full of folly.

Persons that are well affected to religion, that receive instructions of piety with pleasure and satisfaction, often wonder how it comes to pass that they make no greater progress in that religion which they so much admire.

Now the reason of it is this: it is because religion lives only in their head, but **something else has possession of their hearts;** and therefore they continue from year to year mere admirers and praisers of piety, without ever coming up to the reality and perfection of its precepts.

If it be asked why religion does not get possession of their hearts, the reason is this: it is not because they live in gross sins, or debaucheries, for their regard to religion preserves them from such disorders; but it is because their hearts are constantly employed, perverted, and kept in a wrong state by **the indiscreet use of such things as are lawful** to be used. . . .

For our souls may receive an infinite hurt, and be rendered incapable of all virtue, merely by the use of innocent and lawful things.

What is more innocent than rest and retirement? And yet what more dangerous than sloth and idleness? What is more lawful than eating and drinking? And yet what more destructive of all virtue, what more fruitful of all vice, than sensuality and indulgence?

How lawful and praiseworthy is the care of a family! And yet how certainly are many people rendered incapable of all virtue, by a worldly and solicitous temper!

Now it is for want of **religious exactness in the use of these innocent and lawful things**, that religion cannot get possession of our hearts. And it is in the right and prudent management of ourselves, **as to these things**, that all the arts of holy living chiefly consist.

Gross sins are plainly seen and easily avoided by persons that profess religion. But the indiscreet and dangerous use of innocent and lawful things, as it does not shock and offend our consciences, so it is difficult to make people at all sensible of the danger of it. . . .

Flavia and Miranda are two maiden sisters, that have each of them two hundred pounds a year. They buried their parents twenty years ago, and have since that time spent their estate as they pleased.

Flavia has been the wonder of all her friends, for her excellent management, in making so surprising a figure on so moderate a fortune. Several ladies that have twice her fortune are not able to be always so genteel, and so constant at all places of pleasure and expense. She has every thing that is in the fashion, and is in every place where there is any diversion. . . .

When her parents died, she had no thought about her two hundred pounds a year, but that she had so much money to do what she would with, to spend upon herself, and purchase the pleasures and gratifications of all her passions.

And it is this setting out, this false judgment and indiscreet use of her fortune, that has filled her whole life with the same indiscretion, and kept her from thinking of what is right, and wise, and pious, in every thing else.

If you have seen her delighted in plays and romances, in scandal and backbiting, easily flattered, and soon affronted; if you have seen her devoted to pleasures and diversions, a slave to every passion in its turn, nice in every thing that concerned her body or dress, careless of every thing that might benefit her soul, always wanting some new entertainment, and ready for every happy invention in show or dress, it was because she had purchased all these tempers with the yearly revenue of her fortune.

She might have been humble, serious, devout, a lover of good books, an admirer of prayer and retirement, careful of her time, diligent in good works, full of charity and the love of God, but that the imprudent use of her estate forced all the contrary tempers upon her. . . .

More men live regardless of the great duties of piety, through too great a concern for worldly goods, than through direct injustice. . . .

If this woman would make fewer visits, or that not be always talking, they would neither of them find it half so hard to be affected with religion.

For all these things are only little, when they are compared to great sins; and though they are little in that respect, yet they are great, as they are impediments and hindrances of a pious spirit.

For as consideration is the only eye of the soul, as the truths of religion can be seen by nothing else, so whatever raises a levity of mind, a trifling spirit, renders the soul incapable of seeing, apprehending, and relishing the doctrines of piety.

Would we therefore make a real progress in religion, we must not only abhor gross and notorious sins, but we must regulate the innocent and lawful parts of our behaviour, and put the most common and allowed actions of life under the rules of discretion and piety.

CHAPTER VIII.

HOW THE WISE AND PIOUS USE OF AN ESTATE NATUR-
ALLY CARRIETH US TO GREAT PERFECTION IN ALL
THE VIRTUES OF THE CHRISTIAN LIFE; REPRESENTED
IN THE CHARACTER OF MIRANDA.

(How the right use of money helps in the perfecting of Christian character.)

ANY one pious regularity of any one part of our life, is of great advantage, not only on its own account, but as it uses us to live by rule, and think of the government of ourselves.

A man of business, that has brought one part of his affairs under certain rules, is in a fair way to take the same care of the rest.

So he that has brought any one part of his life under the rules of religion, may thence be taught to extend the same order and regularity into other parts of his life. . . .

By rule, must here be constantly understood, a religious rule observed upon a principle of duty to God. . . .

For the smallest rule in these matters is of great benefit, as it teaches us some part of the government of ourselves, as it keeps up a tenderness of mind, as it presents God often to our thoughts, and brings a sense of religion into the ordinary actions of our common life. . . .

It would be easy to show how little and small matters are the first steps and natural beginnings of great perfection.

But the two things which, of all others, most want to be under a strict rule, and which are the greatest blessings both to ourselves and others, when they are rightly used, are our **time** and our **money**. These talents are continual means and opportunities of doing good.

He that is piously strict, and exact in the wise management of either of these, cannot be long ignorant of the right use of the other. And he that is happy in the religious care and disposal of them both, is already ascended several steps upon the ladder of Christian perfection.

Miranda (the sister of Flavia) is a sober, reasonable Christian : as soon as she was mistress of her time and fortune, it was her first thought how she might best fulfil every thing that God required of her in the use of them, and how she might make the best and happiest use of this short life. She depends upon the truth of what our blessed Lord hath said, " One thing is needful," [1] and therefore makes her whole life but one continual labour after it. She has but one reason for doing or not doing, for liking or not liking any thing, and that is, the will of God. She is not so weak as to pretend to add what is called the fine lady to the true Christian ; Miranda thinks too well to be taken with the sound of such silly words ; she has renounced the world, to follow Christ in the exercise of humility, charity, devotion, abstinence, and heavenly affections ; and that is Miranda's fine breeding. . . .

Miranda does not divide her duty between God, her neighbour, and herself ; but she considers all as due to God, and so does every thing in His name, and for His sake. This makes her consider her fortune as the gift of God, that is to be used, as every thing is that belongs to God, for the wise and reasonable ends of a Christian and holy life. Her fortune, therefore, is divided betwixt herself and several other poor people, and she has only her part of relief from it. This is the spirit of Miranda, and thus she uses the gifts of God ; she is only one of a certain number of poor people, that are relieved out of her fortune, and she only differs from them in the blessedness of giving.

[1] Luke xi. 42.

Excepting her victuals, she never spent ten pounds a year upon herself. If you were to see her, you would wonder what poor body it was that was so surprisingly neat and clean. She has but one rule that she observes in her dress, to be always clean and in the cheapest things. Every thing about her resembles the purity of her soul, and she is always clean without, because she is always pure within.

Every morning sees her early at her prayers; she rejoices in the beginning of every day, because it begins all her pious rules of holy living, and brings the fresh pleasure of repeating them. She seems to be as a guardian angel to those that dwell about her, with her watchings and prayers blessing the place where she dwells, and making intercession with God for those that are asleep. . . .

At her table she lives strictly by this rule of holy Scripture, " Whether ye eat, or drink, or whatever ye do, do all to the glory of God."[1] This makes her begin and end every meal, as she begins and ends every day, with acts of devotion : she eats and drinks only for the sake of living, and with so regular an abstinence, that every meal is an exercise of self-denial, and she humbles her body every time that she is forced to feed it. If Miranda was to run a race for her life, she would submit to a diet that was proper for it. But as the race which is set before her is a race of holiness, purity, and heavenly affection, which she is to finish in a corrupt, disordered body of earthly passions, so her everyday diet has only this one end, to make her body fitter for this spiritual race. . . .

To relate her charity, would be to relate the history

[1] 1 Cor. x. 31.

14

of every day for twenty years; for so long has all her fortune been spent that way. She has set up near twenty poor tradesmen that had failed in their business, and saved as many from failing. She has educated several poor children that were picked up in the streets, and put them in a way of an honest employment. As soon as any labourer is confined at home with sickness, she sends him, till he recovers, twice the value of his wages, that he may have one part to give to his family as usual, and the other to provide things convenient for his sickness.

If a family seems too large to be supported by the labour of those that can work in it, she pays their rent, and gives them something yearly towards their clothing. By this means, there are many poor families that live in a comfortable manner, and are from year to year blessing her in their prayers.

If there is any poor man or woman that is more than ordinarily wicked and reprobate, Miranda has her eye upon them; she watches their time of need and adversity; and if she can discover that they are in any great straits, or affliction, she gives them speedy relief. She has this care for this sort of people, because she once saved a very profligate person from being carried to prison, who immediately became a true penitent.

There is nothing in the character of Miranda more to be admired than this temper. For this tenderness of affection towards the most abandoned sinners is the highest instance of a Divine and godlike soul. . . .

Miranda considers that Lazarus was a common beggar, that he was the care of angels, and carried into Abraham's bosom. She considers that our blessed

Saviour and His apostles were kind to beggars; that they spoke comfortably to them, healed their diseases, and restored eyes and limbs to the lame and blind; that Peter said to the beggar that wanted an alms from him, " Silver and gold have I none; but such as I have give I thee: in the name of Jesus Christ of Nazareth, rise up and walk." [1]   Miranda, therefore, never treats beggars with disregard and aversion; but she imitates the kindness of our Saviour and His apostles towards them; and though she cannot, like them, work miracles for their relief, yet she relieves them with that power that she hath; and may say, with the apostle, " Such as I have give I thee, in the name of Jesus Christ."

It may be, says Miranda, that I may often give to those that do not deserve it, or that will make an ill use of my alms.   But what then ?   Is not this the very method of Divine goodness ?   Does not God make " His sun to rise on the evil and on the good " ? [2] Is not this the very goodness that is recommended to us in Scripture, that, by imitating of it, we may be children of our Father which is in heaven, who " sendeth rain on the just and on the unjust " ?   And shall I withhold a little money, or food, from my fellow-creature, for fear he should not be good enough to receive it of me ?   Do I beg of God to deal with me, not according to my merit, but according to His own great goodness; and shall I be so absurd as to withhold my charity from a poor brother, because he may perhaps not deserve it ?   Shall I use a measure towards him, which I pray God never to use towards me ?

[1] Acts iii. 6.   [2] Matt. v. 45.

Besides, where has the Scripture made merit the
rule or measure of charity? On the contrary, the
Scripture saith, "If thy enemy hunger, feed him; if
he thirst, give him drink." [1]

Now this plainly teaches us, that the merit of
persons is to be no rule of our charity; but that we
are to do acts of kindness to those that least of all
deserve it. For if I am to love and do good to my
worst enemies; if I am to be charitable to them,
notwithstanding all their spite and malice; surely
merit is no measure of charity. If I am not to withhold my charity from such bad people, and who are
at the same time my enemies, surely I am not to deny
alms to poor beggars, whom I neither know to be bad
people, nor any way my enemies.

You will perhaps say, that by this means I
encourage people to be beggars. But the same
thoughtless objection may be made against all kinds
of charities, for they may encourage people to depend
upon them. The same may be said against forgiving
our enemies, for it may encourage people to do us
hurt. But when the love of God dwelleth in you,
when it has enlarged your heart, and filled you with
bowels of mercy and compassion, you will make no
more such objections as these.

When you are at any time turning away the poor,
the old, the sick, and helpless traveller, the lame, or
the blind, ask yourself this question, Do I sincerely
wish these poor creatures may be as happy as Lazarus,
that was carried by angels into Abraham's bosom?
Do I sincerely desire that God would make them
fellow-heirs with me in eternal glory? Now, if you

[1] Rom. xii. 20.

search into your soul, you will find that there is none of these notions there; that you are wishing nothing of this. For it is impossible for any one heartily to wish a poor creature so great a happiness, and yet not have a heart to give him a small alms. For this reason, says Miranda, as far as I can, I give to all, because I pray to God to forgive all; and I cannot refuse an alms to those whom I pray God to bless, whom I wish to be partakers of eternal glory, but am glad to show some degree of love to such as, I hope, will be the objects of the infinite love of God. And if, as our Saviour has assured us, it be more blessed to give than to receive, **we ought to look upon those that ask our alms, as so many friends and benefactors**, that come to do us a greater good than they can receive, that come to exalt our virtue, to be witnesses of our charity, to be monuments of our love, to be our advocates with God, to be to us in Christ's stead, to appear for us in the day of judgment, and to help us to a blessedness greater than our alms can bestow on them.

***

CHAPTER IX.

CONTAINING SOME REFLECTIONS UPON THE LIFE OF MIRANDA, AND SHOWING HOW IT MAY, AND OUGHT TO BE IMITATED BY ALL HER SEX.

(The Blessedness of a Life wholly devoted to God.)

NOW this life of Miranda, which I heartily recommend to the imitation of her sex, however

contrary it may seem to the way and fashion of the
world, is yet suitable to the true spirit, and founded
upon the plainest doctrines of Christianity.

To live as she does, is as truly suitable to the
gospel of Christ, as to be baptized, or receive the
Sacrament.

Her spirit is that which animated the saints of
former ages ; and it is because they lived as she does,
that we now celebrate their memories, and praise God
for their examples.

There is nothing that is whimsical, trifling, or unreasonable in her character, but every thing there
described is a right and proper instance of a solid and
real piety.

For all Miranda's rules of living unto God, of
spending her time and fortune, of eating, working,
dressing, and conversing, are as substantial parts of a
reasonable and holy life, as devotion and prayer.

For there is nothing to be said for the wisdom
of sobriety, the wisdom of devotion, the wisdom of
charity, or the wisdom of humility, but what is as
good an argument for the wise and reasonable use of
apparel.

For religion is as deeply concerned in the one as in
the other.

There is therefore nothing right in the use of
clothes, or in the use of any thing else in the world,
but the plainness and simplicity of the gospel. Every
other use of things (however polite and fashionable in
the world) distracts aud disorders the heart, and is
inconsistent with that inward state of piety, that purity
of heart, that wisdom of mind, and regularity of
affection, which Christianity requireth.

If you would be a good Christian, there is but one way,—you must live wholly unto God: and if you would live wholly unto God, you must live according to the wisdom that comes from God; you must act according to right judgments of the nature and value of things; you must live in the exercise of holy and heavenly affections, and use all the gifts of God to His praise and glory.

Some persons, perhaps, who admire the purity and perfection of this life of Miranda, may say, How can it be proposed as a common example? How can we who are married, or we who are under the direction of our parents, imitate such a life?

It is answered, Just as you may imitate the life of our blessed Saviour and His apostles. The circumstances of our Saviour's life, and the state and condition of His apostles, were more different from yours, than those of Miranda's are; and yet their life, the purity and perfection of their behaviour, is the common example that is proposed to all Christians.

It is their spirit, therefore, their piety, their love of God, that you are to imitate, and not the particular form of their life.

Act under God as they did, direct your common actions to that end which they did, glorify your proper state with such love of God, such charity to your neighbour, such humility and self-denial, as they did; and then, though you are only teaching your own children, and St. Paul is converting whole nations, yet you are following his steps, and acting after his example. . . .

As for those who are altogether in their own hands, if the liberty of their state makes them covet the best

gifts, if it carries them to choose the most excellent
ways, if they, having all in their own power, should
turn the whole form of their life into a regular exercise
of the highest virtues, happy are they who have so
learned Christ!

All persons cannot receive this saying. They that
are able to receive it, let them receive it, and bless
that Spirit of God, which has put such good motions
into their hearts.

God may be served and glorified in every state
of life. But as there are some states of life more
desirable than others, that more purify our natures,
that more improve our virtues, and dedicate us unto
God in a higher manner, so those who are at liberty
to choose for themselves seem to be called by God to
be more eminently devoted to His service.

Ever since the beginning of Christianity there have
been two orders, or ranks of people, amongst good
Christians.

The one that feared and served God in the common
offices and business of a secular worldly life:

The other, renouncing the common business, and
common enjoyments of life, as riches, marriage,
honours, and pleasures, devoted themselves to voluntary
poverty, virginity, devotion, and retirement, that by
this means they might live wholly unto God, in the
daily exercise of a Divine and heavenly life.

This testimony I have from the famous ecclesiastical
historian Eusebius, who lived at the time of the first
General Council, when the faith of our Nicene Creed
was established, when the Church was in its greatest
glory and purity, when its bishops were so many holy
fathers and eminent saints.

"Therefore," saith he, "there hath been instituted in the Church of Christ two ways, or manners, of living. The one, raised above the ordinary state of nature, and common ways of living, rejects wedlock, possessions, and worldly goods, and, being wholly separate and removed from the ordinary conversation of common life, is appropriated and devoted solely to the worship and service of God, through an exceeding degree of heavenly love.

"They who are of this order of people seem dead to the life of this world, and, having their bodies only upon earth, are in their minds, and contemplations, dwelling in heaven. From whence, like so many heavenly inhabitants, they look down upon human life, **making intercessions and oblations to Almighty God for the whole race of mankind**. And this not with the blood of beasts, or the fat, or smoke, and burning of bodies, but with the highest exercises of true piety, with cleansed and purified hearts, and with a whole form of life strictly devoted to virtue. These are their sacrifices, which they continually offer unto God, imploring His mercy and favour for themselves and their fellow-creatures.

"Christianity receives this as a perfect manner of life.

"The other is of a lower form, and, suiting itself more to the condition of human nature, admits of chaste wedlock, the care of children and family, of trade and business, and goes through all the employments of life under a sense of piety, and fear of God.

"Now they who have chosen this manner of life have their set times for retirement and spiritual exercises, and particular days are set apart for their hearing and learning the word of God. And this order of people are considered as in the second state of piety." [1]

Thus this learned historian.

If, therefore, persons of either sex, moved with the life of Miranda, and desirous of perfection, should unite themselves into little societies, professing voluntary poverty, virginity, retirement, and devotion, living upon bare necessaries, **that some might be relieved by their charities, and all be blessed with their prayers, and benefited by their example** ; or if, for want of this, they should practise the same manner of life, in as high a degree as they could by themselves ; such persons would be so far from being chargeable with any superstition, or blind devotion, that they might be justly said to restore that piety, which was the boast and glory of the Church, when its greatest saints were alive.

Now, as this learned historian observes, that it was an exceeding great degree of heavenly love that carried these persons so much above the common ways of life to such an eminent state of holiness ; so it is not to be wondered at, that the religion of Jesus Christ should fill the hearts of many Christians with this high degree of love.

For a religion that opens such a scene of glory, that discovers things so infinitely above all the world, that so triumphs over death, that assures us of such mansions of bliss, where we shall so soon be as the angels of God in heaven ; what wonder is it, if such a religion, such truths and expectations, should, in some holy souls, destroy all earthly desires, and make the ardent

[1] Euseb. *Dem. Evan.* l. l. c. 8.

love of heavenly things be the one continual passion of their hearts?

If the religion of Christians is founded upon the infinite humiliation, the cruel mockings and scourgings, the prodigious sufferings, the poor, persecuted life, and painful death of a crucified Son of God; what wonder is it, if many humble adorers of this profound mystery, many affectionate lovers of a crucified Lord, should renounce their share of worldly pleasures, and give themselves up to a continual course of mortification and self-denial, that thus suffering with Christ here, they may reign with Him hereafter?

If truth itself hath assured us that there is but one thing needful, what wonder is it that there should be some amongst Christians so full of faith, as to believe this in the highest sense of the words, and to desire such a separation from the world, that their care and attention to the one thing needful may not be interrupted.

If our blessed Lord hath said, " If thou wilt be perfect, go and sell that thou hast, and give to the poor, and thou shalt have treasure in heaven: and come and follow me;"[1] what wonder is it, that there should be amongst Christians some such zealous followers of Christ, so intent upon heavenly treasure, so desirous of perfection, that they should renounce the enjoyment of their estates, choose a voluntary poverty, and relieve all the poor that they are able?

If the chosen vessel, St. Paul, hath said, " He that is unmarried careth for the things that belong to the Lord, how he may please the Lord: and that there is this difference also between a wife and a virgin; the

[1] Matt. xix. 21.

unmarried woman careth for the things of the Lord, that she may be holy both in body and in spirit;"[1] what wonder is it, if the purity and perfection of the virgin state hath been the praise and glory of the Church in its first and purest ages? that there have always been some so desirous of pleasing God, so zealous after every degree of purity and perfection, so glad of every means of improving their virtue, that they have renounced the comforts and enjoyments of wedlock, to trim their lamps, to purify their souls, and wait upon God in a state of perpetual virginity?

CHAPTER X.

SHOWING HOW ALL ORDERS AND RANKS OF MEN AND WOMEN, OF ALL AGES, ARE OBLIGED TO DEVOTE THEMSELVES UNTO GOD.

(Entire Devotion to God the duty of every Christian.)

I HAVE in the foregoing chapters gone through the several great instances of Christian devotion, and shown that all the parts of our common life, our employments, our talents, and gifts of fortune, are all to be made holy and acceptable unto God by a wise and religious use of every thing, and by directing our actions and designs to such ends as are suitable to the honour and glory of God.

I shall now show that this regularity of devotion, this holiness of common life, this religious use of every

[1] 1 Cor. vii. 32-34.

thing we have, is a devotion that is the duty of all orders of Christian people. . . .

Everybody acknowledges that all orders of men are to be equally and exactly honest and faithful; there is no exception to be made in these duties, for any private or particular state of life. Now, if we would but attend to the reason and nature of things, if we would but consider the nature of God, and the nature of man, we should find the same necessity for every right use of our reason, for every grace, or religious temper of the Christian life; we should find it as absurd to suppose that one man must be exact in piety, and another need not, as to suppose that one man must be exact in honesty, but another need not; for Christian humility, sobriety, devotion, and piety are as great and necessary parts of a reasonable life as justice and honesty. But if we consider mankind in a higher view, as God's order or society of rational beings, that are to glorify Him by the right use of their reason, and by acting comformably to the order of their nature. we shall find that every temper that is equally contrary to reason and order, that opposes God's ends and designs, and disorders the beauty and glory of the rational world, is equally sinful in man, and equally odious to God. . . .

Nothing can be more false than to imagine, that because we are private persons, that have taken upon us no charge or employment of life, therefore we may live more at large, indulge our appetites, and be less careful of the duties of piety and holiness; for it is as good an excuse for cheating and dishonesty. Because he that abuses his reason, that indulges himself in lust and sensuality, and neglects to act the wise and reasonable part of a true Christian, has every thing in his life to render him hateful to God, that is to be found in cheating and dishonesty. . . .

Another argument to prove that all the orders of men are obliged to be thus holy and devout in the common course of their lives, in the use of every thing that they enjoy, may be taken from our obligation to prayer.

It is granted that prayer is a duty that belongs to all states and conditions of men : now, if we inquire into the reason of this, why no state of life is to be excused from prayer, we shall find it as good a reason why every state of life is to be made a state of piety and holiness in all its parts.

For the reason why we are to pray unto God, and glorify Him with hymns, and psalms of thanksgiving, is this, because we are to live wholly unto God, and glorify Him all possible ways. It is not because the praises of words, or forms of thanksgiving, are more particularly parts of piety, or more the worship of God than other things ; but it is because they are possible ways of expressing our dependence, our obedience and devotion to God. Now, if this be the reason of verbal praises and thanksgivings to God, because we are to live unto God all possible ways, then it plainly follows, that we are equally obliged to worship and glorify God in all other actions that can be turned into acts of piety and obedience to Him. And as actions are of much more significance than words, it must be a much more acceptable worship of God, to glorify Him in all the actions of our common life, than with any little forms of words at any particular times.

He that dares not say an ill-natured word, or do an unreasonable thing, because he considers God as everywhere present, performs a better devotion than he that dares not miss the church. To live in the world as a stranger and a pilgrim, using all its enjoyments as if we used them not, making all our actions so many steps towards a better life, is offering a better sacrifice to God than any forms of holy and heavenly prayers. . . .

He that has appointed times for the use of wise and pious prayers, performs a proper instance of devotion; but he that allows himself no times, nor any places, nor any actions, but such as are strictly conformable to wisdom and holiness, worships the Divine nature with the most true and substantial devotion. For who does not know that it is better to be pure and holy, than to talk about purity and holiness? Nay, who does not know that a man is to be reckoned no farther pure or holy, or just, than as he is pure, and holy, and just in the common course of his life? But if this be plain, then it is also plain, that it is better to be holy, than to have holy prayers.

Prayers, therefore, are so far from being a sufficient devotion, that they are the smallest parts of it. We are to praise God with words and prayers, because it is a possible way of glorifying God, who has given us such faculties, as may be so used. But then as words are but small things in themselves, as times of prayer are but little, if compared with the rest of our lives; so that devotion which consists in times and forms of prayer is but a very small thing, if compared to that devotion which is to appear in every other part and circumstance of our lives.

Again: as it is an easy thing to worship God with forms of words, and to observe times of offering them unto Him, so it is the smallest kind of piety.

And, on the other hand, as it is more difficult to
worship God with our substance, to honour Him with
the right use of our time, to offer to Him the
continual sacrifice of self-denial and mortification;
as it requires more piety to eat and drink only for
such ends as may glorify God, to undertake no labour,
nor allow of any diversion, but where we can act in
the name of God; as it is more difficult to sacrifice
all our corrupt tempers, correct all our passions, and
make piety to God the rule and measure of all the
actions of our common life, so the devotion of this
kind is **a much more acceptable service unto God,** than
those words of devotion which we offer to him either
in the church or in our closet. . . .

Bended knees, whilst you are clothed with pride;
heavenly petitions, whilst you are hoarding up treasures upon earth; holy devotions, whilst you live in
the follies of the world; prayers of meekness and
charity, whilst your heart is the seat of spite and resentment; hours of prayer, whilst you give up days
and years to idle diversions, impertinent visits, and
foolish pleasures; are as absurd, unacceptable services
to God, as forms of thanksgiving from a person that
lives in repinings and discontent.

So that, unless **the common course of our lives** be
according to **the common spirit of our prayers,** our
prayers are so far from being a real or sufficient degree of devotion, that they become an empty lip-
labour, or, what is worse, a notorious hypocrisy.

Seeing, therefore, we are to make the spirit and
temper of our prayers the common spirit and temper
of our lives, this may serve to convince us that all
orders of people are to labour and aspire after the

same utmost perfection of the Christian life. For as all Christians are to use the same holy and heavenly devotions, as they are all with the same earnestness to pray for the Spirit of God, so is it a sufficient proof that all orders of people are, to the utmost of their power, to make their life agreeable to that one Spirit, for which they are all to pray.

As certain, therefore, as the same holiness of prayers requires the same holiness of life, so certain is it that all Christians are called to the same holiness of life. . . .

Let young gentlemen be assured, that it is the one only business of a Christian gentleman, to distinguish himself by good works, **to be eminent in the most sublime virtues of the gospel,** to bear with the ignorance and weakness of the vulgar, to be a friend and patron to all that dwell about him, **to live in the utmost heights of wisdom and holiness,** and show through the whole course of his life a true religious greatness of mind. They must aspire after such a gentility, as they might have learnt from seeing the blessed Jesus, and show no other spirit of a gentleman but such as they might have got by living with the holy apostles. They must learn to love God with all their heart, with all their soul, and with all their strength, and their neighbour as themselves; and then they have all the greatness and distinction that they can have here, and are fit for an eternal happiness in heaven hereafter. . . .

For the Son of God did not come from above to add an external form of worship to the several ways of life that are in the world, and so to leave people to live as they did before, in such tempers and enjoyments as the fashion and spirit of the world approves;

15

but as He came down from heaven altogether **Divine
and heavenly** in His own nature, so it was **to call mankind to a Divine and heavenly life; to the highest
change of their own ,nature and temper;** to be born
again of the Holy Spirit; to walk in the wisdom
and light and love of God, and to be like Him to
the utmost of their power; to renounce all the most
plausible ways of the world, whether of greatness,
business, or pleasure; to a mortification of all their
most agreeable passions; and to live in such wisdom,
and purity, and holiness, as might fit them to be
glorious in the enjoyment of God to all eternity. . . .

For as sure as Jesus Christ was wisdom and holiness, **as sure as He came to make us like Himself,** and
to be baptized into His Spirit, so sure is it that none
can be said to keep to their Christian profession, but they
who, **to the utmost of their power,** live a wise and holy
ınd heavenly life. This, and this alone, is Christianity;
an universal holiness in every part of life, a heavenly
wisdom in all our actions, not conforming to the spirit
and temper of the world, but turning all worldly enjoyments into means of piety and devotion to God.

CHAPTER XI.

SHOWING HOW GREAT DEVOTION FILLS OUR LIVES WITH
THE GREATEST PEACE AND HAPPINESS THAT CAN BE
ENJOYED IN THIS WORLD.

(The more exalted our Piety, the greater our Happiness.)

SOME people will perhaps object, that all these rules
of holy living unto God in all that we do, are too

great a restraint upon human life; that it will be made too anxious a state, by thus introducing a regard to God in all our actions; and that by depriving ourselves of so many seemingly innocent pleasures, we shall render our lives dull, uneasy, and melancholy.

To which it may be answered,

First, That these rules are prescribed for, and will certainly procure a quite contrary end. That instead of making our lives dull and melancholy, they will render them full of content and strong satisfactions. That by these rules we only change the childish satisfactions of our vain and sickly passions for the solid enjoyments and real happiness of a sound mind.

Secondly, That as there is no foundation for comfort in the enjoyments of this life, but in the assurance that a wise and good God governeth the world, so the more we find out God in every thing, the more we apply to Him in every place, the more we look up to Him in all our actions, the more we conform to His will, the more we act according to His wisdom, and imitate His goodness, by so much the more do we enjoy God, partake of the Divine nature, and heighten and increase all that is happy and comfortable in human life.

Thirdly, He that is endeavouring to subdue, and root out of his mind, all those passions of pride, envy, and ambition which religion opposes, is doing more to make himself happy, even in this life, than he that is contriving means to indulge them. For these passions are the causes of all the disquiets and vexations of human life: they are the dropsies and fevers of our minds, vexing them with false appetites, and restless cravings after such things as we do not want, and spoiling our taste for those things which are our proper good. . . .

Most people, indeed, confess that religion preserves us from a great many evils, and helps us in many respects to a more happy enjoyment of ourselves; but then they imagine that this is only true of such a moderate share of religion, as only gently restrains us from the excesses of our passions. They suppose that the strict rules and restraints of an exalted piety are such contradictions to our nature, as must needs make our lives dull and uncomfortable.

This objection supposes that religion, moderately practised, adds much to the happiness of life; but that such heights of piety as the perfection of religion requireth, have a contrary effect.

It supposes, also, that the happiness of life consists in a mixture of virtue and vice, a mixture of ambition and humility, charity and envy, heavenly affection and covetousness. All which is as absurd as to suppose that it is happy to be free from excessive pains, but unhappy to be without more moderate pains; or that the happiness of health consisted in being partly sick and partly well.

For if humility be the peace and rest of the soul, then no one has so much happiness from humility, as he that is the most humble. If there is any peace and joy in doing any action according to the will of God, he that brings the most of his actions to this rule does most of all increase the peace and joy of his life. . . .

For, first, Piety requires us to renounce no ways of life, where we can act reasonably, and offer what we do to the glory of God. All ways of life, all satisfactions and enjoyments, that are within these bounds, are no way denied us by the strictest rules of piety. Whatever you can do, or enjoy, as in the presence of God, as His servant, as His rational creature that has received reason and knowledge from Him; all that you can perform conformably to a rational nature, and the will of God, all this is allowed by the laws of piety. And will you think that your life will be uncomfortable unless you may displease God, be a fool, and mad, and act contrary to that reason and wisdom which He has implanted in you? . . .

Who would complain of the severe strictness of a law that, without any exception, forbad the putting of dust into our eyes? Who could think it too rigid, that there were no abatements? Now this is the strictness of religion; it requires nothing of us strictly, or without abatements, but where every degree of the thing is wrong, where every indulgence does us some hurt.

If religion commands an universal charity, to love our neighbour as ourselves, to forgive and pray for all our enemies without any reserve; it is because all degrees of love are degrees of happiness, that strengthen and support the Divine life of the soul, and are as necessary to its health and happiness, as proper food is necessary to the health and happiness of the body.

If religion has laws against laying up treasures upon earth, and commands us to be content with food and raiment, it is because every other use of the world is abusing it to our own vexation, and turning all its conveniences into snares and traps to destroy us. It is because this plainness and simplicity of life secures us from the cares and pains of restless pride and envy, and makes it easier to keep that strait road that will carry us to eternal life.

If religion saith, " Sell that thou hast, and give to the poor," it is because there is no other natural or reasonable use of our riches, no other way of making ourselves happier for them; it is because it is as strictly right to give others that which we do not want ourselves, as it is right to use so much as our own wants require. For if a man has more food than his own nature requires, how base and unreasonable is it to invent foolish ways of wasting it, and make sport for his own full belly, rather than let his fellow-creatures have the same comfort from food which he hath had. It is so far, therefore, from being a hard law of religion, to make this use of our riches, that a reasonable man would rejoice in that religion which teaches him to be happier in that which he gives away, than in that which he keeps for himself; which teaches him to make spare food and raiment be greater blessings to him, than that which feeds and clothes his own body. . . .

If religion calleth us to a life of watching and prayer, it is because we live amongst a crowd of enemies, and are always in need of the assistance of God. If we are to confess and bewail our sins, it is because such confessions relieve the mind, and restore it to ease; as burdens and weights taken off the shoulders, relieve the body, and make it easier to itself. If we are to be frequent and fervent in holy petitions, it is to keep us steady in the sight of our true good, and that we may never want the happiness of a lively faith, a joyful hope, and well-grounded trust in God. If we are to pray often, it is that we may be often happy in such secret joys as only prayer can give; in such communications of the Divine

Presence, as will fill our minds with all the happiness that beings not in heaven are capable of. . . .

If religion commands us to live wholly unto God, and to do all to His glory, it is because every other way is living wholly against ourselves, and will end in our own shame and confusion of face.

As every thing is dark, that God does not enlighten; as every thing is senseless, that has not its share of knowledge from Him; as nothing lives, but by partaking of life from Him; as nothing exists, but because He commands it to be; so there is no glory or greatness, but what is of the glory or greatness of God. . . .

This is the state of all creatures, whether men or angels: as they make not themselves, so they enjoy nothing from themselves: if they are great, it must be only as great receivers of the gifts of God; their power can only be so much of the Divine Power acting in them; their wisdom can be only so much of the Divine Wisdom shining within them; and their light and glory, only so much of the light and glory of God shining upon them.

As they are not men or angels, because they had a mind to be so themselves, but because the will of God formed them to be what they are; so they cannot enjoy this or that happiness of men or angels, because they have a mind to it, but because it is the will of God that such things be the happiness of men, and such things the happiness of angels. But now **if God be thus all** in all; if His will is thus the measure of all things, and all natures; if nothing can be done, but by His power; if nothing can be seen, but by a light from Him; if we have nothing to fear, but from His justice; if we have nothing to hope for, but from

His goodness; if this is the nature of man, thus helpless in himself; if this is the state of all creatures, as
well those in heaven as those on earth; if they are
nothing, can do nothing, can suffer no pain, nor feel
any happiness, but so far, and in such degrees, as the
power of God does all this; if this be the state of
things, then how can we have the least glimpse of joy
or comfort, how can we have any peaceful enjoyment
of ourselves, but by **living wholly unto that God**, using
and doing every thing conformably to His will?   A
life thus **devoted unto God**, looking **wholly unto Him** in
all our actions, and doing all things suitably to His
glory, is so far from being dull and uncomfortable,
that it creates new comforts in every thing that we do.

On the contrary, would you see how happy they
are who live according to their own wills, who cannot
submit to the dull and melancholy business of a life
devoted unto God; look at the man in the parable, to
whom his lord had given one talent.

He could not bear the thoughts of using his talent
according to the will of him from whom he had it,
and therefore he chose to make himself happier in a
way of his own.   "Lord," says he, "I knew thee, that
thou art an hard man, reaping where thou hast not
sown, and gathering where thou hast not strawed:
and I was afraid, and went and hid thy talent in the
earth: lo, there thou hast that is thine."

His lord, having convicted him out of his own
mouth, despatches him with this sentence: "Cast the
unprofitable servant into outer darkness: there shall
be weeping and gnashing of teeth."[1]

Here you see how happy this man made himself,

[1] Matt. xxv. 24, 25, 30.

by not acting wholly according to his lord's will. It was, according to his own account, a happiness of murmuring and discontent: I knew thee, says he, that thou wast an hard man: it was a happiness of fears and apprehensions; I was, says he, afraid: it was a happiness of vain labours and fruitless travels; I went, says he, and hid thy talent; and after having been awhile the sport of foolish passions, tormenting fears, and fruitless labour, he is rewarded with darkness, eternal weeping and gnashing of teeth.

Now this is the happiness of all those who look upon a strict and exalted piety, that is, a right use of their talent, to be a dull and melancholy state of life. . . .

On the other hand, would you see a short description of the happiness of a life rightly employed, **wholly devoted to God**, you must look at the man in the parable to whom his lord had given five talents. " Lord," says he, " thou deliveredst unto me five talents; behold, I have gained beside them five talents more. His lord said unto him, Well done, thou good and faithful servant; thou hast been faithful over a few things, I will make thee ruler over many things: enter thou into the joy of thy lord."

Here you see a life that is wholly intent upon the improvement of the talents, that is devoted **wholly unto God**, is a state of happiness, prosperous labours, and glorious success. Here are not, as in the former case, any uneasy passions, murmurings, vain fears, and fruitless labours. The man is not toiling and digging in the earth for no end or advantage; but his pious labours prosper in his hands, his happiness increases upon him; the blessing of five becomes the blessing of ten talents; and he is received with a

"Well done, good and faithful servant: enter thou into the joy of thy lord."

Now, as the case of these men in the parable left nothing else to their choice, but either to be happy in using their gifts to the glory of the Lord, or miserable by using them according to their own humours and fancies; so the state of Christianity leaves us no other choice.

All that we have, all that we are, all that we enjoy, are only so many talents from God: if we use them to the ends of a pious and holy life, our five talents will become ten, and our labours will carry us into the joy of our Lord; but if we abuse them to the gratifications of our own passions, sacrificing the gifts of God to our own pride and vanity, we shall live here in vain labours and foolish anxieties, shunning religion as a melancholy thing, accusing our Lord as a hard master, and then fall into everlasting misery.

CHAPTER XII.

THE HAPPINESS OF A LIFE WHOLLY DEVOTED TO GOD FARTHER PROVED, FROM THE VANITY, THE SENSUALITY, AND THE RIDICULOUS POOR ENJOYMENTS, WHICH THEY ARE FORCED TO TAKE UP WITH WHO LIVE ACCORDING TO THEIR OWN HUMOURS. THIS REPRESENTED IN VARIOUS CHARACTERS.

(The Emptiness of all Worldly Pleasure.)

WE may still see more of the happiness of a life devoted unto God, by considering the poor contrivances for happiness, and the contemptible ways of life, which they are thrown into, who are not under the directions of a strict piety, but seeking after happiness by other methods.

If one looks at their lives, who live by no rule but their own humours and fancies; if one sees but what it is which they call joy, and greatness, and happiness ; if one sees how they rejoice, and repent, change and fly from one delusion to another; one shall find great reason to rejoice, that God hath appointed a strait and narrow way, that leadeth unto life; and that we are not left to the folly of our own minds, or forced to take up with such shadows of joy and happiness as the weakness and folly of the world has invented. I say invented; because those things which make up the joy and happiness of the world are mere inventions, which have no foundation in nature and reason, are no way the proper good or happiness of man, no way perfect either in his body, or his mind, or carry him to his true end. . . .

Whether we consider the greatness of religion, or the littleness of all other things, and the meanness of all other enjoyments, there is nothing to be found, in the whole nature of things, for a thoughtful mind to rest upon, but a happiness in the hopes of religion.

Consider now with yourself, how unreasonably it is pretended that a life of strict piety must be a dull and anxious state. For can it, with any reason, be said that the duties and restraints of religion must render our lives heavy and melancholy, when they only deprive us of such happiness as has been here laid before you ?

Must it be tedious and tiresome to live in the continual exercise of charity, devotion, and temperance, to act wisely and virtuously, to do good to the utmost of your power, to imitate the Divine perfections, and prepare yourself for the enjoyment of God? Must it be dull and tiresome to be delivered from blindness and vanity, from false hopes and vain fears, to improve in holiness, to feel the comforts of conscience in all your actions, to know that God is your Friend, that all must work for your good, that neither life nor death, neither men nor devils, can do you any harm; but that all your sufferings and doings that are offered unto God, all your watchings and prayers, and labours of love and charity, all your improvements, are in a short time to be rewarded with everlasting glory in the presence of God; must such a state as this be dull and tiresome? . . .

If you were to see a man dully endeavouring all his life to satisfy his thirst, by holding up one and the same empty cup to his mouth, you would certainly despise his ignorance.

But if you should see others of brighter parts, and finer understandings, ridiculing the dull satisfaction of one cup, and thinking to satisfy their own thirst by a variety of gilt and golden empty cups; would you think that these were ever the wiser, or happier, or better employed, for their finer parts?

Now this is all the difference you can see in the happiness of this life.

The dull and heavy soul may be content with one empty appearance of happiness, and be continually trying to hold one and the same empty cup to his mouth all his life. But then let the wit, the great scholar, the fine genius, the great statesman, the polite gentleman, lay all their heads together, and they can only show you more and various empty appearances of happiness; give them all the world into their hands, let them cut and carve as they please, they can only make a greater variety of empty cups. . . .

And if all that is in the world are only so many empty cups, what does it signify which you take, or how many you take, or how many you have?

If you but use yourself to such meditations as these, to reflect upon the vanity of all orders of life without piety, to consider how all the ways of the world are only so many different ways of error, blindness, and mistake; you would soon find your heart made wiser and better by it. These meditations would awaken your soul into a zealous desire of that solid happiness, which is only to be found in recourse to God.

CHAPTER XIII.

THAT NOT ONLY A LIFE OF VANITY, OR SENSUALITY, BUT EVEN THE MOST REGULAR KIND OF LIFE, THAT IS NOT GOVERNED BY GREAT DEVOTION, SUFFICIENTLY SHOWS ITS MISERIES, ITS WANTS AND EMPTINESS, TO THE EYES OF ALL THE WORLD. THIS REPRESENTED IN VARIOUS CHARACTERS.

(The Vanity of Worldly Possessions.)

IT is a very remarkable saying of our Lord and Saviour to His disciples, in these words : " Blessed are your eyes, for they see ; and your ears, for they hear." [1] They teach us two things : first, That the dulness and heaviness of men's minds, with regard to

[1] Matt. xiii. 16.

spiritual matters, is so great, that it may justly be compared to the want of eyes and ears.

Secondly, That God had so filled every thing, and every place, with motives and arguments for a godly life, that they who are but so blessed, so happy as to use their eyes and their ears, must needs be affected with them.

Now, though this was, in a more especial manner, the case of those whose senses were witnesses of the life, and miracles, and doctrines, of our blessed Lord, yet it is as truly the case of all Christians at this time. For the reasons of religion, the calls to piety, are so written and engraved upon every thing, and present themselves so strongly, and so constantly, to all our senses in every thing that we meet, that they can only be disregarded by eyes that see not, and ears that hear not.

What greater motive to a religious life, than the vanity, the poorness of all worldly enjoyments? And yet who can help seeing and feeling this every day of his life.

What greater call to look towards God, than the pains, the sickness, the crosses and vexations of this life? And yet whose eyes and ears are not daily witnesses of them?

What miracles could more strongly appeal to our senses, or what message from Heaven speak louder to us, than the daily dying and departure of our fellow-creatures. So that the one thing needful, or the great end of life, is not left to be discovered by fine reasoning and deep reflections; but is pressed upon us, in the plainest manner, by the experience of all our senses, by every thing that we meet with in life.

Let us but intend to see and hear, and then the whole world becomes a book of wisdom and instruction to us; all that is regular in the order of nature, all that is accidental in the course of things, all the mistakes and disappointments that happen to ourselves, all the miseries and errors that we see in other people, become so many plain lessons of advice to us; teaching us, with as much assurance as an angel from heaven, that we can no ways raise ourselves to any true happiness, but by turning all our thoughts, our wishes, and endeavours, after the happiness of another life.

It is this right use of the world that I would lead you into, by directing you to turn your eyes upon every shape of human folly, that you may thence draw fresh arguments and motives of living to the best and greatest purposes of your creation.

And if you would but carry this intention about you, of profiting by the follies of the world, and of learning the greatness of religion, from the littleness and vanity of every other way of life; if, I say, you would but carry this intention in your mind, you would find every day, every place, and every person, a fresh proof of their wisdom, who choose to **live wholly unto God**. You would then often return home the wiser, the better, and the more strengthened in religion, by every thing that has fallen in your way. . . .

Look now at that condition of life, which draws the envy of all eyes.

Negotius is a temperate, honest man. He served his time under a master of great trade, but has, by his own management, made it a more considerable business than ever it was before.

As money is continually pouring in upon him, so
he often lets it go in various kinds of expense and
generosity, and sometimes in ways of charity.

Negotius is always ready to join in any public con-
tribution. If a purse is making at any place where
he happens to be, whether it be to buy a plate for a
horse-race, or to redeem a prisoner out of gaol, you are
always sure of having something from him. . . .

The generality of people, when they think of
happiness, think of Negotius, in whose life every
instance of happiness is supposed to meet; sober,
prudent, rich, prosperous, generous, and charitable.

Let us now, therefore, look at this condition in
another, but truer light.

Let it be supposed that this same Negotius was a
painful, laborious man, every day deep in variety of
affairs; that he neither drank nor debauched; but
was sober and regular in his business. Let it be
supposed that he grew old in this course of trading;
and that the end and design of all this labour, and
care, and application to business, was only this, that
he might die possessed of more than a hundred
thousand pairs of boots and spurs, and as many
great coats.

Let it be supposed that the sober part of the world
say of him, when he is dead, that he was a great and
happy man, a thorough master of business, and had
acquired a hundred thousand pairs of boots and spurs
when he died.

Now, if this was really the case, I believe it would
be readily granted that a life of such business was as
poor and ridiculous as any that can be invented. But
it would puzzle any one to show that a man has

spent all his time and thoughts in business and hurry,
that he might die, as it is said, worth a hundred
thousand pounds, is any whit wiser than he who has
taken the same pains to have as many pairs of boots
and spurs when he leaves the world.

For if the temper and state of our souls be our
whole state; if the only end of life be to die as free
from sin, and as exalted in virtue, as we can; if
naked as we came, so naked are we to return, and to
stand a trial before Christ and His holy angels, for
everlasting happiness or misery; what can it possibly
signify what a man had, or had not, in this world?
What can it signify what you call those things which
a man has left behind him; whether you call them
his or any one's else; whether you call them trees or
fields, or birds and feathers; whether you call them
a hundred thousand pounds, or a hundred thousand
pairs of boots and spurs? I say, call them; for the
things signify no more,to him than the names.

Now, it is easy to see the folly of a life thus spent,
to furnish a man with such a number of boots and
spurs. But yet there needs no better faculty of
seeing, no finer understanding, to see the folly of a
life spent in making a man a possessor of ten towns
before he dies.

For if, when he has got all his towns, or all his
boots, his soul is to go to its own place among separate
spirits, and his body be laid by in a coffin, till the
last trumpet calls him to judgment; where the inquiry
will be, how humbly, how devoutly, how purely, how
meekly, how piously, how charitably, how heavenly,
we have spoken, thought, and acted, whilst we were in
the body; how can we say that he who has worn out

16

his life in raising a hundred thousand pounds has
acted wiser for himself, than he who has had the
same care to procure a hundred thousand of any
thing else?

But farther: let it now be supposed that Negotius,
when he first entered into business, happening to read
the Gospel with attention, and eyes open, found that
he had a much greater business upon his hands than
that to which he had served an apprenticeship; that
there were things which belong to man, of much more
importance than all that our eyes can see; so glorious,
as to deserve all our thoughts; so dangerous, as to
need all our care; and so certain, as never to deceive
the faithful labourer: let it be supposed that Negotius,
believing these things to be true, entirely devoted
himself to God at his first setting out in the world,
resolving to pursue his business no farther than was
consistent with great devotion, humility, and self-
denial; and for no other ends, but to provide himself
with a sober subsistence, and to do all the good that
he could, to the souls and bodies of his fellow-
creatures; let it therefore be supposed, that instead
of the continual hurry of business, he was frequent in
his retirements, and a strict observer of the hours of
prayers; that, instead of restless desires after more
riches, his soul has been full of the love of God and
heavenly affection, constantly watching against worldly
tempers, and always aspiring after Divine grace; that,
instead of worldly cares and contrivances, he was busy
in fortifying his soul against all approaches of sin:
now, had this been the Christian spirit of Negotius,
can any one say that he had lost the true joy and
happiness of life by thus conforming to the spirit, and

living up to the hopes of the gospel? Can it be said that a life made exemplary by such virtues as these, which keep heaven always in our sight, which both delight and exalt the soul here, and prepare it for the presence of God hereafter, must be poor and dull, if compared to that of heaping up riches, which can neither stay with us, nor we with them?

It would be endless to multiply examples of this kind, to show you how little is lost, and how much is gained, by introducing a strict and exact piety into every condition of human life.

CHAPTER XIV.

CONCERNING THAT PART OF DEVOTION WHICH RELATES TO TIMES AND HOURS OF PRAYER. OF DAILY EARLY PRAYER IN THE MORNING. HOW WE ARE TO IMPROVE OUR FORMS OF PRAYER, AND HOW TO INCREASE THE SPIRIT OF DEVOTION.

(Of Special Times of Prayer.)

HAVING in the foregoing chapters shown the necessity of a devout spirit, or habit of mind, in every part of our common life, in the discharge of all our business, in the use of all the gifts of God; I come now to consider that part of devotion, which relates to times and hours of prayer. . . .

Prayer is the nearest approach to God, and the highest enjoyment of Him, that we are capable of in this life.

It is the noblest exercise of the soul, the most

exalted use of our best faculties, and the highest imitation of the blessed inhabitants of heaven.

When our hearts are full of God, sending up holy
desires to the throne of grace, we are then in our
highest state, we are upon the utmost heights of
human greatness ; we are not before kings and princes,
but in the presence and audience of the Lord of all
the world, and can be no higher, till death is swallowed
up in glory. . . .

The first thing that you are to do, when you are
upon your knees, is to shut your eyes, and with a short
silence let your soul place itself in the presence of
God ; that is, you are to use this, or some other better
method, to separate yourself from all common thoughts,
and make your heart as sensible as you can of the
Divine Presence.

Now, if this recollection of spirit is necessary,—as
who can say it is not ?—then how poorly must they
perform their devotions, who are always in a hurry ;
who begin them in haste, and hardly allow themselves
time to repeat their very form, with any gravity or
attention ! Theirs is properly saying prayers, instead
of praying. . . .

At all the stated hours of prayer, it will be of great
benefit to you to have something fixed, and something
at liberty, in your devotions.

You should have some fixed subject, which is constantly to be the chief matter of your prayer at that
particular time ; and yet have liberty to add such
other petitions, as your condition may then require.

For instance : as the morning is to you the beginning of a new life ; as God has then given you a new
enjoyment of yourself, and a fresh entrance into the

world; it is highly proper that your first devotions should be a praise and thanksgiving to God, as for a new creation; and that you should offer and devote body and soul, all that you are, and all that you have, to His service and glory.

Receive, therefore, every day as a resurrection from death, as a new enjoyment of life; meet every rising sun with such sentiments of God's goodness, as if you had seen it, and all things, new created upon your account: and under the sense of so great a blessing let your joyful heart praise and magnify so good and glorious a Creator.

Let, therefore, praise and thanksgiving, and oblation of yourself unto God, be always the fixed and certain subject of your first prayers in the morning; and then take the liberty of adding such other devotions as the accidental difference of your state, or the accidental difference of your heart, shall then make most needful and expedient for you.

For one of the greatest benefits of private devotion consists in rightly adapting our prayers to those two conditions,—the difference of our state, and the difference of our hearts.

By **the difference of our state** is meant the difference of our external state or condition, as of sickness, health, pains, losses, disappointments, troubles, particular mercies, or judgments, from God; all sorts of kindnesses, injuries, or reproaches from other people.

Now, as these are great parts of our state of life, as they make great difference in it by continually changing; so our devotion will be made doubly beneficial to us, when it watches to receive and sanctify all these changes of our state, and turns them all into

so many occasions of a more particular application
to God of such thanksgiving, such resignation, such
petitions, as our present state more especially requires.

And he that makes every change in his state a
réason of presenting unto God some particular petitions
suitable to that change, will soon find that he has
taken an excellent means not only of praying with
fervour, but of living as he prays.

The next condition, to which we are always to adapt
some part of our prayers, is **the difference of our
hearts**; by which is meant the different state of the
tempers of our hearts, as of love, joy, peace, tranquillity, dulness and dryness of spirit, anxiety, discontent,
motions of envy and ambition, dark and disconsolate
thoughts, resentments, fretfulness, and peevish tempers.

Now, as these tempers, through the weakness of our
nature, will have their succession, more or less, even
in pious minds; so we should constantly make the
present state of our heart the reason of some particular
application to God. . . .

Now, though people of leisure seem called more
particularly to this study of devotion, yet persons of
much business or labour must not think themselves
excused from this, or some better method of improving
their devotion.

For the greater their business is, the more need
they have of some such method as this, to prevent
its power over their hearts, to secure them from
sinking into worldly tempers, and preserve a sense
and taste of heavenly things in their minds. And a
little time regularly and constantly employed to any
one use or end will do great things, and produce
mighty effects.

And it is for want of considering devotion in this light, as something that is to be nursed and cherished with care, as something that is to be made part of our business, that is to be improved with care and contrivance, by art and method, and a diligent use of the best helps ; it is for want of considering .it in this light that so many people are so little benefited by it, and live and die strangers to that spirit of devotion which, by a prudent use of proper means, they might have enjoyed in a high degree.

For though the spirit of devotion is the gift of God, and not attainable by any mere power of our own, yet it is mostly given to, and never.withheld from, those who, by a wise and diligent use of proper means, prepare themselves for the reception of it.

And it is amazing to see how eagerly men employ their parts, their sagacity, time, study, application, and exercise ; how all helps are called to their assistance, when any thing is intended and desired in worldly matters ; and how dull, negligent, and unimproved they are ; how little they use their parts, sagacity, and abilities to raise and increase their devotion !

Mundanus is a man of excellent parts and clear apprehension. He is well advanced in age, and has made a great figure in business. Every part of trade and business that has fallen in his way has had some improvement from him ; and he is always contriving to carry every method of doing any thing well to its greatest height. Mundanus aims at the greatest perfection in every thing. The soundness and strength of his mind, and his just way of thinking upon things, makes him intent upon removing all imperfections.

The one only thing which has not fallen under his

improvement, nor received any benefit from his judicious mind, is his devotion : this is just in the same poor state it was, when he was only six years of age, and the old man prays now in that little form of words which his mother used to hear him repeat night and morning. . . .

All which seems to be owing to a strange, infatuated state of negligence, which keeps people from considering what devotion is. For if they did but once proceed so far as to reflect about it, or ask themselves any questions concerning it, they would soon see that the spirit of devotion was like any other sense or understanding, that is only to be improved by study, care, application, and the use of such means and helps as are necessary to make a man a proficient in any art or science. . . .

Devotion is nothing else but right apprehensions of God, and right affections towards Him.

All practices, therefore, that heighten and improve our true apprehensions of God, all ways of life that tend to nourish, raise, and fix our affections upon Him, are to be reckoned so many helps and means to fill us with devotion.

As prayer is the proper fuel of this holy flame, so we must use all our care and contrivance to give prayer its full power ; as by alms, self-denial, frequent retirements, and holy readings, composing forms for ourselves, or using the best we can get, adding length of time, and observing hours of prayer ; changing, improving, and suiting our devotions to the condition of our lives, and the state of our hearts.

Those who have most leisure seem more especially called to a more eminent observance of these holy rules of a devout life. And they who, by the necessity of their state, and not through their own choice, have but little time to employ thus, must make the best use of that little they have. For this is the certain way of making devotion produce a devout life.

- - - - -

CHAPTER XV.

OF CHANTING, OR SINGING OF PSALMS IN OUR PRIVATE DEVOTIONS. OF THE EXCELLENCY AND BENEFIT OF THIS KIND OF DEVOTION. OF THE GREAT EFFECTS IT HATH UPON OUR HEARTS. OF THE MEANS OF PERFORMING IT IN THE BEST MANNER.

(Of Singing, and beginning the day with Thankfulness and Praise.)

YOU have seen, in the foregoing chapter, what means and methods you are to use, to raise and improve your devotion; how early you are to begin your prayers, and what is to be the subject of your first devotions in the morning.

There is one thing still remaining, that you must be required to observe, not only as fit and proper to be done, but as such as cannot be neglected without great prejudice to your devotions; and that is, to begin all your prayers with a psalm.

This is so right, is so beneficial to devotion, has so much effect upon our hearts, that it may be insisted upon as a common rule for all persons.

I do not mean that you should read over a psalm, but that you should chant or sing one of those psalms, which we commonly call the reading psalms. For

singing is as much the proper use of a psalm as
devout supplication is the proper use of a form of
prayer; and a psalm only read is very much like a
prayer that is only looked over. . . .

You are therefore to consider this chanting of a
psalm as a necessary beginning of your devotions, as
something that is to awaken all that is good and holy
within you, that is to call your spirits to their proper
duty, to set you in your best posture towards heaven,
and tune all the powers of your soul to worship and
adoration.

For there is nothing that so clears a way for your
prayers, nothing that so disperses dulness of heart,
nothing that so purifies the soul from poor and little
passions, nothing that so opens heaven, or carries
your heart so near it, as these songs of praise.

They create a sense and delight in God, they
awaken holy desires, they teach you how to ask, and
they prevail with God to give. They kindle a holy
flame, they turn your heart into an altar, your prayers
into incense, and carry them as a sweet-smelling
savour to the throne of grace. . . .

Secondly, Let us now consider another reason for
this kind of devotion. As singing is a natural effect
of joy in the heart, so it has also a natural power of
rendering the heart joyful.

The soul and body are so united, that they have
each of them power over one another in their actions.
Certain thoughts and sentiments in the soul produce
such and such motions and actions in the body; and,
on the other hand, certain motions and actions of the
body have the same power of raising such and such
thoughts and sentiments in the soul. So that, as

singing is the natural effect of joy in the mind, it is as truly a natural cause of raising joy in the mind.

As devotion of the heart naturally breaks out into outward acts of prayer; so outward acts of prayer are natural means of raising the devotion of the heart.

It is thus in all states and tempers of the mind: as the inward state of the mind produces outward actions suitable to it, so those outward actions have the like power of raising an inward state of mind suitable to them.

As anger produces angry words, so angry words increase anger.

So that, if we barely consider human nature, we shall find that singing or chanting the psalms is as proper and necessary to raise our hearts to a delight in God, as prayer is proper and necessary to excite in us the spirit of devotion. Every reason for one is in all respects as strong a reason for the other.

If, therefore, you would know the reason and necessity of singing psalms, you must consider the reason and necessity of praising and rejoicing in God; because singing of psalms is as much the true exercise and support of the spirit of thanksgiving, as prayer is the true exercise and support of the spirit of devotion. And you may as well think that you can be devout as you ought, without the use of prayer, as that you can rejoice in God as you ought, without the practice of singing psalms: because this singing is as much the natural language of praise and thanksgiving, as prayer is the natural language of devotion. . . .

Now, if you rightly apprehend the union of the soul and body, you will see a great deal into the reason and necessity of all the outward parts of religion.

The union of our souls and bodies is the reason both why we have so little and so much power over ourselves. It is owing to this union that we have so little power over our souls; for as we cannot prevent the effects of external objects upon our bodies, as we cannot command outward causes, so we cannot always command the inward state of our minds; because, as outward objects act upon our bodies without our leave, so our bodies act upon our minds by the laws of the union of the soul and the body: and thus you see it is owing to this union that we have so little power over ourselves.

On the other hand, it is owing to this union that we have so much power over ourselves. For as our souls, in a great measure, depend upon our bodies; and as we have great power over our bodies; as we can command our outward actions, and oblige ourselves to such habits of life as naturally produce habits in the soul; as we can mortify our bodies, and remove ourselves from objects that inflame our passions; so we have a great power over the inward state of our souls. . . .

Now from this you may also see the necessity and benefit of singing psalms, and of all the outward acts of religion; for if the body has so much power over the soul, it is certain that all such bodily actions as affect the soul are of great weight in religion. Not as if there was any true worship, or piety, in the actions themselves, but because they are proper to raise and support that spirit which is the true worship of God.

Though, therefore, the seat of religion is in the heart, yet since our bodies have a power over our hearts; since outward actions both proceed from, and enter into the heart; it is plain that outward actions have a great power over that religion which is seated in the heart.

We are therefore as well to use outward helps, as inward meditation, in order to beget and fix habits of piety in our hearts. . . .

If we would truly prostrate our souls before God, we must use our bodies to postures of lowliness : if we desire true fervours of devotion, we must make prayer the frequent labour of our lips. If we would banish all pride and passion from our hearts, we must force ourselves to all outward actions of patience and meekness. If we would feel inward motions of joy and delight in God, we must practise all the outward acts of it, and make our voices call upon our hearts.

Now, therefore, you may plainly see the reason and necessity of singing of psalms; it is because outward actions are necessary to support inward tempers; and therefore the outward act of joy is necessary to raise and support the inward joy of the mind. . . .

I have been the longer upon this head, because of its great importance to true religion. For there is no state of mind so holy, so excellent, and so truly perfect, as that of thankfulness to God; and consequently nothing is of more importance in religion than that which exercises and improves this habit of mind. . . .

Would you know who is the greatest saint in the world ? it is not he who prays most or fasts most; it is not he who gives most alms, or is most eminent for temperance, chastity, or justice; but it is he who is always thankful to God, who wills every thing that

God willeth, who receives every thing as an instance
of God's goodness, and has a heart always ready to
praise God for it.

All prayer and devotion, fastings and repentance,
meditation and retirement, all sacraments and ordinances, are but so many means to render the soul
thus divine and comfortable to the will of God, and
to fill it with thankfulness and praise for every thing
that comes from God. This is the perfection of all
virtues : and all virtues that do not tend to it, or proceed from it, are but so many false ornaments of a
soul not converted unto God.

You need not, therefore, now wonder that I lay so
much stress upon singing a psalm at all your devotions,
since you see it is to form your spirit to such joy and
thankfulness to God as is the highest perfection of a
divine and holy life.

If any one would tell you the shortest, surest way
to all happiness, and all perfection, he must tell you
to make a rule to yourself, to thank and praise God
for every thing that happens to you. . . .

And although this be the highest temper that you
can aim at, though it be the noblest sacrifice that the
greatest saint can offer unto God, yet it is not tied to
any time, or place, or great occasion, but is always in
your power, and may be the exercise of every day.
For the common events of every day are sufficient to
discover and exercise this temper, and may plainly
show you how far you are governed in all your actions
by this thankful spirit.

And for this reason I exhort you to this method in
your devotion, that every day may be made a day
of thanksgiving, and that the spirit of murmur and

discontent may be unable to enter into the heart which is so often employed in singing the praises of God.

CHAPTER XVI.

RECOMMENDING DEVOTIONS AT NINE O'CLOCK IN THE MORNING, CALLED IN SCRIPTURE THE THIRD HOUR OF THE DAY. THE SUBJECT OF THESE PRAYERS IS HUMILITY.

(Of frequency in Prayer; of praying for Humility.)

I AM now come to another hour of prayer, which in Scripture is called the third hour of the day; but, according to our way of numbering the hours, it is called the ninth hour of the morning.

The devout Christian must at this time look upon himself as called upon by God to renew his acts of prayer, and address himself again to the throne of grace.

There is indeed no express command in Scripture to repeat our devotions at this hour. But then it is to be considered, also, that neither is there any express command to begin and end the day with prayer. So that if that be looked upon as a reason for neglecting devotion at this hour, it may as well be urged as a reason for neglecting devotion both at the beginning and end of the day. . . .

For if you were up at a good time in the morning, your first devotions will have been at a proper distance from this hour; you will have been long enough at other business to make it proper for you to return to

this greatest of all business — the raising your soul
and affections unto God. . . .

For if prayer has power with God, if it looses the
bands of sin, if it purifies the soul, reforms our hearts,
and draws down the aids of Divine grace; how can
that be reckoned a small matter, which robs us of an
hour of prayer? . . .

Now, as this frequency of prayer is founded in the
doctrines of Scripture, and recommended to us by the
practice of the true worshippers of God; so we ought
not to think ourselves excused from it, but where we
can show that we are spending our time in such
business, as is more acceptable to God than these
returns of prayer.

If you are of a devout spirit, you will rejoice at
these returns of prayer which keep your soul in a
holy enjoyment of God; which change your passions
into divine love, and fill your heart with stronger joys
and consolations than you can possibly meet with in
any thing else.

And if you are not of a devout spirit, then you are
moreover obliged to this frequency of prayer, to train
and exercise your heart into a true sense and feeling
of devotion.

Now, seeing the holy spirit of the Christian religion,
and the example of the saints of all ages, call upon
you thus to divide the day into hours of prayer; so it
will be highly beneficial to you to make a right choice
of those matters which are to be the subject of your
prayers, and to keep every hour of prayer appropriated
to some particular subject, which you may alter or
enlarge, according as the state you are in requires.

By this means you will have an opportunity of

being large and particular in all the parts of any virtue or grace, which you then make the subject of your prayers. And by asking for it in all its parts, and making it the substance of a whole prayer once every day, you will soon find a mighty change in your heart; and that you cannot thus constantly pray for all the parts of any virtue every day of your life, and yet live the rest of the day contrary to it.

If a worldly-minded man was to pray every day against all the instances of a worldly temper; if he should make a large description of the temptations of covetousness, and desire God to assist him to reject them all, and to disappoint him in all his covetous designs; he would find his conscience so much awakened, that he would be forced either to forsake such prayers, or to forsake a worldly life. . . .

And because an humble state of soul is the very state of religion, because **humility** is the life and soul of piety, the foundation and support of every virtue and good work, the best guard and security of all holy affections,—I shall recommend humility to you, as highly proper to be made the constant subject of your devotions, at this third hour of the day; earnestly desiring you to think no day safe, or likely to end well, in which you have not thus early put yourself in this posture of humility, and called upon God to carry you through the day, in the exercise of a meek and lowly spirit.

This virtue is so essential to the right state of our souls, that there is no pretending to a reasonable or pious life without it. We may as well think to see without eyes, or live without breath, as to live in the spirit of religion without the spirit of humility. . . .

17

Humility does not consist in having a worse opinion of ourselves than we deserve, or in abasing ourselves lower than we really are; but as all virtue is founded in truth, so humility is founded in a true and just sense of our weakness, misery, and sin. He that rightly feels and lives in this sense of his condition, lives in humility.

The weakness of our state appears from our inability to do any thing as of ourselves. In our natural state we are entirely without any power; we are indeed active beings, but can only act by a power that is every moment lent us from God. . . .

This is the dependent, helpless poverty of our state; which is a great reason for humility. For, since we neither are, nor can do any thing of ourselves, to be proud of any thing that we are, or of any thing that we can do, and to ascribe glory to ourselves for these things, as our own ornaments, has the guilt both of stealing and lying. It has the guilt of stealing, as it gives to ourselves those things which only belong to God; it has the guilt of lying, as it is the denying the truth of our state, and pretending to be something that we are not.

Secondly, Another argument for humility is founded in the **misery** of our condition.

Now the misery of our condition appears in this, that we use these borrowed powers of our nature to the torment and vexation of ourselves, and our fellow-creatures.

God Almighty has entrusted us with the use of reason, and we use it to the disorder and corruption of our nature. We reason ourselves into all kinds of folly and misery, and make our lives the sport of foolish and extravagant passions; seeking after imaginary happiness in all kinds of shapes, creating to ourselves a thousand wants, amusing our hearts with false hopes and fears, using the world worse than irrational animals, envying, vexing, and tormenting one another with restless passions, and unreasonable contentions. . . .

And perhaps there are very few people in the world who would not rather choose to die, than to have all their secret follies, the errors of their judgments, the vanity of their minds, the falseness of their pretences, the frequency of their vain and disorderly passions, their uneasiness, hatred, envies, and vexations made known unto the world.

And shall pride be entertained in a heart thus conscious of its own miserable behaviour? Shall a creature in such a condition, that he could not support himself under the shame of being known to the world in his real state,—shall such a creature, because his shame is only known to God, to holy angels, and his own conscience,—shall he, in the sight of God and holy angels, dare to be vain and proud of himself?

Thirdly, If to this we add the shame and **guilt of sin,** we shall find a still greater reason for humility.

No creature that had lived in innocence would have thereby got any pretence for self-honour and esteem; because, as a creature, all that it is, or has, or does, is from God, and therefore the honour of all that belongs to it is only due to God.

But if a creature that is a sinner, and under the displeasure of the great Governor of all the world, and deserving nothing from Him but pains and punishments for the shameful abuse of his powers; if such a creature pretends to self-glory for any thing that he is or does, he can only be said to glory in his shame. . . .

Have our sins rendered us so abominable and odious to Him that made us, that He could not so much as receive our prayers, or admit our repentance, till the Son of God made Himself man, and became a suffering Advocate for our whole race; and can we, in this state, pretend to high thoughts of ourselves? Shall we presume to take delight in our own worth, who are not worthy so much as to ask pardon for our sins, without the mediation and intercession of the Son of God?

Thus deep is the foundation of humility laid in these deplorable circumstances of our condition; which show that it is as great an offence against truth, and the reason of things, for a man, in this state of things, to lay claim to any degrees of glory, as to pretend to the honour of creating himself. If man will boast of any thing as his own, he must boast of his misery and sin; for there is nothing else but this that is his own pro- perty. . . .

When you have by such general reflections as these convinced your mind of the reasonableness of humility, you must not content yourself with this, as if you were therefore humble, because your mind acknowledges the reasonableness of humility, and declares against pride. But you must immediately enter yourself into the practice of this virtue, like a young beginner, that has all of it to learn, that can learn but little at a time, and with great difficulty. You must consider that you have not only this virtue to learn, but that you must be content to proceed as a learner in it all your time, endeavouring after greater degrees of it, and practising every day acts of humility, as you every day practise acts of devotion.

You would not imagine yourself to be devout, because in your judgment you approved of prayers, and often declared your mind in favour of devotion. Yet how many people imagine themselves humble enough, for no other reason, but because they often commend humility, and make vehement declarations against pride! . . .

All their speeches in favour of humility, and all their railings against pride, are looked upon as so many true exercises and effects of their own humble spirit.

Whereas, in truth, these are so far from being proper acts or proofs of humility, that they are great arguments of the want of it.

For the fuller of pride any one is himself, the more impatient will he be at the smallest instances of it in other people. And the less humility any one has in his own mind, the more will he demand and be delighted with it in other people.

You must therefore act by a quite contrary measure, and reckon yourself only so far humble, as you impose every instance of humility upon yourself, and never call for it in other people,—so far an enemy to pride, as you never spare it in yourself, nor ever censure it in other persons.

Now, in order to do this, you need only consider that pride and humility signify nothing to you, but so far as they are your own ; that they do you neither good nor harm, but as they are the tempers of your heart.

The loving, therefore, of humility, is of no benefit or advantage to you, but so far as you love to see all your own thoughts, words, and actions governed by it. And the hating of pride does you no good, is no perfection in you, but so far as you hate to harbour any degree of it in your own heart.

Now, in order to begin, and set out well, in the practice of humility, you must take it for granted that you are proud, that you have all your life been more or less infected with this unreasonable temper.

You should believe, also, that it is your greatest weakness, that your heart is more subject to it, that it is so constantly stealing upon you, that you have reason to watch and suspect its approaches in all your actions.

For this is what most people, especially new beginners in a pious life, may with great truth think of themselves.

For there is no one vice that is more deeply rooted in our nature, or that receives such constant nourishment from almost every thing that we think or do: there being hardly any thing in the world that we want or use, or any action or duty of life, but pride finds some means or other to take hold of it. So that at what time soever we begin to offer ourselves to God, we can hardly be surer of any thing, than that we have a great deal of pride to repent of.

If, therefore, you find it disagreeable to your mind to entertain this opinion of yourself, and that you cannot put yourself amongst those that want to be cured of pride, you may be as sure as if an angel from heaven had told you that you have not only much, but all your humility to seek.

CHAPTER XVII.

SHOWING HOW DIFFICULT THE PRACTICE OF HUMILITY
IS MADE, BY THE GENERAL SPIRIT AND TEMPER OF
THE WORLD.   HOW CHRISTIANITY REQUIRETH US TO
LIVE CONTRARY TO THE WORLD.

(No Humility without renouncing both Self and the Spirit of the World.)

EVERY person, when he first applies himself to the exercise of this virtue of humility, must, as I said before, consider himself as a learner—that is, to learn something that is contrary to former tempers and habits of mind, and which can only be got by daily and constant practice.

He has not only as much to do as he that has some new art or science to learn, but he has also a great deal to unlearn : he is to forget and lay aside his own spirit, which has been a long while fixing and forming itself ; he must forget and depart from abundance of passions and opinions, which the fashion, and vogue, and spirit of the world have made natural to him.

He must lay aside his own spirit ; because, as we are born in sin, so in pride, which is as natural to us as self-love, and continually springs from it.   And this is the reason why Christianity is so often represented as a new birth, and a new spirit.

He must lay aside the opinions and passions which he has received from the world ; because the vogue and fashion of the world, by which we have been carried away as in a torrent, before we could pass right judgments of the value of things, is, in many respects, contrary to humility ; so that we must unlearn what the spirit of the world has taught us, before we can be governed by the spirit of humility.

Now, according to the spirit and vogue of this world, whose corrupt air we have all breathed, there are many things that pass for great and honourable, and most desirable, which yet are so far from being so, that the true greatness and honour of our nature consists in the not desiring them.

To abound in wealth, to have fine houses, and rich clothes, to be beautiful in our persons, to have titles of dignity, to be above our fellow-creatures, to command the bows and obeisance of other people, to be looked on with admiration, to overcome our enemies with power, to subdue all that oppose us, to set out ourselves in as much splendour as we can, to live highly and magnificently, to eat, and drink, and delight ourselves in the most costly manner, these are the great, the honourable, the desirable things to which the spirit of the world turns the eyes of all people. And many a man is afraid of standing still, and not engaging in the pursuit of these things, lest the same world should take him for a fool. . . .

Notwithstanding the clearness and plainness of these doctrines which thus renounce the world, yet great part of Christians live and die slaves to the customs and temper of the world. . . .

From this quarter arises the greatest difficulty of humility, because it cannot subsist in any mind, but so far as it is dead to the world, and has parted with all desires of enjoying its greatness and honours. So that in order to be truly humble, you must unlearn all those notions which you have been all your life learning from this corrupt spirit of the world.

You can make no stand against the assaults of pride, the meek affections of humility can have no place in your soul, till you stop the power of the world over you, and resolve against a blind obedience to its laws. . . .

Our blessed Lord Himself has fully determined this point in these words : " They are not of this world, as I am not of this world." [1] This is the state of Christianity with regard to this world. If you are not thus out of, and contrary to the world, you want the distinguishing mark of Christianity ; you do not belong to Christ, but by being out of the world as He was out of it.

We may deceive ourselves, if we please, with vain and softening comments upon these words ; but they are, and will be understood in their first simplicity and plainness by every one that reads them in the same spirit that our blessed Lord spoke them. And to understand them in any lower, less significant meaning, is to let carnal wisdom explain away that doctrine by which itself was to be destroyed.

The Christian's great conquest over the world is all contained in the mystery of Christ upon the cross. It was there, and from thence, that He taught all Christians how they were to come out of, and conquer the world, and what they were to do in order to be His disciples. And all the doctrines, sacraments, and institutions of the gospel are only so many explications of the meaning, and applications of the benefit, of this great mystery.

And the state of Christianity implieth nothing else, but an entire, absolute conformity to that spirit which

[1] John xvii. 16.

Christ showed in the mysterious sacrifice of Himself upon the cross. . . .

Thus was the Cross of Christ, in St. Paul's days, the glory of Christians; not as it signified their not being ashamed to own a Master that was crucified, but as it signified their glorying in a religion which was nothing else but a doctrine of the Cross, that called them to the same suffering spirit, the same sacrifice of themselves, the same renunciation of the world, the same humility and meekness, the same patient bearing of injuries, reproaches, and contempts, and the same dying to all the greatness, honours, and happiness of this world, which Christ showed upon the cross.

To have a true idea of Christianity, we must not consider our blessed Lord as suffering in our stead, but as our Representative, acting in our name, and with such particular merit, as to make our joining with Him acceptable unto God.

It was for this reason that the holy Jesus said of His disciples, and in them of all true believers, "They are not of the world, as I am not of the world."[1] Because all true believers, conforming to the sufferings, crucifixion, death, and resurrection of Christ, live no longer after the spirit and temper of this world, but their life is hid with Christ in God.

This is the state of separation from the world, to which all orders of Christians are called. They must so far renounce all worldly tempers, be so far governed by the things of another life, as to show that they are truly and really crucified, dead, and risen with Christ. And it is as necessary for all Christians to conform to this great change of spirit, to be thus in Christ new

[1] John xvii. 14.

creatures, as it was necessary that Christ should suffer, die, and rise again for our salvation. . . .

Now, as it was the spirit of the world that nailed our blessed Lord to the cross; so every man that has the Spirit of Christ, that opposes the world as He did, will certainly be crucified by the world, some way or other.

For Christianity still lives in the same world that Christ did; and these two will be utter enemies, till the kingdom of darkness is entirely at an end.

Had you lived with our Saviour as His true disciple, you had then been hated as He was; and if you now live in His Spirit, the world will be the same enemy to you now, that it was to Him then.

"If ye were of the world," saith the blessed Lord, "the world would love his own; but because ye are not of the world, but I have chosen you out of the world, therefore the world hateth you." [1]

We are apt to lose the true meaning of these words, by considering them only as an historical description of something that was the state of our Saviour and His disciples at that time. But this is reading the Scripture as a dead letter; for they exactly describe the state of true Christians at this, and at all other times, to the end of the world.

For as true Christianity is nothing else but the Spirit of Christ, so, whether that Spirit appear in the person of Christ Himself, or His apostles, or followers in any age, it is the same thing; whoever hath His Spirit will be hated, despised, and condemned by the world, as He was.

For the world will always love its own, and none

[1] John xv. 19.

but its own : this is as certain and unchangeable, as
the contrariety betwixt light and darkness.

When the holy Jesus saith, " If the world hate you,"
He does not add by way of consolation that it may
some time or other cease its hatred, or that it will not
always hate them; but He only gives this as a reason
for their bearing it, " Ye know that it hated Me before
it hated you : " [1] signifying that it was He, that is,
His Spirit, that by reason of its contrariety to the
world, was then, and always would be, hated
by it.

You will perhaps say, that the world has now
become Christian, at least that part of it where we
live; and therefore the world is not now to be considered in the same state of opposition to Christianity
as when it was heathen.

It is granted, the world now professeth Christianity.
But will any one say that this Christian world is of
the spirit of Christ ? Are its general tempers the
tempers of Christ ? Are the passions of sensuality,
self-love, pride, covetousness, ambition, and vain-glory
less contrary to the spirit of the gospel now they are
amongst Christians, than when they were amongst
heathens ? Or will you say that the tempers and
passions of the heathen world are lost and gone ?

Consider, secondly, what you are to mean by the
world. Now this is fully described to our hands by
St. John. " All that is in the world, the lust of the
flesh, the lust of the eyes, and the pride of life," [2] etc.
This is an exact and full description of the world.
Now, will you say that this world is become Christian ?
But if all this still subsists, then the same world is

[1] John xv. 18.   [2] 1 John ii. 16.

now in being, and the same enemy to Christianity, that it was in St. John's days.

It was this world that St. John condemned, as being not of the Father: whether, therefore, it outwardly professeth, or openly persecuteth Christianity, it is still in the same state of contrariety to the true spirit and holiness of the gospel.

And indeed the world, by professing Christianity, is so far from being a less dangerous enemy than it was before, that it has by its favours destroyed more Christians than ever it did by the most violent persecution.

We must therefore be so far from considering the world as in a state of less enmity and opposition to Christianity than it was in the first times of the gospel, that we must guard against it as a greater and more dangerous enemy now than it was in those times.

It is a greater enemy, because it has greater power over Christians by its favours, riches, honours, rewards, and protection, than it had by the fire and fury of its persecutions.

It is a more dangerous enemy, by having lost its appearance of enmity. Its outward profession of Christianity makes it no longer considered as an enemy, and therefore the generality of people are easily persuaded to resign themselves up to be governed and directed by it.

How many consciences are kept at quiet, upon no other foundation, but because they sin under the authority of the Christian world !

How many directions of the gospel lie by unregarded, and how unconcernedly do particular persons

read them, for no other reason but because they seem
unregarded by the Christian world!

How many compliances do people make to the
Christian world, without any hesitation or remorse;
which, if they had been required of them only by
heathens, would have been refused, as contrary to the
holiness of Christianity!

Who could be content with seeing how contrary
his life is to the gospel, but because he sees that he
lives as the Christian world doth?

Who that reads the Gospel would want to be
persuaded of the necessity of great self-denial, humility,
and poverty of spirit, but that the authority of the
world has banished this doctrine of the Cross?

There is nothing, therefore, that a good Christian
ought to be more suspicious of, or more constantly
guard against, than the authority of the Christian
world. . . .

Need a man do more to make his soul unfit for the
mercy of God, than by being greedy and ambitious of
honour? Yet how can a man renounce this temper,
without renouncing the spirit and temper of the world,
in which you now live?

How can a man be made more capable of the
spirit of Christ, than by a wrong value for money?
and yet, how can he be more wrong in his value of
it, than by following the authority of the Christian
world?

———

CHAPTER XVIII.

SHOWING HOW THE EDUCATION WHICH MEN GENERALLY
RECEIVE IN THEIR YOUTH MAKES THE DOCTRINES
OF HUMILITY DIFFICULT TO BE PRACTISED. THE
SPIRIT OF A BETTER EDUCATION REPRESENTED IN
THE CHARACTER OF PATERNUS.

**(How unfavourable the Spirit in which
men are educated is to the growth of
Humility.)**

ANOTHER difficulty in the practice of humility
arises from our education. We are all of us,
for the most part, corruptly educated, and then committed to take our course in a corrupt world; so that
it is no wonder if examples of great piety are so
seldom seen.

Great part of the world are undone by being born
and bred in families that have no religion: where
they are made vicious and irregular, by being like
those with whom they first lived.

But this is not the thing I now mean; the education that I here intend, is such as children generally
receive from virtuous and sober parents, and learned
tutors and governors.

Had we continued perfect, as God created the first
man, perhaps the perfection of our nature had been
a sufficient self-instruction for every one. But as
sickness and diseases have created the necessity of
medicines and physicians, so the change and disorder
of our rational nature have introduced the necessity
of education and tutors.

And as the only end of the physician is to restore

nature to its own state, so the only end of education is to restore our rational nature to its proper state. Education, therefore, is to be considered as a reason borrowed at second-hand, which is, as far as it can, to supply the loss of original perfection. And as physic may justly be called the art of restoring health, so education should be considered in no other light, than as the art of recovering to man the use of his reason.

Now, as the instruction of every art or science is founded upon the discoveries, the wisdom, experience, and maxims of the several great men that have laboured in it; so human wisdom, or right use of our reason, which young people should be called to by their education, is nothing else but the best experience, and finest reasonings, of men that have devoted themselves to the study of wisdom, and the improvement of human nature.

All, therefore, that great saints, and dying men, when the fullest of light and conviction, and after the highest improvement of their reason, all that they have said of the necessity of piety, of the excellency of virtue, of their duty to God, of the emptiness of riches, of the vanity of the world ; all the sentences, judgments, reasonings, and maxims of the wisest of philosophers, when in their highest state of wisdom, should constitute the common lessons of instruction for youthful minds.

This is the only way to make the young and ignorant part of the world the better for the wisdom and knowledge of the wise and ancient.

An education which is not wholly intent upon this, is as much beside the·point, as an art of physic that had little or no regard to the restoration of health.

The youths that attended upon Pythagoras, Socrates, Plato, and Epictetus were thus educated. Their everyday lessons and instructions were so many lectures upon the nature of man, his true end and the right use of his faculties ; upon the immortality of the soul, its relation to God, the beauty of virtue and its agreeableness to the Divine Nature ; upon the dignity of reason, the necessity of temperance, fortitude, and generosity, and the shame and folly of indulging our passions.

Now, as Christianity has, as it were, new created the moral and religious world, and set every thing that is reasonable, wise, holy, and desirable in its true point of light ; so one would expect that the education of youth should be as much bettered and amended by Christianity, as the faith and doctrines of religion are amended by it.

As it has introduced such a new state of things, and so fully informed us of the nature of man, the ends of his creation, the state of his condition ; as it has fixed all our goods and evils, taught us the means of purifying our souls, pleasing God, and becoming eternally happy ; one might naturally suppose that every Christian country abounded with schools for the teaching, not only a few questions and answers of a Catechism, but for the forming, training, and practising youth in such an outward course of life, as the highest precepts, the strictest rules, and the sublimest doctrines of Christianity require.

An education under Pythagoras, or Socrates, had no other end but to teach you to think, judge, act, and follow such rules of life as Pythagoras or Socrates used.

18

And is it not as reasonable to suppose that a Christian education should have no other end, but to teach youth how to think, and judge, and act, and live, according to the strictest laws of Christianity ?

At least one would suppose that in all Christian schools the teaching youth to begin their lives in the spirit of Christianity, in such severity of behaviour, such abstinence, sobriety, humility, and devotion, as Christianity requires, should not only be more, but a hundred times more regarded, than any, or all things else. . . .

But alas! our modern education is not of this kind.

The first temper that we try to awaken in children is pride; as dangerous a passion as that of lust. We stir them up to vain thoughts of themselves, and do every thing we can to puff up their minds with a sense of their own abilities.

Whatever way of life we intend them for, we apply to the fire and vanity of their minds, and exhort them to every thing from corrupt motives. We stir them up to action from principles of strife and ambition, from glory, envy, and a desire of distinction that they may excel others, and shine in the eyes of the world.

And when we have taught them to scorn to be outdone by any, to bear no rival, to thirst after every instance of applause, to be content with nothing but the highest distinctions, then we begin to take comfort in them, and promise the world some mighty things from youths of such a glorious spirit. . . .

That this is the nature of our best education is too plain to need any proof; and I believe there are few parents but would be glad to see these instructions daily given to their children. . . .

You teach a child to scorn to be outdone, to thirst for distinction and applause; and is it any wonder that he continues to act all his life in the same manner?

Now, if a youth is ever to be so far a Christian as to govern his heart by the doctrines of humility, I would fain know at what time he is to begin it; or if he is ever to begin it at all, why we train him up in tempers quite contrary to it? . . .

I know it is said in defence of this method of education, that ambition, and a desire of glory, are necessary to excite young people to industry; and that if we were to press upon them the doctrines of humility, we should deject their minds, and sink them into dulness and idleness.

But those people who say this, do not consider that this reason, if it has any strength, is full as strong against pressing the doctrines of humility upon grown men, lest we should deject their minds, and sink them into dulness and idleness.

For who does not see that middle-aged men want as much the assistance of pride, ambition, and vain-glory, to spur them up to action and industry, as children do? And it is very certain, that the precepts of humility are more contrary to the designs of such men, and more grievous to their minds when they are pressed upon them, than they are to the minds of young persons.

This reason, therefore, that is given why children should not be trained up in the principles of the true humility, is as good a reason why the same humility should never be required of grown men.

Thirdly, Let those people who think that children

would be spoiled, if they were not thus educated, consider this :—

Could they think that, if any children had been educated by our blessed Lord, or His holy apostles, their minds would have been sunk into dulness and idleness ?

Or could they think that such children would not have been trained up in the profoundest principles of a strict and true humility ? Can they say that our blessed Lord, who was the meekest and humblest Man that ever was on earth, was hindered by His humility from being the greatest example of worthy and glorious actions that ever were done by man ?

Can they say that His apostles, who lived in the humble spirit of their Master, did therefore cease to be laborious and active instruments of doing good to all the world ?

Paternus lived about two hundred years ago ; he had but one son, whom he educated himself in his own house. As they were sitting together in the garden, when the child was ten years old, Paternus thus began to him :—

The little time that you have been in the world, my child, you have spent wholly with me ; and my love and tenderness to you has made you look upon me as your only friend and benefactor, and the cause of all the comfort and pleasure that you enjoy ; your heart, I know, would be ready to break with grief if you thought this was the last day that I should live with you.

But, my child, though you now think yourself mighty happy, because you have hold of my hand, you are now in the hands, and under the tender care of a much greater Father and Friend than I am, whose love to you is far greater than mine, and from whom you receive such blessings as no mortal can give. . . .

When you love that which God loves, you act with Him, you join yourself to Him ; and when you love what He dislikes, then you oppose Him, and separate yourself from Him. This is the true and the right way : think what God loves, and do you love it with all your heart.

First of all, my child, worship and adore God, think of Him magnificently, speak of Him reverently, magnify His providence, adore His power, frequent His service, and pray unto Him frequently and constantly.

Next to this, love your neighbour, which is all mankind, with such tenderness and affection as you love yourself. Think how God loves all mankind, how merciful He is to them, how tender He is of them, how carefully He preserves them ; and then strive to love the world, as God loves it.

God would have all men to be happy ; therefore do you will and desire the same. All men are great instances of Divine Love ; therefore let all men be instances of your love.

But above all, my son, mark this : never do any thing through strife, or envy, or emulation, or vainglory. Never do any thing in order to excel other people, but in order to please God, and because it is His will that you should do every thing in the best manner that you can. . . .

Let this, therefore, be your only motive and spur to all good actions, honest industry, and business, to do every thing in as perfect and excellent a manner as you can, for this only reason, because it is pleasing to God, who desires your perfection, and writes all your actions in a book. When I am dead, my son, you will be master of all my estate, which will be a great deal more than the necessities of one family require. Therefore, as you are to be charitable to the souls of men, and wish them in the same happiness with you in heaven, so be charitable to their bodies, and endeavour to make them as happy as you upon earth. . . .

But, my son, observe this as a most principal thing, which I shall remember you of as long as I live with you :—

Hate and despise all human glory, for it is nothing else but human folly. It is the greatest snare, and the greatest betrayer, that you can possibly admit into your heart.

Love humility in all its instances; practise it in all its parts, for it is the noblest state of the soul of man; it will set your heart and affections right towards God, and fill you with every temper that is tender and affectionate towards men.

Let every day, therefore, be a day of humility; condescend to all the weaknesses and infirmities of your fellow-creatures, cover their frailties, love their excellencies, encourage their virtues, relieve their wants, rejoice in their prosperities, compassionate their distress, receive their friendship, overlook their unkindness, forgive their malice, be a servant of servants, and condescend to do the lowest offices to the lowest of mankind. . . .

Remember that there is but one man in the world, with whom you are to have perpetual contention, and be always striving to exceed him, and that is yourself. . . .

Thus did Paternus educate his son.

Can any one now think that such an education as this would weaken and deject the minds of young people, and deprive the world of any worthy and reasonable labours?

It is so far from that, that there is nothing so likely to ennoble and exalt the mind, and prepare it for the most heroical exercise of all virtues.

For who will say that a love of God, a desire of pleasing Him, a love of our neighbour, a love of truth, of reason, and virtue, a contemplation of eternity, and the rewards of piety, are not stronger motives to great and good actions than a little uncertain popular praise?

On the other hand, there is nothing in reality that more weakens the mind, and reduces it to meanness and slavery, nothing that makes it less master of its own actions, or less capable of following reason, than a love of praise and honour.

CHAPTER XIX.

SHOWING HOW THE METHOD OF EDUCATING DAUGHTERS MAKES IT DIFFICULT FOR THEM TO ENTER INTO THE SPIRIT OF CHRISTIAN HUMILITY. HOW MISERABLY THEY ARE INJURED AND ABUSED BY SUCH AN EDUCATION. THE SPIRIT OF A BETTER EDUCATION, REPRESENTED IN THE CHARACTER OF EUSEBIA.

(How in the Education of our Daughters the Spirit of Pride is fostered.)

THAT turn of mind which is taught and encouraged in the education of danghters, makes it exceedingly difficult for them to enter into such a sense and practice of humility, as the spirit of Christianity requires.

The right education of this sex is of the utmost importance to human life. There is nothing that is more desirable for the common good of all the world. For though women do not carry on the trade and business of the world, yet as they are mothers, and mistresses of families, that have for some time the care of the education of their children of both sorts, they are entrusted with that which is of the greatest consequence to human life. For this reason, good or bad women are likely to do as much good or harm in the world, as good or bad men in the greatest business of life.

For, as the health and strength or weakness of our bodies is very much owing to their methods of treating us when we were young; so the soundness or folly of our minds are not less owing to those first tempers and ways of thinking, which we eagerly receive from the love, tenderness, authority, and constant conversation of our mothers. . . .

They are not indeed suffered to dispute with us the proud prizes of arts and sciences, of learning and eloquence, in which I have much suspicion they would often prove our superiors ; but we turn them over to the study of beauty and dress, and the whole world conspires to make them think of nothing else. Fathers and mothers, friends and relations, seem to have no other wish towards the little girl, but that she may have a fair skin, a fine shape, dress well, and dance to admiration. . . .

And what makes this matter still more to be lamented is this, that women are not only spoiled by this education, but we spoil that part of the world, which would otherwise furnish most instances of an eminent and exalted piety.

For I believe it may be affirmed, that for the most part there is a finer sense, a clearer mind, a readier apprehension, and gentler dispositions in that sex than in the other.

All which tempers, if they were truly improved by proper studies and sober methods of education, would in all probability carry them to greater heights of piety, than are to be found amongst the generality of men.

For this reason, I speak to this matter with so much openness and plainness, because it is much to be lamented, that persons so naturally qualified to be great examples of piety, should, by an erroneous education, be made poor and gaudy spectacles of the greatest vanity. . . .

For personal pride and affectation, a delight in beauty and fondness of finery, are tempers that must either kill all religion in the soul, or be themselves killed by it; they can no more thrive together than health and sickness.

Some people that judge hastily will perhaps here say, that I am exercising too great a severity against the sex: but more reasonable persons will easily observe, that I entirely spare the sex, and only arraign their education; that I not only spare them, but plead their interest, assert their honour, set forth their perfections, commend their natural tempers, and only condemn that education which is so injurious to their interests, so debases their honour, and deprives them of the benefit of their excellent natures and tempers.

Their education, I profess, I cannot spare; but the

only reason is, because it is their greatest enemy;
because it deprives the world of so many blessings, and
the Church of so many saints, as might reasonably
be expected from persons so formed by their natural
tempers to all goodness and tenderness, and so fitted
by the clearness and brightness of their minds to con-
template, love, and admire every thing that is holy,
virtuous, and divine.

How possible it is to bring up daughters in the
more excellent way, let the following character declare:

Eusebia is a pious widow, well-born, and well-bred,
and has a good estate for five daughters, whom she
brings up as one entrusted by God to fit five virgins
for the Kingdom of heaven.   Her family has the
same regulation as a religious house, and all its
orders tend to the support of a constant regular
devotion. . . .

Eusebia brings them up to all kinds of labour that
are proper for women, as sewing, knitting, spinning,
and all other parts of housewifery; not for their
amusement, but that they may be serviceable to themselves and others, and be saved from those temptations
which attend an idle life.

She tells them, she had rather see them reduced to
the necessity of maintaining themselves by their own
work, than to have riches to excuse themselves from
labour.   For though, says she, you may be able to
assist the poor without your labour, yet by your labour
you will be able to assist them more.

If Eusebia has lived as free from sin as it is possible for human nature, it is because she is always
watching and guarding against all instances of pride.
And if her virtues are stronger and higher than other

people's, it is because they are all founded in a deep humility.

My children, says she, when your father died I was much pitied by my friends, as having all the care of a family and the management of an estate fallen upon me.

But my own grief was founded upon another principle; I was grieved to see myself deprived of so faithful a friend, and that such an eminent example of Christian virtues should be taken from the eyes of his children, before they were of an age to love and follow it.

But as to worldly cares, which my friends thought so heavy upon me, they are most of them of our own making, and fall away as soon as we know ourselves. . . .

But, my children, there are things in the world which pass for wisdom, politeness, grandeur, happiness, and fine breeding, which show as great ignorance of ourselves, and might as justly pass for thorough madness, as when a man fancies himself to be glass or ice. . . .

Every thing that you call yours, beside this spirit, is but like your clothing; something that is only to be used for a while, and then to end, and die, and wear away, and to signify no more to you, than the clothing and bodies of other people.

But, my children, you are not only in this manner spirits, but you are fallen spirits, that began your life in a state of corruption and disorder, full of tempers and passions that blind and darken the reason of your mind, and incline you to that which is hurtful.

Your bodies are not only poor and perishing like your clothes, but they are like infected clothes, that fill you with all diseases and distempers, which oppress the soul with sickly appetites and vain cravings.

So that all of us are like two beings, that have, as it were, two hearts within us; with the one we see, and taste, and admire reason, purity, and holiness: with the other we incline to pride, and vanity, and sensual delights.

This internal war we always feel within us more or less: and if you would know the one thing necessary to all the world, it is this; to preserve and perfect all that is rational, holy, and divine in our nature, and to mortify, remove, and destroy all that vanity, pride, and sensuality which springs from the corruption of our state. . . .

As to your bodies, you are to consider them as poor, perishing things, that are sickly and corrupt at present, and will soon drop into common dust. You are to watch over them as enemies that are always trying to tempt and betray you, and so never follow their advice and counsel; you are to consider them as the place and habitation of our souls, and so keep them pure, and clean, and decent; you are to consider them as the servants and instruments of action, and so give them food, and rest, and raiment, that they may be strong and healthful to do the duties of a charitable, useful, pious life.

Whilst you live thus, you live like yourselves; and whenever you have less regard to your souls, or more regard to your bodies, than this comes to; whenever you are more intent upon adorning your persons, than upon the perfecting your souls, you are much more beside yourselves than he that had rather have a laced coat than an healthful body.

For this reason, my children, I have taught you nothing that was dangerous for you to learn; I have kept you from every thing that might betray you into weakness and folly; or make you think any thing fine, but a fine mind; any thing happy, but the favour of God; or any thing desirable, but to do all the good you possibly can. . . .

Consider often how powerfully you are called to a virtuous life, and what great and glorious things God has done for you, to make you in love with every thing that can promote His glory. . . .

Whether married, therefore, or unmarried, consider yourselves as mothers and sisters, as friends and relations, to all that want your assistance; and never allow yourselves to be idle, whilst others are in want of any thing that your hands can make for them.

This useful, charitable, humble employment of yourselves, is what I recommend to you with great earnestness, as being a substantial part of a wise and pious life. And besides the good you will thereby do to other people, every virtue of your own heart will be very much improved by it.

For next to reading, meditation, and prayer, there is nothing that so secures our hearts from foolish passions, nothing that preserves so holy and wise a frame of mind, as some useful, humble employment of ourselves.

Never, therefore, consider your labour as an amusement that is to get rid of your time, and so may be as trifling as you please; but consider it as something that is to be serviceable to yourselves and others, that is to serve some sober ends of life, to save and redeem your time, and make it turn to your account when the works of all people shall be tried by fire. . . .

What would you think of the wisdom of him that should employ his time in distilling of waters, and making liquors which nobody could use, merely to amuse himself with the variety of their colour and clearness, when with less labour and expense he might satisfy the wants of those who have nothing to drink ? Yet he would be as wisely employed as those that are amusing themselves with such tedious works as they neither need, nor hardly know how to use when they are finished; when with less labour and expense they might be doing as much good as he that is clothing the naked, or visiting the sick.

Be glad, therefore, to know the wants of the poorest people, and let your hands be employed in making such mean and ordinary things for them, as their necessities require. By thus making your labour a gift and service to the poor, your ordinary work will be changed into a holy service, and made as acceptable to God as your devotions.

And charity is the greatest of all virtues, as it always was the chief temper of the greatest saints ; so nothing can make your own charity more amiable in the sight of God, than this method of adding your labour to it.

The humility also of this employment will be as beneficial to you as the charity of it. It will keep you from all vain and proud thoughts of your own state and distinction in life, and from treating the poor as creatures of a different species. By accustoming yourselves to this labour and service for the poor, as the representatives of Jesus Christ, you will soon find your heart softened into the greatest meekness and lowliness towards them. You will reverence their estate and condition, think it an honour to serve them, and never be so pleased with yourselves as when you are most humbly employed in their service.

Christianity has then had its most glorious effects upon your hearts, when it has thus changed your spirit, removed all the pride of life from you, and made you delight in humbling yourselves beneath the lowest of all your fellow-creatures. . . .

Love poverty, and reverence poor people; as for many reasons, so particularly for this, because our blessed Saviour was one of the number, and because you may make them all so many friends and advocates with God for you.

Visit and converse with them frequently; you will often find simplicity, innocence, patience, fortitude, and great piety among them; and where they are not so, your good example may amend them.

Rejoice at every opportunity of doing an humble action, and exercising the meekness of your minds, whether it be, as the Scripture expresses it, in washing the saints' feet, that is, in waiting upon and serving those that are below you; or in bearing with the haughtiness and ill-manners of those that are your equals, or above you. For there is nothing better than humility; it is the fruitful soil of all virtues; and every thing that is kind and good naturally grows from it.

Therefore, my children, pray for, and practise humility, and reject every thing in dress, or carriage, or conversation that has any appearance of pride. . . .

Never, therefore, allow yourselves to despise those

who do not follow your rules of life; but force your hearts to love them, and pray to God for them; and let humility be always whispering it into your ears, that you yourselves would fall from those rules tomorrow, if God should leave you to your own strength and wisdom. . . .

A very ordinary knowledge of the spirit of Christianity seems to be enough to convince us that no education can be of true advantage to young women, but that which trains them up in humble industry, in great plainness of life, in exact modesty of dress, manners, and carriage, and in strict devotion. For what should a Christian woman be, but a plain, unaffected, modest, humble creature, averse to every thing in her dress and carriage that can draw the eyes of beholders, or gratify the passions of lewd and amorous persons? . . .

I have considered the nature and necessity of humility, and its great importance to a religious life. I have shown you how many difficulties are formed against it from our natural tempers, the spirit of the world, and the common education of both sexes.

These considerations will, I hope, instruct you how to form your prayers for it to the best advantage, and teach you the necessity of letting no day pass, without a serious, earnest application to God, for the whole spirit of humility: fervently beseeching Him to fill every part of your soul with it, to make it the ruling, constant habit of your mind, that you may not only feel it, but feel all your other tempers arising from it; that you may have no thoughts, no desires, no designs, but such as are the true fruits of a humble, meek, and lowly heart.

That you may look for nothing, claim nothing, resent nothing; that you may go through all the actions and accidents of life, calmly and quietly, as in the presence of God, looking **wholly unto Him**, acting **wholly for Him**: neither seeking vain applause, nor resenting neglects or affronts, but doing and receiving every thing in the meek and lowly spirit of our Lord and Saviour Jesus Christ.

CHAPTER XX.

RECOMMENDING DEVOTION AT TWELVE O'CLOCK, CALLED IN SCRIPTURE THE SIXTH HOUR OF THE DAY. THIS FREQUENCY OF DEVOTION EQUALLY DESIRABLE BY ALL ORDERS OF PEOPLE. UNIVERSAL LOVE IS HERE RECOMMENDED TO BE THE SUBJECT OF PRAYER AT THIS HOUR. OF INTERCESSION, AS AN ACT OF UNIVERSAL LOVE.

(Much Prayer equally desirable for all. Of Universal Love.)

IT will perhaps be thought by some people, that these hours of prayer come too thick; that they can only be observed by people of great leisure, and ought not to be pressed upon the generality of men, who have the cares of families, trades, and employments; nor upon the gentry, whose state and figure in the world cannot admit of this frequency of devotion. And that it is only fit for monasteries and nunneries, or such people as have no more to do in the world than they have.

To this it is answered,

19

First, That this method of devotion is not pressed upon any sort of people, as absolutely necessary, but recommended to all people, as the best, the happiest, and most perfect way of life.

And if a great and exemplary devotion is as much the greatest happiness and perfection of a merchant, a soldier, or a man of quality, as it is the greatest happiness and perfection of the most retired contemplative life, then it is as proper to recommend it without any abatements to one order of men, as to another; because happiness and perfection are of the same worth and value to all people.

It is certainly very honest and creditable for people to engage in trades and employments; it is reasonable for gentlemen to manage well their estates and families, and take such recreations as are proper to their state. But then every gentleman and tradesman loses the greatest happiness of his creation, is robbed of something that is greater than all employments, distinctions, and pleasures of the world, if he does not live more to piety and devotion, than to any thing else in the world.

Here are, therefore, no excuses made for men of business and figure in the world. First, Because it would be to excuse them from that which is the greatest end of living; and be only finding so many reasons for making them less beneficial to themselves, and less serviceable to God and the world.

Secondly, Because most men of business and figure engage too far in worldly matters; much farther than the reasons of human life, or the necessities of the world require.

Merchants and tradesmen, for instance, are generally ten times farther engaged in business than they need;

which is so far from being a reasonable excuse for
their want of time for devotion, that it is their crime,
and must be censured as a blameable instance of
covetousness and ambition. . . .

If a merchant, having forborne from too great
business, that he might quietly attend in the service
of God, should therefore die worth twenty instead of
fifty thousand pounds, could any one say that he
had mistaken his calling, or gone a loser out of
the world?

If a tradesman, by aspiring after Christian perfection, and retiring himself often from his business,
should, instead of leaving his children fortunes to
spend in luxury and idleness, leave them to live by
their own honest labour, could it be said that he had
made a wrong use of the world, because he had shown
his children that he had more regard to that which is
eternal, than to this which is so soon to be at an
end? . . .

Any devotion that is not to the greater advantage
of him that uses it than any thing that he can do in
the room of it; any devotion that does not procure an
infinitely greater good than can be got by neglecting
it, is freely yielded up; here is no demand of it. . . .

You would think it very absurd for a man not to
value his own health, because he was not a physician;
nor the preservation of his limbs, because he was not
a bone-setter. Yet it is more absurd for you, Claudius,
to neglect the improvement of your soul in piety,
because you are not an apostle, or a bishop.

Consider this text of Scripture: "If ye live after
the flesh, ye shall die; but if ye through the Spirit do
mortify the deeds of the body, ye shall live. For as

many as are led by the Spirit of God, they are the sons of God." [1] Do you think that this Scripture does not equally relate to all mankind ? Can you find any exception here for men of figure and estates ? Is not a spiritual and devout life here made the common condition on which all men are to become sons of God ? Will you leave hours of prayer and rules of devotion to particular states of life, when nothing but the same spirit of devotion can save you, or any man, from eternal death ? . . .

Again, consider this doctrine of the apostle : " For none of us," that is, of us Christians, " liveth to himself, and no man dieth to himself. For whether we live, we live unto the Lord ; and whether we die, we die unto the Lord. For to this end Christ both died, and rose, and revived, that He might be Lord both of the dead and living." [2]

Now, are you excepted out of the doctrine of this text ? Will you, because of your condition, leave it to any particular sort of people, to live and die unto Christ ? If so, you must leave it to them to be redeemed by the death and resurrection of Christ. For it is the express doctrine of the text, that for this end Christ died and rose again, that none of us should live to himself. It is not that priests, or apostles, or monks, or hermits, should live no longer to themselves ; but that none of us, that is, no Christian of what state soever, should live unto himself.

If, therefore, there be any instances of piety, any rules of devotion, which you can neglect, and yet live as truly unto Christ as if you observed them, this text calls you to no such devotion. But if you forsake

[1] Rom. viii. 13, 14.   [2] Rom. xiv. 7, 8, 9.

such devotion, as you yourself know is expected from some particular sorts of people ; such devotion as you know becomes people that live **wholly unto Christ,** that aspire after great piety; if you neglect such devotion for any worldly consideration, that you may live more to your own temper and taste, more to the fashions and ways of the world, you forsake the terms on which all Christians are to receive the benefit of Christ's Death and Resurrection. . . .

And if you leave it to others to live in such piety and devotion, in such self-denial, humility, and temperance, as may render them able to glorify God in their body, and in their spirit; you must leave it to them also, to have the benefit of the Blood of Christ. . . .

I now proceed to consider the nature and necessity of universal love, which is here recommended to be the subject of your devotion at this hour. You are here also called to intercession, as the most proper exercise to raise and preserve that love.

By intercession is meant a praying to God, and interceding with Him for our fellow-creatures.

Our blessed Lord hath recommended His love to us, as the pattern and example of our love to one another. As, therefore, He is continually making intercession for us all, so ought we to intercede and pray for one another.

" A new commandment," saith He, " I give unto you, That ye love one another, as I have loved you. By this shall all men know that ye are My disciples, if ye have love one to another." [1]

The newness of this precept did not consist in this, that men were commanded to love one another; for

[1] John xiii. 34, 35.

this was an old precept, both of the law of Moses, and of nature. But it was new in this respect, that it was to imitate a new, and till then unheard-of example of love; it was to love one another, as Christ had loved us. . . .

There is no principle of the heart that is more acceptable to God, than an universal fervent love to all mankind, wishing and praying for their happiness; because there is no principle of the heart that makes us more like God, who is love and goodness itself, and created all beings for their enjoyment of happiness.

The greatest idea that we can frame of God, is when we conceive Him to be a Being of infinite love and goodness; using an infinite wisdom and power for the common good and happiness of all His creatures.

The highest notion, therefore, that we can form of man is when we conceive him as like to God, in this respect, as he can be; using all his infinite faculties, whether of wisdom, power, or prayers, for the common good of all his fellow-creatures; heartily desiring they may have all the happiness they are capable of, and as many benefits and assistances fron him, as his state and condition in the world will permit him to give them.

And, on the other hand, what a baseness and iniquity is there in all instances of hatred, envy, spite, and ill-will; if we consider that every instance of them is so far acting in opposition to God, and intending mischief and harm to those creatures which God favours, and protects, and preserves, in order to their happiness! An ill-natured man, amongst God's creatures, is the most perverse creature in the world, acting contrary to that love by which himself subsists, and which alone gives subsistence to all that variety of beings, that enjoy life in any part of the creation.

"Whatsoever ye would that men should do to you, do ye even so to them."[1]

Now, though this is a doctrine of strict justice, yet it is only an universal love that can comply with it. For as love is the measure of our acting towards ourselves, so we can never act in the same manner towards other people, till we look upon them with that love with which we look upon ourselves.

If we had any imperfection in our eyes, that made us see any one thing wrong, for the same reason they would show us an hundred things wrong.

So, if we have any temper of our hearts, that makes us envious, or spiteful, or ill-natured towards any one man, the same temper will make us envious, and spiteful, and ill-natured towards a great many more.

If, therefore, we desire this Divine virtue of love, we must exercise and practise our hearts in the love of all, because it is not Christian love, till it is the love of all.

Acts of love, that proceed not from a principle of universal love, are but like acts of justice that proceed from a heart not disposed to universal justice.

A love which is not universal may indeed have tenderness and affection, but it hath nothing of righteousness or piety in it; it is but humour, and temper, or interest, or such a love as publicans and heathens practise.

Who, therefore, whose heart has any tendency towards God, would not aspire after this Divine temper,

[1] Matt. vii. 12.

which so changes and exalts our nature into an union
with Him ?

How should we rejoice in the exercise and practice
of this love, which, so often as we feel it, is so often
an assurance to us, that God is in us, that we act
according to His Spirit, who is Love itself ! But we
must observe that love has then only this mighty
power of uniting us to God, when it is so pure and
universal as to imitate that love which God beareth to
all His creatures.

God willeth the happiness of all beings, though it
is no happiness to Himself. Therefore we must desire
the happiness of all beings, though no happiness
cometh to us from it.

God equally delighteth in the perfections of all His
creatures ; therefore we should rejoice in those perfections, wherever we see them, and be as glad to have
other people perfect as ourselves. . . .

To proceed now to another motive to this universal
love.

Our power of doing external acts of love and goodness is often very narrow and restrained. There are,
it may be, but few people to whom we can contribute
any worldly relief.

But though our outward means of doing good are
often thus limited, yet if our hearts are but full of
love and goodness, we get, as it were, an infinite
power ; because God will attribute to us those good
works, those acts of love, and tender charities which
we sincerely desired, and would gladly have performed,
had it been in our power.

You cannot heal all the sick, relieve all the poor ;
you cannot comfort all in distress, nor be a father to

all the fatherless; you cannot, it may be, deliver many from their misfortunes, or teach them to find comfort in God.

But if there is a love and tenderness in your heart, that delight in these good works, and excite you to do all that you can; if your love has no bounds, but continually wishes and prays for the relief and happiness of all that are in distress; you will be received by God as a benefactor to those who have had nothing from you but your good will and tender affections.

You cannot build hospitals for the incurable; you cannot erect monasteries for the education of persons in holy solitude, continual prayer, and mortification: but if you join in your heart with those that do, and thank God for their pious designs; if you are a friend to these great friends to mankind, and rejoice in their eminent virtues; you will be received by God as a sharer of such good works as, though they had none of your hands, yet had all your heart. . . .

Now, there is nothing that so much exalts our souls, as this heavenly love: it cleanses and purifies like a holy fire, and all ill tempers fall away before it. It makes room for all virtues, and carries them to their greatest height. Every thing that is good and holy grows out of it, and it becomes a continual source of all holy desires and pious practices. By love, I do not mean any natural tenderness, which is more or less in people, according to their constitutions; but I mean a larger principle of the soul, founded in reason and piety, which makes us tender, kind, and benevolent to all our fellow-creatures, as creatures of God, and for His sake.

It is this love, that loves all things in God, as His

WHOLLY FOR GOD

298

creatures, as the images of His power, as the creatures
of His goodness, as parts of His family, as members of
His society, that becomes a holy principle of all great
and good actions.

The love, therefore, of our neighbour is only a
branch of our love to God. For when we love God
with all our hearts, and with all our souls, and with
all our strength, we shall necessarily love those beings
that are so nearly related to God, that have every
thing from Him, and are created by Him to be objects
of His own eternal love. If I hate or despise any one
man in the world, I hate something that God cannot
hate, and despise that which He loves.

And can I think that I love God with all my heart,
whilst I hate that which belongs only to God, which
has no other master but Him, which bears His image,
is part of His family, and exists only by the continuance
of His love towards it ?

It was the impossibility of this that made St. John
say, that " if any man saith he loveth God, and hateth
his brother, he is a liar." [1]

These reasons sufficiently show us that no love is
holy or religious till it becomes universal.

For if religion require me to love all persons, as
God's creatures, that belong to Him, that bear His
image, enjoy His protection, and make parts of His
family and household; if these are the great and
necessary reasons why I should live in love and
friendship with **any one man** in the world; they are
the same great and necessary reasons why I should live
in love and friendship with **every man** in the world ;
and, consequently, I offend against all these reasons,

[1] 1 John iv. 20.

and break through all these ties and obligations, whenever I want love towards any one man. The sin, therefore, of hating, or despising any one man, is like the sin of hating all God's creation; and the necessity of loving any one man is the same necessity of loving every man in the world. And though many people may appear to us ever so sinful, odious, or extravagant in their conduct, we must never look upon that as the least motive for any contempt or disregard of them; but look upon them with the greater compassion, as being in the most pitiable condition that can be.

As it was the sins of the world that made the Son of God become a compassionate suffering Advocate for all mankind, so no one is of the spirit of Christ, but he that has the utmost compassion for sinners. Nor is there any greater sign of your own perfection, than when you find yourself all love and compassion towards them that are very weak and defective. And, on the other hand, you have never less reason to be pleased with yourself, than when you find yourself most angry and offended at the behaviour of others. All sin is certainly to be hated and abhorred, wherever it is; but then we must set ourselves against sin, as we do against sickness and diseases, by showing ourselves tender and compassionate to the sick and diseased.

All other hatred of sin, which does not fill the heart with the softest, tenderest affections towards persons miserable in it, is the servant of sin, at the same time that it seems to be hating it.

And there is no temper which even good men ought more carefully to watch and guard against, than this.

For it is a temper that lurks and hides itself under the cover of many virtues, and, by being unsuspected, does the more mischief.

A man naturally fancies that it is his own exceeding love of virtue that makes him not able to bear with those that want it. And when he abhors one man, despises another, and cannot bear the name of a third, he supposes it all to be a proof of his own high sense of virtue, and just hatred of sin.

And yet, one would think that a man needed no other cure for this temper than this one reflection:

That if this had been the spirit of the Son of God, if He had hated sin in this manner, there had been no redemption of the world; that if God had hated sinners in this manner, day and night, the world itself had ceased long ago. . . .

You will perhaps say, How is it possible to love a good and a bad man in the same degree?

Just as it is possible to be as just and faithful to a good man, as to an evil man. Now, are you in any difficulty about performing justice and faithfulness to a bad man? Are you in any doubts, whether you need be so just and faithful to him, as you need be to a good man? Now, why is it that you are in no doubt about it? It is because you know that justice and faithfulness are founded upon reasons that never vary nor change, that have no dependence upon the merits of men, but are founded in the nature of things, in the laws of God, and therefore are to be observed with an equal exactness towards good and bad men. . . .

But now, if the want of a true and exact charity be so great a want, that, as St. Paul saith, it renders our greatest virtues but empty sounds and tinkling cymbals, how highly does it concern us to study every art, and practise every method of raising our souls to this state of charity! It is for this reason that you are here desired not to let this hour of prayer pass without a full and solemn supplication to God for all the instances of an universal love and benevolence to all mankind; such daily constant devotion being the only likely means of preserving you in such a state of love as is necessary to prove you to be a true follower of Jesus Christ.

CHAPTER XXI.

OF THE NECESSITY AND BENEFIT OF INTERCESSION, CON-SIDERED AS AN EXERCISE OF UNIVERSAL LOVE. HOW ALL ORDERS OF MEN ARE TO PRAY AND INTERCEDE WITH GOD FOR ONE ANOTHER. HOW NATURALLY SUCH INTERCESSION AMENDS AND REFORMS THE HEARTS OF THOSE THAT USE IT.

Of Intercession, and the Blessing it brings to those who engage in it.

THAT intercession is a great and necessary part of Christian devotion, is very evident from Scripture.

The first followers of Christ seem to support all their love, and to maintain all their intercourse and correspondence, by mutual prayers for one another.

St. Paul, whether he writes to churches or particular persons, shows his intercession to be perpetual for them; that they are the constant subject of his prayers. . . .

This was the ancient friendship of Christians, uniting and cementing their hearts, not by worldly considerations or human passions, but by the mutual communication of spiritual blessings, by prayers and thanksgiving to God for one another.

It was this holy intercession that raised Christians to such a state of mutual love, as far exceeded all that had been praised and admired in human friendship. And when the same spirit of intercession is again in the world, when Christianity has the same power over the hearts of people that it then had, this holy friendship will be again in fashion, and Christians will be again the wonder of the world, for that exceeding love which they bear to one another.

For a frequent intercession with God, earnestly beseeching Him to forgive the sins of all mankind, to bless them with His providence, enlighten them with His Spirit, and bring them to everlasting happiness, is the divinest exercise that the heart of man can be engaged in.

Be daily, therefore, on your knees, in a solemn, deliberate performance of this devotion, praying for others in such forms, with such length, importunity, and earnestness as you use for yourself; and you will find all little, ill-natured passions die away, your heart grow great and generous, delighting in the common happiness of others, as you used only to delight in your own.

For he that daily prays to God, that all men may be happy in heaven, takes the likeliest way to make him wish for, and delight in their happiness on earth. And it is hardly possible for you to beseech and entreat God to make any one happy in the highest enjoyments of His glory to all eternity, and yet be troubled to see him enjoy the much smaller gifts of God in this short and low state of human life.

For how strange and unnatural would it be to pray to God to grant health and a longer life to a sick man, and at the same time to envy him the poor pleasure of agreeable medicines!

Yet this would be no more strange or unnatural than to pray to God that your neighbour may enjoy the highest degrees of His mercy and favour, and yet at the same time envy him the little credit and figure he hath amongst his fellow-creatures.

When, therefore, you have once habituated your heart to a serious performance of this holy intercession, you have done a great deal to render it incapable of spite and envy, and to make it naturally delight in the happiness of all mankind.

This is the natural effect of a general intercession for all mankind. But the greatest benefits of it are then received, when it descends to such particular instances as our state and condition in life more particularly require.

For there is nothing that makes us love a man so much as praying for him; and when you can once do this sincerely for any man, you have fitted your soul for the performance of every thing that is kind and civil towards him. This will fill your heart with a generosity and tenderness that will give you a better and sweeter behaviour than any thing that is called fine breeding and good manners.

By considering yourself as an advocate with God for your neighbours and acquaintance, you would never find it hard to be at peace with them yourself.

It would be easy to you to bear with and forgive those for whom you particularly implored the Divine mercy and forgiveness.

Such prayers as these amongst neighbours and acquaintance would unite them to one another in the strongest bonds of love and tenderness. It would exalt and ennoble their souls, and teach them to consider one another in a higher state, as members of a spiritual society, that are created for the enjoyment of the common blessings of God, and fellow-heirs of the same future glory. . . .

Ouranius is a holy priest, full of the spirit of the gospel, watching, labouring, and praying for a poor country village. Every soul in it is as dear to him as himself; and he loves them all, as he loves himself, because he prays for them all, as often as he prays for himself.

If his whole life is one continual exercise of great zeal and labour, hardly ever satisfied with any degrees of care and watchfulness, it is because he has learned the great value of souls, by so often appearing before God as an intercessor for them. . . .

When Ouranius first entered into Holy Orders, he had a haughtiness in his temper, a great contempt and disregard for all foolish and unreasonable people; but he has prayed away this spirit, and has now the greatest tenderness for the most obstinate sinners; because he is always hoping that God will, sooner or later, hear those prayers that he makes for their repentance.

The rudeness, ill-nature, or perverse behaviour of any of his flock, used at first to betray him into impatience; but now it raises no other passion in him, than a desire of being upon his knees in prayer to God for them.

Thus have his prayers for others altered and amended the state of his own heart. . . .

All these noble thoughts and divine sentiments are the effects of his great devotion; he presents every one so often before God in his prayers, that he never thinks he can esteem, reverence, or serve those enough, for whom he implores so many mercies from God.

Ouranius is mightily affected with this passage of holy Scripture: "The effectual fervent prayer of a righteous man availeth much." [1]

This makes him practise all the arts of holy living, and aspire after every instance of piety and righteousness, that his prayers for his flock may have their full force, and avail much with God.

For this reason, he has sold a small estate that he had, and has erected a charitable retirement for ancient poor people, to live in prayer and piety, that his prayers, being assisted by such good works, may pierce the clouds, and bring down blessings upon those souls committed to his care.

Ouranius reads how much God Himself said unto Abimelech, concerning Abraham: "He is a prophet; he shall pray for thee, and thou shalt live." [2]

And again, how He said of Job: "And My servant Job shall pray for you: for him will I accept." [3]

From these passages Ouranius justly concludes, that the prayers of men eminent for holiness of life have an extraordinary power with God; that He grants to other people such pardons, reliefs, and

[1] James v. 16.   [2] Gen. xx. 7.   [3] Job xlii. 8.

blessings, through their prayers, as would not be granted to men of less piety and perfection. This makes Ouranius exceeding studious of Christian perfection, searching after every grace and holy temper, purifying his heart all manner of ways, fearful of every error and defect in his life, lest his prayers for his flock should be less availing with God, through his own defects in holiness.

This makes him careful of every temper of his heart, give alms of all that he hath, watch, and fast, and mortify, and live according to the strictest rules of temperance, meekness, and humility, that he may be in some degree like an Abraham or a Job in his parish, and make such prayers for them, as God will hear and accept.

These are the happy effects which a devout intercession hath produced in the life of Ouranius.

And if other people, in their several stations, were to imitate this example, in such a manner as suited their particular state of life, they would certainly find the same happy effects from it. . . .

If all people, when they feel the first approaches of resentment, envy, or contempt, towards others; or if in all little disagreements and misunderstandings whatever, they should, instead of indulging their minds with little low reflections, have recourse, at such times, to a more particular and extraordinary intercession with God, for such persons as had raised their envy, resentment, or discontent; this would be a certain way to prevent the growth of all uncharitable tempers.

If you were also to form your prayer or intercession at that time, to the greatest degree of contrariety to that temper which you were then in, it would be an excellent means of raising your heart to the greatest state of perfection. . . .

This would be such a triumph over yourself, would so humble and reduce your heart into obedience and order, that the devil would even be afraid of tempting you again in the same manner, when he saw the temptation turned into so great a means of amending and reforming the state of your heart. . . .

For such devotion must necessarily either destroy such tempers, or be itself destroyed by them: you cannot possibly have any ill temper, or show any unkind behaviour to a man, for whose welfare you are so much concerned, as to be his advocate with God in private. . . .

You think it a small matter to ridicule one man, and despise another; but you should consider whether it be a small matter to want that charity towards these people, which Christians are not allowed to want towards their most inveterate enemies.

For you cannot possibly despise and ridicule that man, whom your private prayers recommend to the love and favour of God. . . .

Intercession is not only the best arbitrator of all differences, the best promoter of true friendship, the best cure and preservative against all unkind tempers, all angry and haughty passions, but is also of great use to discover to us the true state of our own hearts.

There are many tempers which we think lawful and innocent, which we never suspect of any harm; which, if they were to be tried by this devotion, would soon show us how we have deceived ourselves. . . .

I have laid before you the many and great advan-

tages of intercession. You have seen what a divine
friendship it must needs beget amongst Christians;
how dear it would render all relations and neighbours
to one another; how it tends to make clergymen,
masters, and parents, exemplary and perfect in all the
duties of their station; how certainly it destroys all
envy, spite, and ill-natured passions; how speedily it
reconciles all differences; and with what a piercing
light it discovers to a man the true state of his heart.

These considerations will, I hope, persuade you to
make such intercession as is proper for your state, the
constant, chief matter of your devotion, at this hour
of prayer.

CHAPTER XXII.

RECOMMENDING DEVOTION AT THREE O'CLOCK, CALLED
    IN SCRIPTURE THE NINTH HOUR OF THE DAY.
    THE SUBJECT OF PRAYER AT THIS HOUR IS
    RESIGNATION TO THE DIVINE PLEASURE. THE
    NATURE AND DUTY OF CONFORMITY TO THE WILL
    OF GOD, IN ALL OUR ACTIONS AND DESIGNS.

(Of Prayer for entire Resignation to the Will of God.)

I HAVE recommended certain subjects to be made
    the fixed and chief matter of your devotions, at
all the hours of prayer that have been already
considered.

As thanksgiving and oblation of yourself to God, at
your first prayers in the morning; at nine, the great
virtue of Christian humility is to be the chief part of
your petitions. At twelve, you are called upon to

pray for all the graces of universal love, and to raise it in your heart by such general and particular intercessions as your own state and relation to other people seem more particularly to require of you.

At this hour of the afternoon, you are desired to consider the necessity of **resignation and conformity to the will of God**, and to make this great virtue the principal matter of your prayers.

There is nothing wise, or holy, or just, but the great will of God. This is as strictly true, in the most rigid sense, as to say, that nothing is infinite and eternal but God.

No beings, therefore, whether in heaven or on earth, can be wise, or holy, or just, but so far as they conform to this will of God. It is **conformity to this will** that gives virtue and perfection to the highest services of angels in heaven; and it is **conformity to the same will** that makes the ordinary actions of men on earth become an acceptable service unto God.

The whole nature of virtue consists in conforming to, and the whole nature of vice in declining from, the will of God. All God's creatures are created to fulfil His will; the sun and moon obey His will, by the necessity of their nature; angels conform to His will, by the perfection of their nature: if, therefore, you would show yourself not to be a rebel and apostate from the order of the creation, you must act like beings both above and below you; it must be the great desire of your soul, that God's will may be done by you on earth, as it is done in heaven. It must be **the settled purpose and intention of your heart, to will nothing,** design nothing, do nothing, but so far as you

have reason to believe that it is the will of God that
you should so desire, design, and do.

It is as just and necessary to live in this state of
heart, to think thus of God and yourself, as to think
that you have any dependence upon Him. And it
is as great a rebellion against God, to think that your
will may ever differ from His, as to think that you
have not received the power of willing for Him.

You are therefore to consider yourself as a being
that has no other business in the world, but to be that
which God requires you to be; to have no tempers, no
rules of your own, to seek no self-designs or self-
ends, but to fill some place, and act some part, in
strict conformity and thankful resignation to the
Divine pleasure.

To think that you are your own, or at your own
disposal, is as absurd as to think that you created and
can preserve yourself. It is as plain and necessary
a first principle, to believe you are thus God's, that
you thus belong to Him, and are to act and suffer all
in a thankful resignation to His pleasure, as to believe
that in Him you "live, and move, and have your
being."[1]

Resignation to the Divine will signifies a cheerful
approbation, and thankful acceptance of everything
that comes from God. It is not enough patiently to
submit, but we must thankfully receive, and fully
approve of everything, that by the order of God's
providence happens to us. . . .

This resignation to the Divine will may be considered
in two respects : First, as it signifies a thankful approbation of God's general providence over the world;

[1] Acts xvii. 28.

Secondly, as it signifies a thankful acceptance of His particular providence over us.

First, Every man is, by the law of his creation, by the first article of his creed, obliged to consent to, and acknowledge the wisdom and goodness of God in His general providence over the whole world. He is to believe that it·is the effect of God's great wisdom and goodness, that the world itself was formed at such a particular time, and in such a manner; that the general order of nature, the whole frame of things, is contrived and formed in the best manner. He is to believe that God's providence over states and kingdoms, times and seasons, is all for the best; that the revolutions of states and changes of empire, the rise and fall of monarchies, persecutions, wars, famines, and plagues, are all permitted and conducted by God's providence to the general good of man in this state of trial.

A good man is to believe all this, with the same fulness of assent as he believes that God is in every place, though he neither sees nor can comprehend the manner of His presence.

This is a noble magnificence of thought, a true religious greatness of mind, to be thus affected with God's general providence, admiring and magnifying His wisdom in all things; never murmuring at the course of the world, or the state of things, but looking upon all around, at heaven and earth, as a pleased spectator, and adoring that invisible Hand, which gives laws to all motions, and overrules all events to ends suitable to the highest wisdom and goodness.

It is very common for people to allow themselves great liberty in finding fault with such things as have only God for their cause.

Every one thinks he may justly say, what a wretched abominable climate he lives in. This man is frequently telling you, what a dismal cursed day it is, and what intolerable seasons we have. Another thinks he has very little to thank God for, that it is hardly worth his while to live in a world so full of changes and revolutions. But these are tempers of great impiety, and show that religion has not yet its seat in the heart of those that have them. . . .

As, therefore, when we think of God Himself, we are to have no sentiments but of praise and thanksgiving; so, when we look at those things which are under the direction of God, and governed by His providence, we are to receive them with the same tempers of praise and gratitude. . . .

You cannot therefore look upon this as an unnecessary high pitch of perfection, since the want of it implies the want, not of any high notions, but of a plain and ordinary faith in the most certain doctrines both of natural and revealed religion.

Thus much concerning resignation to the Divine will, as it signifies a thankful approbation of God's general providence: it is now to be considered as it signifies a thankful acceptance of God's particular providence over us. . . .

It is as much by the counsel and eternal purpose of God that you should be born in your particular state, and that Isaac should be the son of Abraham, as that Gabriel should be an angel, and Isaac a man. . . .

Had you been anything else than what you are, you had, all things considered, been less wisely provided for than you are now: you had wanted some circumstances and conditions that are best fitted to make you happy yourself, and serviceable to the glory of God.

Could you see all that which God sees, all that happy chain of causes and motives which are to move and invite you to a right course of life, you would see something to make you like that state you are in, as fitter for you than any other.

But as you cannot see this, so it is here that your Christian faith and trust in God is to exercise itself, and render you as grateful and thankful for the happiness of your state, as if you saw every thing that contributes to it with your own eyes.

But now, if this be the case of every man in the world, thus blessed with some particular state that is most convenient for him, how reasonable is it for every man to will that which God has already willed for him; and by a pious faith and trust in the Divine goodness, thankfully to adore and magnify that wise Providence, which he is sure has made the best choice for him of those things which he could not choose for himself! . . .

So that, whether we consider the infinite goodness of God, that cannot choose amiss for us, or our own great ignorance of what is most advantageous to us, there can be nothing so reasonable and pious, as to have no will but that of God's, and to desire nothing for ourselves, in our persons, our state, and condition, but that which the good providence of God appoints us.

Farther, as the good providence of God thus introduces us into the world, into such states and conditions of life as are most convenient for us, so the same unerring wisdom orders all events and changes in the whole course of our lives, in such a manner, as to render them the fittest means to exercise and improve our virtue.

Nothing hurts us, nothing destroys us, but the ill use of that liberty with which God has entrusted us. . . .

For the providence of God is not more concerned in the government of night and day, and the variety of seasons, than in the common course of events that seem most to depend upon the mere wills of men. So that it is strictly right to look upon all worldly accidents and changes, all the various turns and alternations in your own life, to be as truly the effects of Divine providence, as the rising and setting of the sun, or the alternations of the seasons of the year. As you are, therefore, always to adore the wisdom of God in the direction of these things; so it is the same reasonable duty always to magnify God, as an equal Director of every thing that happens to you in the course of your own life.

This holy resignation and conformity of your will to the will of God being so much the true state of piety, I hope you will think it proper to make this hour of prayer a constant season of applying to God for so great a gift; that by thus constantly praying for it, your heart may be habitually disposed towards it, and always in a state of readiness to look at **every thing** as God's, and to consider Him in **every thing**; that so **every thing** that befalls you may be received in the spirit of piety, and made a means of exercising some virtue.

There is nothing that so powerfully governs the heart, that so strongly excites us to wise and reasonable actions, as a true sense of God's presence. But as we cannot see or apprehend the essence of God, so nothing will so constantly keep us under a lively sense of the presence of God, as this holy resignation which attributes every thing to Him, and receives every thing as from Him.

Could we see a miracle from God, how would our thoughts be affected with an holy awe and veneration of His presence! But if we consider every thing as God's doing, either by order or permission, we shall then be affected with common things, as they would be who saw a miracle.

For as there is nothing to affect you in a miracle, but as it is the action of God, and bespeaks His presence; so, when you consider God as acting in all things, and all events, then all things will become venerable to you, like miracles, and fill you with the same awful sentiments of the Divine presence.

Now, you must not reserve the exercise of this pious temper to any particular times or occasions, or fancy how resigned you will be to God, if such or such trials should happen. For this is amusing yourself with the notion or idea of resignation, instead of the virtue itself.

Do not therefore please yourself with thinking how piously you would act and submit to God in a plague, or famine, or persecution, but be intent upon the perfection of the present day; and be assured, that the best way of showing a true zeal is to make little things the occasions of great piety.

Begin therefore in the smallest matters, and most ordinary occasions, and accustom your mind to the daily exercise of this pious temper, in the lowest occurrences of life. And when a contempt, an affront,

a little injury, loss, or disappointment, or the smallest
events of every day, continually raise your mind to
God in proper acts of resignation, then you may justly
hope that you shall be numbered amongst those that
are resigned and thankful to God in the greatest trials
and afflictions.

CHAPTER XXIII.

OF EVENING PRAYER. OF THE NATURE AND NECESSITY OF EXAMINATION. HOW WE ARE TO BE PARTICULAR IN THE CONFESSION OF ALL OUR SINS. HOW WE ARE TO FILL OUR MINDS WITH A JUST HORROR AND DREAD OF ALL SIN.

(Of the particular Confession of Sin.)

I AM now come to six o'clock in the evening, which,
according to the Scripture account, is called the
twelfth, or last hour of the day. This is a time so
proper for devotion, that I suppose nothing need be
said to recommend it as a season of prayer to all people
that profess any regard to piety.

As the labour and action of every state of life is
generally over at this hour, so this is the proper time
for every one to call himself to account and review all
his behaviour from the first action of the day. The
necessity of this examination is founded upon the
necessity of repentance. For if it be necessary to
repent of all our sins, if the guilt of unrepented sins
still continue upon us, then it is necessary, not only
that all our sins, but the particular circumstances and
aggravations of them, be known, and recollected, and
brought to repentance.

The Scripture saith, "If we confess our sins, He is faithful and just to forgive us our sins, and to cleanse us from all unrighteousness." [1] Which is as much as to say, that then only our sins are forgiven, and we cleansed from the guilt and unrighteousness of them, when they are thus confessed and repented of.

There seems therefore to be the greatest necessity, that all our daily actions be constantly observed and brought to account, lest by a negligence we load ourselves with the guilt of unrepented sins. . . .

You would, I suppose, think yourself chargeable with great impiety, if you were to go to bed without confessing yourself to be a sinner and asking pardon of God; you would not think it sufficient that you did so yesterday. And yet if, without any regard to the present day, you only repeat the same form of words that you used yesterday, the sins of the present day may justly be looked upon to have had no repentance. For if the sins of the present day require a new confession, it must be such a new confession as is proper to itself. For it is the state and condition of every day that is to determine the state and manner of your repentance in the evening; otherwise the same general form of words is rather an empty formality that has the appearance of a duty, than such a true performance of it as is necessary to make it truly useful to you.

Let it be supposed that on a certain day you have been guilty of these sins; that you have told a vain lie upon yourself, ascribing something falsely to yourself, through pride; that you have been guilty of detraction, and indulged yourself in some degree of

[1] 1 John i. 9.

intemperance.   Let it be supposed, that on the next
day you have lived in a contrary manner: that you
have neglected no duty of devotion, and been the rest
of the day innocently employed in your proper business.   Let it be supposed, that on the evening of both
these days you only use the same confession in general,
considering it rather as a duty that is to be performed
every night, than as a repentance that is to be suited to
the particular state of the day.

Can it with any reason be said, that each day has
had its proper repentance ?   Is it not as good sense
to say, there is no difference in the guilt of these
days, as to say that there need be no different repentance at the end of them ?   Or how can each of them
have its proper repentance, but by its having a repentance as large, and extensive, and particular as the
guilt of each day ? . . .

And I have entered into all these particulars, only
to show you, in the plainest manner, that examination
and a careful review of all the actions of the day, is
not only to be looked upon as a good rule, but as
something as necessary as repentance itself.

If a man is to account for his expenses at night,
can it be thought a needless exactness in him, to take
notice of every particular expense in the day ?

And if a man is to repent of his sins at night, can it
be thought too great a piece of scrupulosity in him, to
know and call to mind what sins he is to repent of ? . . .

In order to make this examination still farther
beneficial, every man should oblige himself to a certain
method in it.   As every man has something particular
in his nature, stronger inclinations to some vices than
others, some infirmities that stick closer to him, and

are harder to be conquered than others; and as it is as easy for every man to know this of himself, as to know whom he likes or dislikes; so it is highly necessary that these particularities of our natures and tempers should never escape a severe trial at our evening repentance: I say, a severe trial, because nothing but a rigorous severity against these natural tempers is sufficient to conquer them.

They are the right eyes that are not to be spared; but to be plucked out and cast from us. For as they are the infirmities of nature, so they have the strength of nature, and must be treated with great opposition, or they will soon be too strong for us.

He, therefore, who knows himself most of all subject to anger and passion, must be very exact and constant in his examination of this temper every evening. He must find out every slip that he has made of that kind, whether in thought, or word, or action; he must shame, and reproach, and accuse himself before God, for every thing that he has said or done in obedience to his passion. He must no more allow himself to forget the examination of this temper, than to forget his whole prayers. . . .

Consider next your own particular share in the guilt of sin. And if you would know with what zeal you ought to repent yourself, consider how you would exhort another sinner to repentance; and what repentance and amendment you would expect from him whom you judged to be the greatest sinner in the world.

Now this case every man may justly reckon to be his own. And you may fairly look upon yourself to be the greatest sinner that you know in the world.

For though you may know abundance of people to be guilty of some gross sins, with which you cannot

charge yourself, yet you may justly condemn yourself
as the greatest sinner that you know. And that for
these following reasons:

First, Because you know more of the folly of your
own heart, than you do of other people's; and can
charge yourself with various sins, that you only know
of yourself, and cannot be sure that other sinners are
guilty of them. So that, as you know more of the folly,
the baseness, the pride, the deceitfulness and negligence
of your own heart, than you do of any one's else, so you
have just reason to consider yourself as the greatest
sinner that you know; because you know more of the
greatness of your own sins, than you do of other people's.

Secondly, The greatness of our guilt arises chiefly
from the greatness of God's goodness towards us, from
the particular graces and blessings, the favours, the
lights and instructions that we have received from Him.

Now, as these graces and blessings, and the multitude
of God's favours towards us, are the great aggravations
of our sins against God, so they are only known to
ourselves. And therefore every sinner knows more
of the aggravations of his own guilt, than he does of
other people's; and consequently may justly look upon
himself to be the greatest sinner that he knows.

How good God has been to other sinners, what light
and instruction He has vouchsafed to them; what blessings and graces they have received from Him; how
often He has touched their hearts with holy inspirations,
you cannot tell. But all this you know of yourself;
therefore you know greater aggravations of your own
guilt, and are able to charge yourself with greater
ingratitude, than you can charge upon other people....

God Almighty knows greater sinners, it may be, than

you are; because He sees and knows the circumstances of all men's sins: but your own heart, if it is faithful to you, can discover no guilt so great as your own; because it can only see in you those circumstances on which great part of the guilt of sin is founded.

You may see sins in other people that you cannot charge upon yourself; but then you know a number of circumstances of your own guilt that you cannot lay to their charge.

And perhaps that person that appears at such a distance from your virtue, and so odious in your eyes, would have been much better than you are, had he been altogether in your circumstances, and received all the same favours and graces from God that you have.

This is a very humbling reflection, and very proper for those people to make, who measure their virtue by comparing the outward course of their lives with that of other people's. . . .

A serious and frequent reflection upon these things will mightily tend to humble us in our own eyes, make us very apprehensive of the greatness of our own guilt, and very tender in censuring and condemning other people.

CHAPTER XXIV.

THE CONCLUSION. OF THE EXCELLENCY AND GREATNESS OF A DEVOUT SPIRIT.

(Great Devotion the noblest Temper of the noblest Souls.)

I HAVE now finished what I intended in this treatise. I have explained the nature of devotion, both as it signifies a life devoted to God, and as it signifies a

21

regular method of daily prayer. I have now only to add a word or two in recommendation of a life governed by this spirit of devotion.

For though it is as reasonable to suppose it the desire of all Christians to arrive at Christian perfection, as to suppose that all sick men desire to be restored to perfect health; yet experience shows us, that nothing wants more to be pressed, repeated, and forced upon our minds, than the plainest rules of Christianity.

Voluntary poverty, virginity, and devout retirement, have been here recommended as things not necessary, yet highly beneficial to those that would make the way to perfection the most easy and certain. But Christian perfection itself is tied to no particular form of life; but is to be attained, though not with the same ease, in every state of life.

So that the whole of the matter is plainly this: Virginity, voluntary poverty, and such other restraints of lawful things, are not necessary to Christian perfection; but are much to be commended in those who choose them as helps and means of a more safe and speedy arrival at it.

It is only in this manner, and in this sense, that I would recommend any particularity of life; not as if perfection consisted in it, but because of its great tendency to produce and support the true spirit of Christian perfection.

But the thing which is here pressed upon all, is a life of a great and strict devotion; which, I think, has been sufficiently shown to be equally the duty and happiness of all orders of men. Neither is there any thing in any particular state of life, that can be justly pleaded as a reason for any abatements of a devout spirit.

But because in this polite age of ours, we have so lived away the spirit of devotion, that many seem afraid even to be suspected of it, imagining great devotion to be great bigotry : that it is founded in ignorance and poorness of spirit ; and that little, weak, and dejected minds are generally the greatest proficients in it :

It shall here be fully shown, that great devotion is the noblest temper of the greatest and noblest souls ; and that they who think it receives any advantage from ignorance and poorness of spirit, are themselves not a little, but entirely ignorant of the nature of devotion, the nature of God, and the nature of themselves. . . .

And first, who reckons it a sign of a poor, little mind, for a man to be full of reverence and duty to his parents, to have the truest love and honour for his friend, or to excel in the highest instances of gratitude to his benefactor ?

Are not these tempers in the highest degree, in the most exalted and perfect minds ?

And yet what is high devotion, but the highest exercise of these tempers, of duty, reverence, love, honour, and gratitude to the amiable, glorious Parent, Friend, and Benefactor of all mankind ?

Is it a true greatness of mind, to reverence the authority of your parents, to fear the displeasure of your friend, to dread the reproaches of your benefactor ? And must not this fear, and dread, and reverence be much more just, and reasonable, and honourable, when they are in the highest degree towards God ?

Now, as the higher these tempers are, the more are they esteemed amongst men, and are allowed to be so much the greater proofs of a true greatness of mind ; so the higher and greater these same tempers are towards God, so much the more do they prove the nobility, excellence, and greatness of the mind.

So that, so long as duty to parents, love to friends, and gratitude to benefactors, are thought great and honourable tempers; devotion, which is nothing else but duty, love, and gratitude to God, must have the highest place amongst our highest virtues. . . .

And, on the other hand, it shall here be made appear by variety of arguments, that indevotion is founded on the most excessive ignorance.

And first, our blessed Lord, and His apostles, were eminent instances of great and frequent devotion. Now, if we will grant (as all Christians must grant) that their great devotion was founded in a true knowledge of the nature of devotion, the nature of God, and the nature of man; then it is plain, that all those that are insensible of the duty of devotion, are in this excessive state of ignorance, they neither know God, nor themselves, nor devotion.

For if a right knowledge in these three respects produces great devotion, as in the case of our Saviour and His apostles; then a neglect of devotion must be chargeable upon ignorance. . . .

If there be any things that concern us more than others, if there be any truths that are more to us than all others, he that has the fullest knowledge of these things, that sees these truths in the clearest, strongest light, has, of all others, as a rational creature, the clearest understanding, and the strongest parts.

If, therefore, our relation to God be our greatest relation, if our advancement in His favour be our highest advancement, he that has the highest notions of the excellence of this relation, he that most strongly perceives the highest worth, and great value of holiness and virtue, that judges every thing little, when compared with it, proves himself to be master of the best and most excellent knowledge. . . .

If a gentleman should fancy that the moon is no bigger than it appears to the eye, that it shines with its own light, that all the stars are only so many spots of light: if, after reading books of astronomy, he should still continue in the same opinion, most people would think he had but a poor apprehension.

But if the same person should think it better to provide for a short life here, than to prepare for a glorious eternity hereafter ; that it was better to be rich, than to be eminent in piety ; his ignorance and dulness would be too great to be compared to any thing else.

There is no knowledge that deserves so much as the name of it, but that which we call judgment.

And that is the most clear and improved understanding, which judges best of the value and worth of things. All the rest is but the capacity of an animal, it is but mere seeing and hearing.

And there is no excellence of any knowledge in us, till we exercise our judgment, and judge well of the value and worth of things. . . .

If, therefore, God be our greatest good ; if there can be no good but in His favour, nor any evil but in departing from Him ; then it is plain, that he who judges it the best thing he can do to please God to the utmost of his power, who worships and adores Him with all his heart and soul, who would rather have a pious mind than all the dignities and honours in the world, shows himself to be in the highest state of human wisdom.

To proceed : We know how our blessed Lord acted

in a human body: it was His meat and drink to do
the will of His Father which is in heaven.

And if any number of heavenly spirits were to leave
their habitations in the light of God, and be for a
while united to human bodies, they would certainly
tend towards God in all their actions, and be as
heavenly as they could, in a state of flesh and blood.

They would certainly act in this manner, because
they would know that God was the only good of all
spirits; and that whether they were in the body, or out
of the body, in heaven or on earth, they must have every
degree of their greatness and happiness from God alone.

All human spirits, therefore, the more exalted they
are, the more they know their Divine Original, the
nearer they come to heavenly spirits; by so much the
more will they live to God in all their actions, and
make their whole life a state of devotion.

Devotion, therefore, is the greatest sign of a great and
noble genius; it supposes a soul in its highest state of
knowledge; and none but little and blinded minds, that
are sunk into ignorance and vanity, are destitute of it.

If a human spirit should imagine some mighty
prince to be greater than God, we should take him for
a poor, ignorant creature; all people would acknowledge such an imagination to be the height of stupidity.

But if this same human spirit should think it
better to be devoted to some mighty prince, than to be
devoted to God, would not this still be a greater proof
of a poor, ignorant, and blinded nature?

Yet this is what all people do, who think any thing
better, greater, or wiser, than a devout life.

So that which way soever we consider this matter, it
plainly appears, that devotion is an instance of great judg-

ment, of an elevated nature; and the want of devotion is a certain proof of the want of understanding. . . .

For if there is an infinitely wise and good Creator, in whom we live, move, and have our being, whose providence governs all things in all places, surely it must be the highest act of our understanding to conceive rightly of Him; it must be the noblest instance of judgment, the most exalted temper of our nature, to worship and adore this universal providence, to conform to its laws, to study its wisdom, and to live and act everywhere, as in the presence of this infinitely good and wise Creator.

Now, he that lives thus, lives in the spirit of devotion.

And what can show such great parts, and so fine an understanding, as to live in this temper?

For if God is wisdom, surely he must be the wisest man in the world, who most conforms to the wisdom of God, who best obeys His providence, who enters farthest into His designs, and does all he can, that God's will may be done on earth, as it is done in heaven.

A devout man makes a true use of his reason: he sees through the vanity of the world, discovers the corruption of his nature, and the blindness of his passion. He lives by a law which is not visible to vulgar eyes; he enters into the world of spirits; he compares the greatest things, sets eternity against time; and chooses rather to be for ever great in the presence of God when he dies, than to have the greatest share of worldly pleasure whilst he lives.

There is nothing, therefore, that shows so great a genius, nothing that so raises us above vulgar spirits, nothing that so plainly declares an heroic greatness of mind, as great devotion.

Lastly; courage and bravery are words of a great sound, and seem to signify an heroic spirit; but yet humility, which seems to be the lo⸳ est, meanest part of devotion, is a more certain argument of a noble and courageous mind.

For humility contends with greater enemies, is more constantly engaged, more violently assaulted, bears more, suffers more, and requires greater courage to support itself, than any instances of worldly bravery.

A man that dares be poor and contemptible in the eyes of the world, to approve himself to God; that resists and rejects all human glory, that opposes the clamour of his passions, that meekly puts up all injuries and wrongs, and dares stay for his reward till the invisible hand of God gives to every one their proper places, endures a much greater trial, and exerts a nobler fortitude, than he that is bold and daring in the fire of battle. . . .

I have made this digression, for the sake of those who think a great devotion to be bigotry and poorness of spirit; that by these considerations they may see how poor and mean all other tempers are, if compared to it ; that they may see, that all worldly attainments, whether of greatness, wisdom, or bravery, are but empty sounds; and **there is nothing wise, or great, or noble, in an human spirit, but rightly to know and heartily worship and adore the great God, that is the support and life of all spirits, whether in heaven or on earth.**

ABOUT THE AUTHORS

WILLIAM LAW

WILLIAM LAW was an English clergyman who lived just before the time of the American revolution. He studied at Immanuel College, Cambridge, and was ordained and elected a fellow of that college in 1711. Because of his refusal to take an oath of allegiance to King George he lost his position, and was, in effect blacklisted by the state church. The subsequent enforced inactivity proved to be the doorway into a life of meditation and prayer. From the years of his holy solitude emerged some of the most perceptive thought ever penned concerning the nature and practice of intimacy with God. The book for which he is best known is *A Serious Call to a Devout and Holy Life.*

ANDREW MURRAY

ANDREW MURRAY was born in 1828 in South Africa, the son of a minister of Scotch ancestry. He was educated in Scotland and Holland. In 1864 he returned to Capetown to take up ministry there. He was a pastor, evangelist, teacher, convention speaker of wide reputation, and the author of several books. He died peacefully in 1917, in his 89th year, after 69 years of preaching, teaching and writing. So memorable were his experiences and his insights that his books are still widely read.

OTHER QUALITY BOOKS FROM BETHANY FELLOWSHIP

BY ANDREW MURRAY

_____Be Perfect $1.45

_____Day By Day $1.45

_____Holy in Christ $2.45

_____How to Raise Your Children for Christ $3.50

_____Jesus Christ: Prophet-Priest . . . . $ .95

_____Like Christ $1.45

_____New Life $1.45